LEADERSHIP IS EMPOWERING PEOPLE

Paul R. Britton
John W. Stallings

88-1650

UNIVERSITY
PRESS OF
AMERICA

LANHAM • NEW YORK • LONDON

Copyright © 1986 by

University Press of America,® Inc.

4720 Boston Way
Lanham, MD 20706

3 Henrietta Street
London WC2E 8LU England

Library of Congress Cataloging in Publication Data

Britton, Paul R., 1933-
  Leadership is empowering people.

  Bibliography: p.
  1. Leadership.   2. Employee motivation.   3. Job
enrichment.   4. Job satisfaction.   I. Stallings,
John W., 1923-   II. Title.
HD57.7.B75   1986   658.3'14   86-9193
ISBN 0-8191-5409-1 (alk. paper)
ISBN 0-8191-5410-5 (pbk. : alk. paper)

All University Press of America books are produced on acid-free
paper which exceeds the minimum standards set by the National
Historical Publications and Records Commission.

DEDICATION

To Todd and Katrina Britton, and Julie Anne, John Kim and Sharon Lynn Stallings.

ACKNOWLEDGEMENTS

We thank many people for helping us to make this book possible. We are indebted to past authors who have maintained that effective leaders and managers must give deep respect and dignity to employees as well as to meet the organization's production goals. A few of these writers are: William Ouchi, Richard Tanner, Anthony Athos, Thomas Peters, Robert Waterman, John Naisbitt, Paul Hersey, Kenneth Blanchard and Roland Campbell. Building on many of these authors' concepts, we have tried to combine inspirational illustrations with technical descriptions to show how to lead and manage for respect, dignity and productivity. Illustrations and ideas have been gleaned from a wide variety of sources such as speakers at management conferences, video and audio cassettes and publications. We are particularly indebted to the following people and publications for illustrations: William Tice, Bob Moawad, Dennis Waitley, William Daniels, Earl Nightingale, "Bits and Pieces," "Orbin's Comedy," AEsop's Fables and The Bible. Most important of all, we thank our wives, Rosalind and Dina, for their invaluable help and inspiration. Last, Toni Sandell's incisive suggestions for our rough draft manuscript are deeply appreciated.

SUMMARY TABLE OF CONTENTS

PART I: THE EMPLOYEE: PREDICT, CHALLENGE AND CHANNEL BEHAVIOR

PART II: THE MANAGER: HUMANISTIC POWER TECHNIQUES, AND ERADICATION OF VICTORIAN BOSS HABITS

PART III: A PHILOSOPHICAL BASE FOR UNDERSTANDING THE PAST, PRESENT AND FUTURE

DETAILED TABLE OF CONTENTS

Conclusion

VI   THE GUTS OF POWER   181

- Ignore Some People
- Play Favorites
- Show Selfishness
- Hold the Good Back
- Be Sly
- Be Insensitive
- Vacillate
- Make Numbers Everything
- Say Nay
- Lower Your Standards
- Be Excessively Reflective

Finally: No More "Good Old Days"

INTRODUCTION

The future is here. We live in a new age with strong challenges, intense frustrations and rapid changes. In this age one of the basic problems for managers is that employees and society have changed dramatically while management practices in many organizations have remained nearly static. For example, many managers look at their new-age employees and say, "Am I really supposed to supervise those people? They don't know what responsibility is; they just want to do their own thing." On the other hand, employees look at managers today, and think (and sometimes even say), "They're crazy if they think I'm going to do that. It's degrading, or meaningless and unnecessary."

Some managers accept these challenges. They find this an exciting time to be alive. Others are discouraged, disgruntled and dispirited. This book is designed to help both kinds of managers to deal with the challenges of this new age. Although it is primarily a book of strategies, with many lists and hundreds of simple suggestions to help you manage new-age employees along the lines of what has recently been labeled Japanese, and then Theory Z management, it also has a philosophical orientation that ties these discrete suggestions together. The reason a philosophical base has been included is because we believe that one of the basic causes of manager/personnel problems today is that outmoded philosophies guide many managers' actions. If actions are to change, managers' perceptions and thinking have to change. Therefore, we urge you to read the introduction in which foundations are laid for the rest of the book, before you move on to the first chapter where you will begin to read about strategies for specific situations.

CRISES

There are two related crises in contemporary American management. The first and most visible is the productivity crisis. The second, more subtle and devastating because it controls the first, is the crisis of relationships--relationships of manager to employee, employees to themselves, employees and managers to their organizations, and people to their ideas, their culture and their world.

The problem of relationships is a matter of connectedness, of understanding and being concerned with the whole as much as the part. It means some commitment to all of one's society and not just one's own organization or self. And it presupposes on the part of managers a dedication to the internal needs of employees as well as to external needs of productivity.

Even though relationships have always been important for humane management, they have not always been integral to productivity itself at times when resources were plentiful, when workers were intimidated and divided, and when the church and small communities took care of spiritual needs and relationships. Times have changed, however. As resources have begun to run out, cooperation has become essential. As workers have gained security and unity, power developed with people has become necessary. And, as communities and churches have taken care of fewer and fewer spiritual needs, personal identity and job meaning for employees have emerged as basic to effective management. In short, employees, resources and society have changed dramatically while management practices have remained nearly static. The result is a crisis of productivity due to the crisis of relationships. This is as much a problem for non-profit service organizations as for profit making businesses and industries.

By way of contrast to the crisis in American productivity, the Japanese have been immensely productive. The Japanese rank first among nations in several areas: the number of inventions made and patents granted each year, the number of novels published each year, high school completion rate, mastery of foreign languages by high school and college students, test scores in science and mathematics among school children, rate of real economic growth and productivity increase, and the quality of goods and services in such industries as transportation, communication, consumer products and electronics. Japan's GNP was the third highest in the world in 1980, and is predicted to be number one by the year 2,000.[1] Japan's size is about equal to the state of Montana, and yet it supports 115 million people, about half as many in all of the U.S. Japan's has almost no physical resources, and still it exports $75 million more in goods than it imports. Japan has become dominant over other countries of the world in one industry after another. It has overtaken the English in motorcycle production, the Germans and Americans in automobiles, the Swiss and Germans in watches, cameras and optical instruments, and the Americans in businesses as diverse as steel, shipbuilding, pianos, zippers, and consumer electronics.[2] Certainly the Japanese have some substantial advantages over the Americans by having a relatively homogeneous population and certain cultural practices, but there seems to be no simple way to explain Japan's success through these factors alone.

One of the major explanations for Japanese superiority today lies in the subtle complexities of Japanese management. Reduced to perhaps its simplest terms, Japanese managers seem to differ from most American managers by seeing the organization as an interconnected part of society. The organization is a social unit as well as a profit or service oriented enterprise. Both quality of life and productivity are essential. Making the individual feel a part of the organization is synonomous with making the organization successful. Providing meaning for employees is a company objective as much as ensuring top-level production. Management techniques must foster individual satisfaction as well as organizational productivity; there must be a balance of productive harmony between the individual and the organization.

It all makes sense, for we all spend a large proportion of our time at work. Many of us develop at least the beginnings of our significant relationships there. And almost all of us decide how committed we will be to our work on the basis of how personally fulfilling it is. Why then do we managers often neglect the development of the personal, inner dimension?

We believe that fundamental culprits are excessive selfishness, exploitation and hostility. While these human characteristics will be discussed in more detail in Chapter IX, suffice it to say now that we believe that these qualities are wide-spread and detrimental in American workplaces largely because of dichotomies, or fragmentations, in our culture, and the ways power is used in our society.

If this is true, it would seem that we should replace dichotomies and fragmentation with a sense of connectedness and wholeness, and we should exchange excessive selfishness and exploitation for cooperation and power with people.

DICHOTOMIES AND CONNECTEDNESS

In contrast to China and Japan, Western countries have developed dichotomies in their societies. In Western society, the church emerged as the conservator of peoples' faith and spirituality, while government and business became the providers of their worldly existence. We Westerners have developed societies that separate our spiritual lives from our work lives. We call one philosophical and the other practical. We often infer that the philosophical and spiritual are less important than the practical. Western organizational theory evolved to justify this duality as natural. This contributed to the feeling that one's spiritual and social life really existed outside of work. This idea has continued in Western societies, and it is likely that it is one of the fundamental forerunners, as well as present irritants, of our management problems today.

The dualities of church and state, spiritual and temporal, have made it easy to legitimize the dichotomies of business and other work organizations. Even though human beings have a driving need for inner meaning and identity in their lives, managers have felt no responsibility for this, for those things were the function of another realm--the church.

The Industrial Revolution was a major event in

xxii

building Western perspectives of people in relation to organizations and society. The proliferation of mass production diminished the importance of individuals and their skills and social affiliations. Human beings no longer were integral parts of the organic whole of a community or society, except as they belonged to special groups or small communities. Individuals became standardized and expendable components of mass production. The word anonymous took on a new meaning. Anonymity, in the interests of productivity, was easily justified, for the interchangeability of people in mass production was deemed important to producing goods, which in turn were important to greater creature comforts.

Anonymity also has recently been rationalized in the interests of greater individual freedom and ever greater individual autonomy. The reasoning has been that individuals could fulfill themselves better without binding and blinding expectations of demanding families and communities than they could with these encumbrances.

What has actually happened has been something less than ideal. Managers have easily exploited people in widespread selfishness and greed. Employees have retaliated against these degradations by banding together in unions for strength to counter-exploit. Both managers and employees have been intensely frustrated, sometimes unknowingly, by the emptiness of anonymity. Not surprisingly, hostilities have stultified production.

Part of this state of affairs is explained by the dilemma of independence vs. interdependence, which is basic to Western culture. Although we are thoroughly dependent on each other, we tend to uphold independence as the ultimate form of living. We see ourselves at the center of the universe; we are narcissistic and think of the world principally in terms of ourselves. To explain a person who is having difficulty we often say that the person doesn't know himself, whereas in Japan the explanation is most likely to revolve around not belonging. The American psychologist, Harry Stack Sullivan, has proposed that the idea of "the individual" has created considerable trouble for

Westerners. He maintains that it is simply not very helpful to consider the individual separately from his or her relationships, in spite of the fact that much psychotherapy recently has focused excessively on individuals "doing their own thing".[3] Some of the most significant American contributions to psychotherapy in the last two decades have come from working with people as interdependent beings--couples, families, groups in school or at work.

One of the basic premises of this book is that we are all connected in one way or another, and one of the major tasks of the manager is to understand and use this connectedness for the maximum advantage of all. This does not mean that our Western strong sense of self should be discarded, but rather that our ways of thinking about ourselves should be broadened to include a commitment to helping others even when no immediate selfish returns are available. It means learning to "go along" with some outcomes not fully congruent with our own view, and to develop the ability to find a common ground, taking others' points and using them creatively.

Connectedness in management also includes getting people to share values with significant meanings. These values provide a compass for work and socializing employees. They may be like IBM's threefold goals of respect for individuals, service to customers, and excellence in productivity. They may be similar to Delta Airline's family feeling. Or, they may be Matsushita's social goals of restoring Japan's prestige, advancing the country's standard of living, and contributing to each employee's personal growth over his lifetime. Connectedness in management means getting all the "players in the orchestra" to follow the same tempo and to play much better than they could without a conductor. The important things with these values are that these are known to everyone, constantly and visibly used, that they address needs of personal meaning as well as productivity, and that the players' dignity is maximized.

Above all, connectedness for the manager means focusing on relationships. American managers have been socialized to be independent of each other and of employees. Independent judgment, independent action, and even separateness and isolation have been highly valued. In a sense, the historical needs of a frontier society are still prized even though they retain little value. Japanese managers, on the other hand, tend to think in terms of being interdependent with others, of being integral parts of a larger unity where dependencies are nurtured. Westerners seem deeply preoccupied with self, separate categories of friends, relatives, and subordinates while the Japanese are concerned with cooperative rings of relationships. Although Westerners tend to repress dependency as an aspect of infancy, the Japanese seem cognizantly to develop it.

What the authors of this book are proposing is not that Americans suddenly and indiscriminately become dependent, but rather that we emphasize the best of both dependence and independence, dedicating ourselves in the workplace to the development of group harmony, team spirit, unity and excellence. For managers, this means steady personal contact and self-interest pursued in terms of real collective interest. Among a host of other things, it means sensitivity in helping to solve human problems and dilemmas--problems such as the conflicts and tensions between individuals and the organization, managers and employees, and the needs of all both for cooperation and competition.

POWER

Central to management problems in America today is the use of power. In a country where independence, short-term employment of executives, and cut-throat competition exist, raw power is exalted. Even in public service organizations such as a school district one frequently hears assumptions about the use of power which are detrimental to developing cooperative and productive work groups.

Managers frequently make statements such as: "Don't surrender your power." "Are you going to let teachers dictate to you?" "I don't have any stress, I make it." Or, "If we let those teachers get by without enforcing this policy, we may just as well never try to enforce another policy again." Certainly no effective manager is going to surrender power, let others dictate, be forced to be a bystander, or be immobilized by subordinates. The problem is simply that we Americans suffer sorely from "erroneous zones" of thinking. Wayne Dyer gave this label of "erroneous zones" to thinking that is injurious to self-development.[4] This same principle applies to manager practices which are harmful to organizational growth. One of the primary "erroneous zones" of managers is to believe that the best way to be a boss is to maintain chest-thumping power over others, when what is really needed is power and accountability with others. This certainly does not mean all positive reinforcement and soft ball; it can also mean a performance orientation that includes knuckle rapping and hard ball. Above all, it means the kind of genuine nurturing of employees by managers which results in widespread employee belief that criticism is for personal development, not for testing, or power displays.

Professors Pascale and Athos, in **The Art of Japanese Management**, state that one reason for Japanese success in personnel management is the acceptance of ambiguity, uncertainty and imperfection in organizational life.[5] In American managerial life, however, (not only in the military but also in business and even in public service organizations), ambiguity, uncertainty and imperfections are to be eradicated at almost any cost. These conditions are considered to result in vacillating and waffling, and they are to be annihilated.

American managers are trained to be firm, decisive and explicit, even though this means beating at icicles tossed in tropical rains. We often flail away at those problems which will melt away in fairly short order. We are foiled by our own intransigence and perfectionism, and we miss many of the possibilities in life.

By being excessively oriented to ends, we easily neglect to focus enough on means which paradoxically might actually enhance the final product. By being simplistically preoccupied with logic and legalism we curiously lock ourselves out of the richness of experience necessary to give weight to our rational arguments. And by idealizing kinetic drives to fast decisions we often inhibit the deep perceptions necessary for wise actions.

Pascale and Athos say, "The inherent preferences of organizations are clarity, certainty and perfection. The inherent nature of human relationships involves ambiguity, uncertainty, and imperfection. How one honors, balances and integrates the needs of both is the trick of management."[6] This is what power _with_ people and _empowering_ them is all about.

ORGANIZATION OF THIS BOOK

Part I focuses on the _employee_. You will see how to predict, change and channel the behavior of employees through "spiritual" management. This includes trust, a central belief system, participative management, communication, conflict resolution and motivation.

Part II tells you, the _manager_, how to develop and use humanistic power strategies and to eradicate Victorian boss habits.

Part III gives a philosophical base for understanding the past, present and future. Three major problems of the workplace--selfishness, exploitation and hostility are discussed. The evolution of management systems is briefly described. Last, you will read a summary of Leadership is Empowering People, and be challenged to ask yourself what _you_ will do.

SELF-IMPROVEMENT

One of the most difficult things for a leader to do is to become a learner, particularly when this involves changing personal habits. Yet this is necessary if managers and leaders are to be effective in today's changing world. You need to understand some theory related to these changes. You may need to move beyond your own training or culture. And it is possible that you will need to change some old-guard, self-defeating boss habits. Now, of course, self-defeating behaviors, and ways to overcome them, are touchy things to write about. Saying that you are open to looking at yourself in depth is one thing; diligently doing it is another. Personal change is fantastically difficult. Most people resist change with all kinds of rationalizations. All of us develop perceptions, practices and habits which have been built on many past experiences and thoughts. Mental and emotional maps have been developed of what is and what isn't, what can be and what can't be. Some of these maps may be incorrect, but we persist in following them, because even when we're lost it's human nature to block out discovering where we are by ignoring data, deluding ourselves or by distorting information to make it congruent with our past maps. When we lock ourselves onto these incorrect maps, we lock ourselves out of opportunities.

This book is about correcting these mistaken maps, giving up self-defeating habits, and beginning new practices. Almost everything we are has been learned, or has been modified by learning, and thus is changeable. We hope you will find insights in this book which will help you to identify some aspects of management which need to be changed, and we trust that some of these strategies will help you to make those changes.

PART ONE

THE EMPLOYEE

PREDICT, CHALLENGE AND CHANNEL BEHAVIOR

How to predict, challenge and channel the behavior of employees through communication, conflict resolution, "spiritual" management, and motivation.

"SPIRITUAL MANAGEMENT"

To produce things and rear them,
To produce, but not to take possession of them,
To act, but only to rely on one's own ability,
To lead them, but not to master them -
This is called profound and secret virtue.

Lau Tzu, 6th Century B.C.

INTRODUCTION

In spite of much national attention in the last five years focused on improving management, there are still many problems. We all know that there is low productivity and high tension in many workplaces. Feelings of inadequacy and of not being in control are widespread. Increasing demands are made on managers while resources and authority are diminished. Perhaps most important, there is still extensive confrontation at a time when pervasive cooperation is needed. Even though there have been many serious attempts by American management during the last fifty years to improve, clearly much is lacking.

It is also clear that there is much frustration. Henry Kissinger put it this way: "Utopia was seen not as a dream, but as our logical destination if we only traveled the right road. Our generation is the first to find that the road is endless, that in traveling it, we find not Utopia, but ourselves."

While at first glance this quotation by Henry Kissinger might seem to be pessimistic, it is meant to be used as a springboard to an optimistic future.

There are no utopias. There are no "business messiahs." Our national character is both "righteous" and "sinful." Society's saviors can be ourselves.

From shattered dreams we can now begin to engineer a society with workplaces which are equally beneficial to individuals as well as to organizations. Instead of continuing to perceive management as a lot of separate cause and effect acts, where exploitation in one place won't carry over to another and boomerang, we are in a good position to grasp the interrelatedness of almost all acts, because in one way or another, the beads on the string are all tied together. We can now begin to build organizations where the emphasis is on trust and service much more than fear and punishment, where there is a unity of belief and cooperation rather than narrow financial objectives and cut throat competition to meet these objectives. We are now in a position to build management systems which foster deep respect among almost all employees. We can now be highly results oriented, both for our company product and for individual employees. We can coach and reassign employees when mistakes are made rather than to do them in. We can also now involve people importantly in decisions about their work and their company rather than to manipulate them in demeaning ways.

Ten years ago most managers probably would have thought that the term spiritual management in conjunction with management was flaky. Now, however, more and more managers are finding it not only acceptable, but desirable because they are beginning to see that it results in both higher productivity **and** employee satisfaction.

Pascale and Athos, in **The Art of Japanese Management**, point out that even though the term "spiritual" at first thought seems to be a complete misnomer for corporate life, nothing else can really explain contradictions such as the following which are commonplace in Japanese management:

      -- Criticism is perceived as training,
      -- Job transfers are seen as character developers,
      -- Pushes for efficiency are correlated with

a genuine desire to win people over, and
-- Business profitability is tied to the
social good.1

In short, work is a belief system, and not a
system to be beaten.

One way to illustrate spiritual management for
Americans is to look back to the best coach or teacher
you ever had. Think about that person for a minute.
The chances are that you have thought of a person who
had high expectations for you, captured and stretched
your imagination, and gave you the kind of guidance
which made you feel as though you had your own special
mentor. Although you made mistakes and received
reprimands, you somehow knew that you were accepted
with an unconditional kind of love. Even when you were
being pushed to your limit, you felt that it was for
your own self-development as well as that of the team.
You may even have learned the magic of being alive to
your own senses, while also being sympathetic to the
sensitivities of others.

On the other hand, think about those coaches or
teachers (or managers) who stifled imagination, gave
little guidance, communicated dislike or seemed to push
you mainly for their own glory. These people didn't
seem to like you, didn't think you were very capable,
and didn't want to help you solve problems. You may
have felt alone in hostile fights for survival.

As a manager, you may find it difficult to see
yourself as a teacher or coach, for you may feel that
an executive title demands a more exalted image.
Actually, however, these roles open doors to the
development of limitless **empowerment** of people, of
infinite employee and product growth.

TRUST

*"As contagion of sickness makes sickness,
contagion of trust can make trust."*

Marianne Moore

TRUST QUOTIENT

How much trust is there in your own organization? In order to get an idea, answer these thirteen questions on a scale of 1-5 (5 being high). Answer on the basis of how a person not too friendly to you would feel, not on the basis of how a protege would respond.

1. How willingly is information shared among workers and managers?   (1 2 3 4 5)

2. How much does the giver of information trust the receiver to use the information for the good of the giver as well as the receiver?   (1 2 3 4 5)

3. How free do people feel to be themselves even in competitive struggles?   (1 2 3 4 5)

4. How much mutual support do your employees give each other?   (1 2 3 4 5)

5. How much mutual respect do your employees have?   (1 2 3 4 5)

6. How much empathetic understanding of others' positions is there?   (1 2 3 4 5)

7. To what extent do people reserve judgment while respecting complexity and subtlety?   (1 2 3 4 5)

8. To what extent is there an openness to look at motives?   (1 2 3 4 5)

9. How much are helpful (non-manipulative) motives prized?   (1 2 3 4 5)

10. How much of an attempt is there to flatten

the traditional hierarchical line and staff
structure?   (1 2 3 4 5)

11. Are people and profits (or the mission of the
    organization) seen as compatible?   (1 2 3 4 5)

12. To what extent is stability of jobs a goal of
    the company?   (1 2 3 4 5)

13. How much bureaucratic inflexibility is there?   (1 2 3 4 5)

If your total score is 85, skip to the beginning
of "Central Belief System" in this chapter. Otherwise,
why not see if you can get something from this section?
You know that you can no longer get employees to trust
you and work well simply by telling them what to do.
If they are to break the barriers of ordinary
productivity, they also have to have trust. They need
to believe that fellow employees are not out to harm
them, and that others are to be respected for both
their fairness and competence. In fact, your ability
to build genuine trust and cooperation in the midst of
competition and apprehension will to a large extent
govern your success in modern organizations.

This is a very big order, and it begins with a
solid foundation. If you, the manager, don't begin
this foundation, it will never be laid. If it's never
laid, your management will be built on soft sand, and
both your own authority and employee productivity will
be unstable. With trust, however, you can begin to
build unshakable authority and productivity.

A PERSPECTIVE ON TRUST

Trust is not merely openness, not honesty, nor
what things seem to be at first glance. It is very
complex. Regardless of the complexities in trust,
however, it all really boils down to your point of view
and whether or not you want to build trust. You can
build a contagion of trust, or you can build a
contagion of disease. It ultimately depends on whether
you believe that the worst single characteristic in
employees and organizations is untrustworthiness, or if
you consider distrust natural and inevitable. Before

you settle on untrustworthiness as normal, and the best life can offer, look carefully at its consequences.

With distrust, relationships degenerate into conflict and wasted energy, whereas with trust, the sky's the limit. Without substantial trust, paranoia is likely to rule. Jungle laws of survival override civilized arts of cooperation. Exploitation becomes commonplace. Hostility builds. Sabotage results--either passive or active--and productivity is reduced. The best thing for the conventional manager with the conventional workplace to do then is to clamp on more control, so there is at least a modicum of mediocre productivity.

Life in almost any workplace involves much interdependence. People have to rely on each other. The only way to do this efficiently is through trust. Without basic trust there can never be a breakthrough kind of productivity. For managers and workers will spend much time using negative energy in covering their own asses rather than in positive initiative in making the organization go forward.

Trust is central to synergy. The first reason for firing should be untrustworthiness. The second, incompetence. Not that either should be tolerated, but untrustworthiness reduces otherwise competent people to incompetence. It not only weakens; it destroys. Ouchi, in **Theory Z**, says, "I would guess that most poor productivity is the result of inputs not received, machinery not repaired, designs poorly coordinated by uncooperative men competing against each other."[2] Tragically, many managers continue to pit submanagers and employees against one another, thinking that this is the path to good competition and productivity.

Another reason for building trust is that if productivity is to be increased by work groups such as the recently popularized Quality Circle teams, trust is imperative. There is no way that "semi-autonomous" work teams can be productive without trust.

One of the problems with the workplace is that our whole American society has abused trust. We have more or less come to accept it as one accepts an affliction.

An Opinion Research Corporation study, summarized in the 1980 January/February issue of the Harvard Business Review, revealed some startling research about trust:

-- In the 1950's, nearly 80% of managers thought their companies fair; now, less than 50% gave their companies good marks.

-- In the 1950's, about 70% of clerical workers gave their firms a "good or very good" fairness rating; by the late 70's this figure had dropped to approximately 20%.[3]

In spite of the fact that most U.S. citizens are probably basically honest, duplicity seems to have become increasingly commonplace, as we have adjusted to widespread expectations of dishonesty. Watergate, Abscam, and the IRS seem almost as synonymous with deception as Quisling* is to traitors. Even the prestigious institutions of medicine, law and higher education have suffered the stains of deception. Surgeons have prescribed needless operations, lawyers have bilked large companies as well as private citizens, and universities have cheated on academics in order to win in athletics.

It is not hard to see why there is widespread distrust and suspicion. Selfishness and exploitation surround us. External pressures for personal and commercial achievement bombard us. Relaxed morality involving dishonesty lures us. Advertising which blurs the truth, inures us. Anonymity, where the deceived don't have to be faced, ensnares us.

Does this description mean something to you? Is your workplace similar?

WHAT IS TRUST?

Full, mutual trust is contingent first upon things such as full communication of wants, need-satisfactions, changes of feelings, hopes and fears. Full trust also depends on living up to

*A Norwegian politician who sold out to the Germans in W.W.II.

agreements, and even sharing reluctances to live up to agreements--with re-negotiations following reluctances. It even presupposes such superior fairness as initiating relationship "repairs" when there are upset feelings. While this kind of trust might seem improbable in the workplace, a modified version **is** possible. A modified version of trust includes honoring the complexity of ambiguity. Whenever you have teams of people working together, certain things such as performance and trust, will be somewhat uncertain. Still, if you focus on the importance of trust, ambiguity can be reduced.

Trust involves subtlety, intimacy, and intuition. William Ouchi believes that above all, it means getting people to realize that they matter as people, not just as parts.[4] While exams were in progress at Hunter College, President Donna Shalaha not only agreed to the administration serving a midnight breakfast to studying students, but even served bacon and eggs herself. When questioned as to whether or not this would weaken her power, she maintained that on the contrary, it would "humanize" the institution. It would mean that students, and their exam performances really mattered.

DEVELOPING AND MAINTAINING TRUST

FOUR MAIN PRINCIPLES & MANY TECHNIQUES

We suggest four main principles in outlining a basic path to follow for building trust. These are:

1. Make a commitment to people.

2. Reward trust and penalize distrust.

3. Don't take advantage of managerial positions.

4. Build individual cooperation **and** independence.

It should be pointed out that the development of trust needs to start at the top. It is next to impossible for lower level managers to develop and maintain trust unless the chief executive also prizes and emphasizes it.

1. COMMITMENT TO PEOPLE.

It's often the little things that count, for actions speak louder than words. The little things begin with your reactions to people. Do you run them down, even ever so subtly? If you do, teamwork and morale will suffer. It's human nature to grumble if someone irritates you. But this is not wise, because as a manager, you may be taken more seriously than you intended. Particularly employees who are competitive are apt to latch onto your critical comments and non-verbal innuendoes--a lift of the eyebrows or a shrug of the shoulder. Subordinates pattern their attitudes according to the esteem they **think** you hold for another person. This means less trust or cooperation if they believe John or Sally is out of favor with you. The bottom line is, of course, lower morale, trust and teamwork.

A certain amount of distrust is natural among peers. One of the manager's problems is to overcome this, and to develop a smooth working team by building trust through learning to react to people and phrase things appropriately. Even if you want to build trust, how well do you do in your every day contacts--your "automatic" phrases and response, in your receiving of criticism, and in your giving of advice? Most managers have trouble. Because of this, we have included some phrases to steer clear of.

Automatic Responses and Trust Killers: Trust is fragile. Certain words which many of us use automatically are profoundly destructive to trust. These we have called "trust killer" phrases. The following is a list of some of these destructive phrases. **Test yourself**. Opposite the statement, put a check by any statement you use. After you finish, count the number of checks and see your score at the end of the list.

CHECK IF YOU USE

1. "It's a great idea, but . . ."

2. "No good, it won't work."

3. "We don't have the time."

4. "There are better ways."

5. "Let's talk about it some other time."

6. "Why start something new?"

7. "We never did it that way before."

8. "We are not ready for that."

9. "Someone would have thought of it before if it was any good."

10. "It's too new."

11. "It's too old-fashioned."

12. "You don't understand the problem."

13. "We have too much going on at present."

14. "You are really saying . . ."

15. "It is not practical enough."

16. "Let's just keep it in mind for awhile."

17. "You had better do this or else."

18. "It would be best for you if . . ."

19. "The only and best solution is . . ."

20. "You usually have good judgment."

21. "You'll feel different tomorrow."

22. "You think you've got problems."[5]

<u>Your Score =</u> _____

Your number of checks: 0-2 = Outstanding
                                 2-4 = Better than most
                                 5-10 = Average, but not good
                                 10 or more = Awful

Receiving Criticism: Our trust level with others can be influenced by the way in which we both receive criticism and give advice. It is a well known fact that all of us can learn a great deal from our associates and that in turn we can all help our associates to be more effective. The important thing is, do we demonstrate to others that we want them to help us, and do we accept the responsibility to help others?

Following is a list of questions that can be helpful in receiving criticism.

Check if Answer is Yes

1. Do you let people know that you welcome constructive criticism?

2. Do you demonstrate by your actions that you want suggestions for improvement?

3. Are you negative or defensive? Do you respond positively?

4. Do you ask for information whenever people are giving you constructive criticism?

5. Are you an attentive listener?

6. Do you ask for specifics about what people think?

7. Do you let your emotions get in the way of accepting criticism?

8. Do you listen for consistency of the same criticism?

9. Do you take criticism and modify it to your style?

10. Do you develop a strategy for change?

11. Do you divide the behavior to be changed into a series of steps?

12. Are you careful and honest in evaluating yourself with the help of others?[6]

Your total number of checks: 10-12 = Outstanding
                                7 - 9 = Better than most
                                4 - 7 = Average, but not good
                                0 - 3 = Need work badly

Giving Advice:

Check for each Yes

1. Do you make it a point almost always to give advice <u>only</u> just before it can be used? (If yes, give yourself 5 points.)

2. Do you always establish a climate of respect and acceptance before giving advice?

3. Do you select the time and place carefully?

4. Do you show that you empathize with others' problems or feelings?

5. Do you make sure that the other person understands your criticism, and more importantly, the reason for it?

6. Do you make your criticism as specific as possible?

7. Are you sure the behavior you are criticizing can be changed?

8. Do you avoid threats or accusations?

9. Do you commit yourself to share in helping the other person?

10. Do you let negative or emotional feelings color your words? Do you watch the tone of your voice and avoid gestures such as scowls, pointed fingers, and clenched fists?

11. Do you preach or belabor a point? It is so easy to "tune out" people.

12. Do you give recognition and praise? If not, follow up and try to help in other ways.[7]

Your total number of checks: 10-12 = Outstanding
                                7 - 9 = Good
                                4 - 6 = Average, but not good
                                0 - 3 = Unlikely to survive
                                        except with lots of
                                        henchmen.

Giving advice is very tricky. Unless you give it just **before** it can be used, and unless a climate of trust and respect has been established, most people will see it as punitive, even though you give it with the best intent, even when you are trying to save the person from falling off the world. Not only is advice given under other circumstances likely to be perceived as negative, the advicee is likely to think you petty and stupid--you may well even be hated.

All three of these categories--your automatic responses, receiving of criticism and your giving of advice--are crucial in building and maintaining trust. These might be called small things that count so much.

Finally, if you're really committed to people, you won't be too narrow in your judgment of them. You'll realize that many can have talents and personalities which are very different from yours. To illustrate this, there is the story about the time that one of America's most papers printed that Henry Ford was an ignoramus. Ford brought legal action seeking proof. During the trial, Ford was asked dozens of formal education questions such as the dates of national wars. Ford's forte was not formal education and he did very poorly in answering the questions. He finally became impatient and blurted out that he used his energy to think, not to memorize information that was useless to him when he could find answers to those questions if the remote need rose.

2. REWARD TRUST AND PENALIZE SOWERS OF DISTRUST.

One of Aesop's fables is about Mercury and the Woodman. The woodman, an honest and hardworking, but very poor man, accidentally dropped his main tool, an ax, into the river. Mercury saw him, and offered to help. Mercury dove into the swift stream twice, first pulling up an ax of gold, and next, of silver. He asked each time if this was the right ax. The woodman replied no each time. Mercury dove once more, this time bringing up a replica of the woodman's ax. The owner straightforwardly admitted that this was his ax. Mercury was so happy with the owner's honesty that he gave him the gold and silver axes as rewards.

One of the woodman's neighbors, who heard of this good fortune, threw his ax into the river and then sat down and began to moan about his loss. Mercury again appeared and dove into the water, fetching a gold ax. When asked if this was his ax, the neighbor replied "yes." Mercury then told the neighbor that because he was lying, the ax would be denied him, and in addition, that his own ax would be left at the bottom of the river.[8]

While many people tacitly believe that honesty and trust are important, they also find them hard to practice. They may not actually lie very much, but they may engage in insidious practices such as collusion with others to get their own way, thus causing distrust. They may withhold information, in ploys of selfish power, and believe that this is really good for them, at least. They may believe that adversary relations help to develop the kind of keen edge of competition which makes an organization thrive.

Some managers reinforce gossip, not even realizing the personal destruction that they are participating in. An eagle, a wildcat, and a sow lived in the same tree--the eagle in the high branches, the wildcat in the hollow trunk, and the sow in a burrowed hole beneath the tree's roots. For some time, all three families lived peaceably, until the wildcat began to gossip, whispering first to the eagle, that even with "the highest respect for the sow below," continued digging would cause the tree to crash down. The wildcat continued that, "it's probably what she had in mind so she can feed our babies to her litter." Mother eagle became worried, stayed home, and no longer soared after food. Meanwhile, the gossiping wildcat gossiped to the sow, saying, "I'm no gossip, but if I were you, I'd leave home today, for I overheard the eagle talking to her children that they were going to have pork for for dinner." So, the eagle and sow both stayed home. The wildcat sneaked out looking for food.

It is possible that both families would have been weakened to starvation, while governing their own territory, had not the wildcat gotten caught in a hunter's trap, leaving the eagle and sow to be reunited in open and caring trust for their offspring.[9]

One of the worst things a manager can do is to allow gossip in the workplace. For as gossips and other neurotics are listened to, the power of people who are honest and healthy is weakened, and positive, cooperative energy sources are poisoned.

3. NEVER TAKE ADVANTAGE OF YOUR POSITION.

A commitment to do so is a good way to begin to build a contagion of trust. Of course, one need not be a manager to destroy trust.

Often employees, through grievances or union power, take unfair advantages and make unreasonable demands in exercising the power they have.

Among the greedy and silly advantage takers are both managers and employees. One such manager was a media supervisor at a junior college. Just call her Puff, the Abominable Dragon. Although Puff may seem simple and even absurd, she illustrates how ludicrous so much advantage taking is. Who's fooling whom?

Puff gave an "ironclad" order that all A.V. equipment absolutely must be handed into her assistant by 12:00 p.m. on Friday before Spring holidays, even though some employees needed the equipment past that time. Then Puff, herself, went on "sick leave" two days before the holidays began so that she could clandestinely self-actualize herself and fly home to New York. Even though the sick leave was highly suspect (Puff's toe hurt), the Abominable Dragon was so greedy and insensitive that she actually saw nothing wrong with sticking it to others while taking advantage herself. Sad, but true--there are countless dragons out there who can't understand what all the clamor is about when they take advantage.

But the point here is, we believe that managers should take the first steps in breaking the cycle of, "They take advantage, so why shouldn't I?" One example of breaking this cycle is the microelectronics firm, Tandem, where the executives have foregone some simple perks of executives such as "reserved parking spaces on up." Perhaps even more importantly, James Freybig, the founder of Tandem, "frees up 100% of his personal time to work on people projects. Tandem's people oriented management style includes Friday afternoon beer parties, employee stock options, flexible work hours . . . a company swimming pool that is open from 6:00 a.m. to 8:00 p.m., and sabbatical leave every four years--which all employees are required to take."[10]

4. BUILD INDIVIDUALS' COOPERATION **AND** INDEPENDENCE.

Trust thrives when the manager helps his or her employees to self-actualize themselves; cooperation is then likely to result. You know that good coaches help team members to be both cooperative and somewhat independent. They build an atmosphere of trust where there is desire, enthusiasm and responsibility, as well as independence and cooperation.

One rule you can use to develop a high level of both independence and cooperation is to vary the way you help your employees according to what they need. Maximize your help when people are low in skills and/or acceptance of responsibility and initiative. As employees reach higher levels of these traits, however, minimize your help and "let them fly." In this process of helping your employees to develop, keep in mind the following principles, which are listed in sequential order as they should usually be used.

FOUR STEPS IN DEVELOPING INDEPENDENCE AND COOPERATION:

1. Show How. Know how to explain and demonstrate what needs to be done. Then involve your employees in doing those things.

2. Check Up. Dwight Eisenhower indicated that even in the presidency one of the greatest problems was following up to be sure that jobs were done. This happens in all kinds of jobs; people easily get deterred from mutually agreed upon goals unless, at least in the initial stages, someone persistently follows up. The price of effectiveness is diligence.

3. Build Initiative. When things are going **reasonably well**, keep out of the way. Learn to step back. Avoid over-supervision. Simply observe what is going on so that you'll be informed, and so that you can deftly intervene if necessary. Make only brief and casual suggestions. Usually, you'll want to keep the help minimal and indirect. Let subordinates savor success.

4. Work Together. At this point the scene is set for "independent cooperation." Emphasize the mutual benefits of working together as a team. Help to satisfy both emotional and intellectual needs of employees.

In summary, when individuals and the group are still low in acceptance of responsibility or initiative, or in skills, maximize your help. As they reach higher levels of responsibility, initiative and skills, minimize your help and let them be independently cooperative.

To build trust, communicate to your employees a feeling of doing everything for their benefit and development as well as for the organization. Don't just probe to find out what's wrong, like an investigator or monitor. Don't just give directions. But do probe to find out how to help and get excellence from each person on the team.

ELEVEN ONE LINERS FOR BUILDING TRUST

In addition to these four main strategies, here are short suggestions for building trust.

1. Trust yourself, for if you do not, you will never spread trust among others.

3. Be sure that your decisions can withstand the scrutiny of "right thinking" critics, or don't make them.

4. Never exploit employees.

5. In decision making, give all people who are going to be affected by a decision a real opportunity for input into that decision. And, don't be satisfied simply to give superficial opportunities.

6. Work for consensus; try to stay away from mere votes, for they tend to promote a kind of adversarial relationship. Promote the belief that "If we can't agree on most things, it must be because we don't have the same information; otherwise, we wouldn't still disagree."

7. Promote happiness among employees, for although it is not an ironclad rule, happiness, trust and high productivity tend to go hand in hand.

8. Know your employees well enough that you can sense things that are important to them, whether they be work oriented or not. Trust can be greatly enhanced by the feeling that, "My boss really understands me," as long as there is also the feeling that, "He wants to help me." On the other hand, trust is easily decreased when the managers communicate somehow that they don't really realize what is important to employees.

9. If you model kindness, openness, and under-standing, even in the midst of hostility, narrowness and nonsense, trust is likely to be improved.

10. Trust can be improved in gradual stages. Solve one problem at a time.

11. Never take trust for granted.

Finally, where trust exists, it is sure to be one of the greatest assets possible to any manager. High trust is the greatest ingredient in spiritual management, and it begins by example.

One very fine day, a mother crab and her child were making their way along the beach; the mother crab was busy scolding her offspring.

"Why in the world, child, do you not walk as the other children do, forward instead of backward?"

"Mother dear," replied the little crab, "do but set the example yourself, and I will follow you."[11]

CENTRAL BELIEF SYSTEMS (CBS)

"I think you will find that [any great organization] owes resilience not to its form of organization or administrative skills, but to the power of what we call beliefs *. . . if an organization is to meet the challenge of a changing world, it must be prepared to change everything about itself except those beliefs. . . . Many things weigh heavily in success. But they are, I think, transcended by how strongly the people in the organization believe in its basic* precepts *and how faithfully they carry them out."* [12]

Thomas J. Watson

What do you think about the following three statements? Force yourself to agree or disagree.

Agree   Disagree

———   ———   - "We don't have time to discuss philosophy or ideals. We don't get on with the real work."

———   ———   - "Employees and other managers would laugh at belief or value systems; what they want is something practical."

———   ———   - "What we need is a guiding set of quotas, not philosophical guidance."

If you agree substantially with all of these statements, you probably also agree with most American managers. The majority of American managers want hard data; they want facts, rules, budgets, organizational structures, and strategies, but they do not seem to realize the importance of philosophies or value systems. They pride themselves on being tough minded and keeping professors and "philosophers" on track, and they regard even simple statements of organizational philosophy as vague and soft.

When one of the authors was a small boy, his father, who was a minister, preached a sermon titled, "An army with Banners is More Powerful Than One With Weapons." In spite of nuclear warfare, this may still be the case today for workplaces as well as armies. Although some generals and CEO's maintain that raw power over people, "kill ratios," and tables of numbers are more powerful than values or beliefs, we believe that in the long run there is more power in the direction and momentum of a Central Belief System (CBS). There are practical reasons for this.

SEVEN REASONS FOR A CENTRAL BELIEF SYSTEM (CBS)

1. **Performance**: Organizations with strong and well-practiced philosophies seem to outperform other workplaces. A study by Kennedy and Phillips showed that virtually all of the better performing companies which they looked at had a well defined set of beliefs. The institutions which performed less well had one of two qualities. Many had no coherent beliefs; others seemed to get charged up only for objectives which were quantified--i.e. financial. The paradox is that the workplaces which seemed most narrowly focused with precisely quantifiable objectives did not do as well as those with broader statements of purpose and quality.[13] Peters and Waterman believe that the main reason for this is that the organizations with real belief systems somehow impart zest to a vast majority of employees, whereas those with more narrow and precise objectives motivate the top employee, but do not reach down far enough with their motivation.[14]

2. **Adaptability**: There is likely to be adaptability to change when there is a deeply practiced common philosophy which includes the interests of employees and their society, as well as the organization. This may at first seem contradictory since many of us believe that people who have strong

common beliefs tend to be inflexible. This, of course, depends on the beliefs. What seems to happen is that while there is a solid commitment to the Central Belief System when it involves organizational goals, employee needs and the society, there is also a flexibility concerning the survival of these crucial aspects. Employees learn through their Central Belief System that the interest of themselves, the company and society are best served by changing some short term practices within the boundaries of the long term belief system. They learn how to be stable and flexible at the same time.

3. **Decision Making**: Decisions can be made independently in thousands of instances from just a few guides. While almost all workplaces have an "atmosphere" which results in certain decisions and behaviors, few have carefully thought out and integrated statements which are well known by employees, and which systematically guide the actions of employees on the assembly line as well as top executives. With an active Central Belief System (CBS), decision making can be made easier for more employees, and both productivity and job satisfaction can be raised.

4. **Cooperation and Coordination**: Simultaneously with this independence in decision making, there also seems to be a natural cooperation and coordination because people have agreed upon central values which have the best interests at heart of the employees and society. Without a CBS, employees are left to ferret out the value systems, and in the process they often learn to beat the work system rather than to join it. A positive and integrated set of ideals which is internalized by the "bottom" as well as the "top" persons in any institution is likely to add tremendous vigor to that organization.

5. **Long Range Plans**: These can be made more easily by focusing on relatively unalterable beliefs than on overriding concerns with short term financial objectives. Short term financial objectives can easily result in pursuits which may even undercut long term plans.

A Central Belief System can help to guide subtle and complex analyses of problems so that plans will be made for the long range as well as for the immediate future. The important elements are: (1) that there is a clear belief system, (2) that people who give input for long range goals share a common set of values and language, and (3) that people who are involved in decision making look at the many complexities of an issue.

6. **Socialization**: Employees can be systematically socialized to the values of the organization. Behaviors of employees are more likely to be consistently rewarded by different managers if there is a Central Belief System, than if individual managers are left to their own beliefs. This in turn can lead to more trust, inasmuch as some untrustworthiness seems to result from differences in aspects of socialization such as understanding, perception and values.

7. **Meaning**: Life can gain enriched meaning with a central philosophy. Ideals can become focused. Employees can grow and become more than they could otherwise by finding something bigger and more important than themselves to believe in. They can put their hearts and souls into endeavors which help the company as well as themselves. This is particularly crucial at a time when the influence of traditional institutions such as the family, church and community seems to be waning.

How to Build a Central Belief System

To build a Central Belief System, first look at a model to get an idea what some exemplary belief systems look like. Second, analyze eight fundamental ingredients. Third, beware of three general **pitfalls**. Fourth, **start writing** your CBS using three basic steps.

Look at a CBS Model for a School District

If you figure out what your organization stands for and then get 90% of your people to live by these values as described in a CBS, you can move mountains. Ouchi has printed several model company philosophies.[15] There are none, however, for public service organizations in any of the recent management bestsellers. Here is a Model Central Belief System which could be used as a model for non-profit institutions; it is particularly designed for school districts. In this model, we emphasize aspects of the best companies which are often overlooked in public service institutions. These are to treat students, parents and community members as though they are paying customers for a business, and to treat employees as though they are partners who want to be best, not simply public servants who have tenure and just want to get by.

CRONAN* SCHOOL DISTRICT CENTRAL BELIEF SYSTEM

INTRODUCTION

The central objective of the Cronan Unified School District is to be the best, and to be recognized as being best in providing education to students in a suburban school district with a diverse population. If we achieve this, all individuals in the district--both employees and citizens of the community--will share in this success because the achievements of any school district are the results of the combined work of employees and constituents.

For any institution to be great, it means that almost all workers are committed to working toward common objectives which are realistic, clearly understood by everyone, and which describe the institution's fundamental character. For a school district to be great, it means that students and parents will be treated as valuable clients, employees as precious resources, and the total community as a part of the main body of schools. It means also that both the immediate and long term success of individual students and of a democratic society will be sought.

STUDENTS AND PARENTS AS CLIENTS

- **Service**: All employees should treat students and parents with responsiveness, honesty and integrity as

*Denotes fictitious name.

though they are paying customers for a business enterprise.

- **Variety**: Education will be provided to meet the wide variety of existing individual student needs.

- **Basic Core**: A basic core of education will be provided for all students. This will meet the needs of democracy, individual career, self-development and environment. It will also include a heavy dose of "basic" subject skills such as critical thinking and responsibility to society as well as reading, writing, mathematics and technology.

- **Results Oriented and Hard Work**: Hard work and high results in student achievement are something for admiration and pride. Although the emphasis in education has often been on the process of teaching, we believe the main emphasis should be on the progress of the student.

EMPLOYEES

Trust, Creativity, Innovativeness and Initiative: These are perhaps the most important qualities in a workplace. The sky is the limit both in job satisfaction and productivity with them; without them, conflict, wasted energy and apathy are likely to result. All employees (managers and all others) are urged to help produce an atmosphere which encourages these traits.

Participation in Management: We want all employees to be involved and participating in their work at Cronan. We want not only for the district to care about employees, but for employees to care about their district. "Assumed responsibility" is urged. This is where when something needs to be done, employees assume responsibility to help get it done regardless of whose "formal" job it is.

Ethical Behavior: High standards of ethical behavior, including integrity and objectivity unencumbered by conflicting interests are expected.

Employee Development and Advancement: Opportunities to

develop full potential should be provided to all employees as much as possible. Even though it means that some employees will transfer to another district, advancement and development will be emphasized.

Better Ways: We want all employees to constantly look for new and better ways to do things and to help get these better ways into practice.

Enthusiasm: There is very little place for half-hearted people in a great organization. Both management and other employees are expected to be enthusiastic.

Humaneness and Fairness: The school district "must always be considered fair by the employee. Even though an employee may not consider his immediate superior or his associates fair, everything must be done to see that the employee knows by his own experience of others that the organization is always fair with its employees. . . . An individual with the least understanding of people can fire anybody if he has the authority, but it takes a confident individual with much tolerance, consideration and understanding of human beings to help an unfortunate employee to overcome a situation and develop that employee to a point where he will be a satisfied, happy and contented employee." [16]

MANAGEMENT

Freedom vs. Constraint: We want to foster the best initiative and creativity by allowing maximum freedom to act within the boundaries of Cronan's philosophy and goals. It is not the policy of Cronan to have a military-like organization, but rather to have clear overall goals which are agreed to, and then to give all people the greatest freedom possible in working toward those goals.

Develop Trust: A bulwark of Cronan's management belief system is to assume that all but a very small percentage of employees will respond very positively to trust and cooperation. "I got ya" kinds of management should never be practiced. Managers are to look for ways to help people, not to catch them.

Criticism: Managers must recognize, accept and correct their mistakes; they must be self-critical.

Openness: Constructive and open discussion, and even disagreement, on both problems and possibilities is invited among all employees, from top to bottom. Covering up of problems is not acceptable.

Organization and Details: Even though Cronan emphasizes creativity and innovation, detailed planning and organization are also essential to being the best.

Developing Subordinates: Site managers, in conjunction with district managers, are responsible for maximizing the development of their subordinates.

Teams: Outstanding team performance at Cronan is vital. There are three kinds of teams: (1) Formal-- i.e. the long term Secondary Principals' Council; (2) Informal Task Force Teams--i.e. the short term Teachers' Council on Improving Primary Education, and (3) Informal "Rise to the Occasion Teams"--i.e. an ad hoc group that sees a problem and gets together to solve it. Team objectives almost always take precedence over individual objectives. There will usually be a certain amount of ambiguity in the responsibility of teams under the principle of assumed responsibility. The reason for this is to rely on the principle of fast response and flexibility in dealing with problems and potential. The alternative would be to have long standing teams which would result in wasted time and money, static productivity and duplication of talents.

"Simultaneous Loose-Tight Properties": This is a term used by Peters and Waterman. It is one of their "eight basics" of excellent management. It describes the "co-existence of firm central direction and maximum individual autonomy."[17] Cronan is committed to this.

COMMUNITY, ENVIRONMENT AND CITIZENSHIP

It is recognized that any currently great workplace--even business--will be sensitive to the needs of the community and environment. In fact, the Dayton-Hudson Corporation even takes 5% of its federally taxable income to improve the quality of life in the communities they are a part of. Cronan emphasizes the following community beliefs:

Partners in Education: Business and industry, local non-profit organizations, and education have important common goals; we will work together to foster these through both formal and informal means.

Other Cooperation with Community: Cronan will work cooperatively with business, civic and government groups to improve the community environment; this includes joint use of recreational, fine arts and classroom facilities.

EIGHT FUNDAMENTAL INGREDIENTS IN A CENTRAL BELIEF SYSTEM

You've just read seven reasons for a CBS, and you've looked at a model for one. Now look at what we believe to be the most important major ingredients in any CBS.

When you write a Central Belief System, you should include at least something about (1) Customers or Clients, (2) Employees, (3) Management and (4) the Relationship of the Organization to Society and the Community. You should also work into the CBS a guiding philosophy about operating procedures and the character of the organization.

More specifically, Peters and Waterman name seven most important central areas in a values' system. These are: (1) being best, (2) the importance of details, (3) the importance of people, (4) superior quality and service, (5) innovation and its corollary, some failure, (6) informality and (7) growth and profits. [18]

We have chosen to describe the following eight ingredients of a CBS; we are not, however, suggesting that these eight items be included with a specific subtopic heading, as they are here, only that these ingredients should somehow find their way into your CBS.

1. **Excellence and Success**: The humanistic entrepreneur seeks equal success in both profit and people. These double targets are illustrated by Hewlett-Packard's "Statement of Corporate Objectives."

- Profit. "To achieve sufficient profit to finance company growth and to provide the resources we need to achieve our other corporate objectives."[19]

- Customers. "To provide products and services of the greatest possible value to our customers, thereby gaining and holding their respect and loyalty."[20]

Intel makes clear in several ways its commitment to both business and people success.

- Being Best. The first point that Intel makes in its belief statement is ". . . to be and be recognized as the best, the leader, #1, in both technology and business."[21] Further along in the "Intel Informal Culture" statement is found, "Intel is a results oriented company. The focus is on substance vs. form, quality vs. quantity."[22] ". . . a bottom line emphasis prevails. . . ."[23]

- People. "Commitments to customers are considered sacred." "We seek to create an environment that allows the employee to enjoy his/her work while achieving his/her goals."[24]

2. **Subjective Terms**: Instead of precise, objective descriptions, terms of quality are generally used. For example, Hewlett-Packard says, regarding "Fields of Interest," that their objective is, "To enter new fields only when the ideas we have, together with our technical, manufacturing and marketing skills, assure that we can make a needed and profitable contribution to the field."[25]

Intel Corporation organizes its Central Belief System around four main areas. These are: Technology/

Business, Management Style, Work Ethic/Environment and Teams. Under "Management Style" there is the statement that **Management is self-critical.** The leaders must be capable of recognizing and accepting their mistakes and to learn from them."[26]

These are all broad terms of ambition and excellence; they are not narrow descriptions of quantity.

3. **Transcending Purposes**: Central Belief Systems emphasize a transcendence over narrow or short term goals, and focus on "greater" purposes. An example of this is Intel's: "The concept of assumed responsibility is accepted. (If a task needs to be done, assume you have the responsibility to get it done.)"[27]

Delta Airlines with its "family feeling" even goes so far as to say, "At Delta, you don't just join an airline, you join an objective."[28]

4. **Tap the Talents and Vigor of Low Echelon Workers**: Once again, look at Intel's model. "We desire to have **all** employees involved and participative in their relationship with Intel. We want employees to care about their company. To aid in achieving this end, we stress good communication, and attempt to organize the company in smallest possible groups to allow a sense of identity and closeness."[29]

5. **Humaneness and Fairness**: Eli Lilly Co.'s "Basic Personnel Policies" state that employees must know that their company is fair. The Lilly statement goes on to describe that any manager can fire people, but only the confident, tolerant and understanding manager can help employees to develop self-fulfillment.[30]

6. **Creativity and Innovation**: Intel's "Informal Culture" says, Innovativeness and creativity are stressed in our technology, productivity and approach to the business. ... In some cases, this leads to high exposure to failure.[31] Hewlett-Packard's main objective for management is "To foster initiative and creativity, by allowing the individual great freedom of action in attaining well defined objectives."[32]

Implicit in both of these statements is the importance of employee job security, for if the organization wants broad creativity, it must also give broad protection for appropriate risks.

7. **Informality**: It's hard to see how much trust and on-line productivity can be maintained without a relatively high degree of informality. Intel's statement says, "Open (constructive) confrontation is encouraged at all levels of the corporation, and is viewed as a method of problem solving, conflict resolution. Hiding problems is not acceptable. Covert political activity is strongly discouraged."[33]

8. **Organization and Details**: No matter how creative an organization is, it will fail if there is not a high regard for what are sometimes called the nuts and bolts--organization and detail. Dayton-Hudson's philosophy describes how to maintain a balance between operating autonomy and flexibility by specifying the responsibilities of the following: (1) the corporation, (2) the operating companies, (3) the corporate staff and (4) what the corporation will insist on.[34]

Intel's statement says that "A high degree of organizational skills and discipline are demanded . . . and a high degree of planning is required."[35]

Summing Up Ingredients. Finally, regarding the ingredients of a Central Belief System, we believe that it must help to give meaning to people's lives, impetus to cooperation, standards for decision making and the rewarding behavior, and adaptability to change. If you're committed to those things, try a CBS, but beware of the pitfalls as outlined in the next section.

THREE GENERAL PITFALLS IN COMPOSING A CBS

1. **Authoritarians**: If you're an extremely authoritarian boss, don't even waste time trying to compose a Central Belief System, for in order for a CBS to work, there have to be basic feelings of security, trust, openness and cooperation.

2. **Objectives vs. CBS**: Don't confuse work objectives for a central belief system. Financial and other

quantifiable objectives are simply not a CBS.

3. **Beliefs only**: The mere description of beliefs is not to produce action. Ways to accomplish the belief must also be included in a Central Belief System--ways which can be understood and translated into action by all employees. People at the bottom of the organization as well as those at the top, must feel committed to the central belief system and be inspired by it on a daily basis. This requires some descriptions of how to make beliefs work which tie in with important values.

USE THREE BASIC STEPS TO COMPOSE A CENTRAL BELIEF SYSTEM

The three main steps in composing a Central Belief System are: (1) describe the present guiding principles for decision making, whether written or unwritten, (2) choose your 4-8 main areas of belief, and (3) write an integrated Central Belief System in language which matches the style and substance of your organization.

Step I: Describe Present Beliefs. First, determine what the organization's belief system is presently. This does **not mean** to describe what you **want** to value, but what you do value now. Do this by using the following exercise for the three areas of (a) significant decisions, (b) value contradictions, and (c) people values. While you're engaged in these three exercises, keep in mind how strategies are arrived at and carried out, how people communicate and what resources are available to carry out your organization's goals. You will also need to include all levels of employees in this; otherwise, you may come up with inaccurate descriptions.

a. Significant Decisions: List 3-5 significant decisions which have been made in your work organization in the last two years. Tell which have succeeded and which have not. Next, analyze the values which governed those decisions. For example, your company may have been faced with declining sales. In response to this, were people laid off rather indiscriminantely, were new markets found, were hours cut, or was some other solution found? How are long vs. short term dilemmas resolved? Is a balance sought which will involve central values of the organization, such as dilemmas which sometimes develop between job security for employees and profitability for the organization during slumps in business?

Decisions	Success or Failure	Inherent Values
1.		
2.		
3.		
4.		
5.		

   b. Value Contradictions: Identify 3-5 paradoxes of values in your organization. Find differences between what is written into goals, and what is actually practiced. Any organization, whether it be company or country, has some contradictions, such as preaching respect to employees and yet distrust in employees, emphasizing creativity and yet reinforcing dull routine, or stressing people over profits, and yet discovering that profits always take precedence. See how these inconsistencies are resolved. On which side of the paradoxes are the resolutions made?

Paradox	Resolution
1.	
2.	
3.	
4.	
5.	

   c. People Values: Look carefully at people values. Which practices of your company are clearly humanistic? Do you actually practice job security (not

indiscriminate protection of incompetents)? Are
promotions built more on short term exploitation that
long term cooperation? Do you find that people have
been rewarded who were cantankerous and adversarial as
long as they fought for their own narrow turf? Have
people been prized who hindered cooperation by a divide
to conquer attitude? Does your evaluation system
promote long term cooperation?

What are the roles of competition in your
organization? Are individuals likely to be pitted
against each other? Are serious jealousies considered
natural? Are rumors and gossip fed, or at least easily
allowed? How do winners emerge from competition? Are
they humble or arrogant? How often does the judging of
competition ever seem capricious? When competition **is**
used, to what extent are individuals most often pitted
against themselves, or groups against rather distant
groups, in order to lessen weakening distrust? How
important are trust and openness in your organization?

Now, name 3-5 strongly practiced people values.

1.

2.

3.

4.

5.

Step II: Choosing Areas of Major Beliefs. You've
looked at how decisions have actually been made on
important issues, what value contradictions exist, and
what people values are currently practiced and which
people values should be practiced. Now choose the
values you want to emphasize. At this point, you can
use one of several means to make the choices.

1. **Which Way to Choose.** At one end of the
continuum of choices, the owner of the company will
simply choose what to include. At the other end, all
levels of employees will have a chance go give input.

Still, whether initial values are chosen by the chief executive officer or the common employee, we believe that the important things are to make the connection of the organization with employees and society, and to include the eight fundamental ingredients of a CBS described in this section. It is also imperative that if the Board or top executives set the principles for a belief system that others in the organization debate, and help to shape those values as well as to accept them in the end.

2. <u>Idealized Image</u>. Karen Horney, the famous New York psychologist, popularized this phrase in regard to individuals in the 1950's. In the 1980's, this is an important part of the workplace. What is your idealized image? With some companies there are certain singular themes which clearly stand out. Delta Airlines stresses "Service" and "Family Feeling." IBM emphasizes respect for individuals, customer service, and excellence. Hewlett-Packard makes clear that job security and service to customers and society are top priorities.

<u>**Step III: Writing Your CBS**</u>. Whether the wording is formal or informal, language is a function of the style of the organization itself. Intel has a statement which reflects informality; in fact, the title is even "Informal Culture."[36] At Intel, conversation clearly reflects this informality with the first names being the order of the day. On the other hand, IBM has a more formal statement, and in IBM, last names are frequently used, prefaced by Mr. and Mrs. even in conversation. Both companies are outstanding in productivity and humane emphases.

The Central Belief System statement should never be too long nor complex. It should be internally consistent, and it should emerge as a simple yet eloquent description of what the organization stands for.

IMPLEMENTING A CENTRAL BELIEF SYSTEM: SIX CRUCIAL ELEMENTS

There are six crucial elements in implementing and making a belief system work.

1. **Manager Modeling**: If a humanistic belief system is to work there has to be a congruence between values and actions, and this congruence must begin with modeling by managers. The late Mayor La Guardia was one manager who modeled his values. He also liked to keep in contact with the various departments of his city government by trying his hand at lower level jobs.

One winter evening, he decided to fill in for the judge at a night court. A poor, nervous man had been charged with the theft of some bread. The man said the reason he had stolen was that his family was starving.

La Guardia fined him ten dollars, declaring that he had to fine him as he could not make any exceptions to the law. As he passed sentence, however, he put $10.00 of his own money in his own hat and passed it around the courtroom. The tearful father was sent home with $47.50.

Managers who are not worried about a false dignity of their position can find it easy to move about in this way. These managers are not afraid to try their talents at low level jobs again. They're not just mayor, or vice president of this or that; they're human, and they're part of the team.

2. **Looking at Complexities Through Clear General Goals**: This is a second ingredient in implementing a CBS. General standards for actions and decisions must be clear, well-known by all levels of employees, and broad enough to cover many situations. But the really important thing is to get people looking at the many complexities involved in organizational decision making through these general goals. All people should be aware of the basic ramifications of actions, and how these may affect resources, people, politics or profits.

3. **Psychological Responsibilities**: The third crucial element in making a CBS work is difficult to define. Still, psychological responsibilities need to be understood by managers and employees. These psychological responsibilities include trust, cooperation, openness and mutual support and mutual

define. Still, psychological responsibilities need to
be understood by managers and employees. These
psychological responsibilities include trust,
cooperation, openness and mutual support and mutual
accountability. In a sense, psychological responsibility can be summed up as a willingness to go the
second mile to help.

If people only work on the basis of precise items
in job descriptions, the company loses productivity and
employees lose deep rewards of excitement from
creativity and helping others. Going the second mile
means transcending mere job descriptions. When this is
done, psychological responsibilities are taking over.
While they are not things that can be precisely
described, measured, nor demanded, if they are not
focused on, they will fail to be much used. If they
are little used, employees, organization and society
suffer in the long run.

4. **Employee Control and Enthusiasm**: One of the
fundamental reasons for having a CBS is to maximize
employee energy, but if enthusiasm and initiative are
to be unleashed, there must be maximum employee control
to accomplish clear goals for which employees are
accountable. The more freedom you can give people to
do a clear job the way they want to do it, and the
fewer narrow expectations you cramp them with, the more
satisfaction they'll usually get from it, and the more
excellent results you will ordinarily get.

Employee control means reinforcing work climates
in which employees have the freedom to get the
information **they** need and to act on it, not the
information someone else may erroneously think they
need.   The famous mathematician Einstein, when
questioned as to how many feet are in a mile, replied
that he didn't know and didn't want to clutter his
mind with that kind of information when he could easily
get the information, should it be needed.

If you are a manager who messes with the processes
of your employees by having narrow expectations, you
probably also limit their productivity. One of the
best ways to get enthusiasm is to give your employees
esteem by giving them control. As you communicate that

5. **Connections**: A Central Belief System is not likely to mean much unless it integrates the major aspect of employees' lives. We believe that if the basic needs of any of the following three groups-- employee, organization and society--are not met, an imbalance occurs which in the long run results either in excessive apathy or aggression, neither of which is beneficial to any of the groups. Therefore, as a balance in meeting these needs is addressed in a belief statement, and then carried out, the better off all groups will be.

6. **Trust**: Only in an atmosphere of basic trust and cooperation will it be possible for a Central Belief System to become dynamic.

EVALUATING PROGRESS, AND DETERMINING WHERE TO GO FROM A CENTRAL BELIEF SYSTEM POINT OF VIEW

Once a year managers and employees need to sit down and answer honestly the following four questions:

1. Where were we?

2. Where are we now?

3. How well have we done?

4. Where do we need to go by when?

These questions need to be answered simply and with candor for all major goals. Here is an easy-to-use form which will be effective if you're honest.

CENTRAL BELIEF SYSTEM EVALUATION FORM

Major Goals (Simple & Short)	Where were we two years ago?	Where are we now?	Self Rating 1 -3 -5 - 10 Low High	Where do we go by when?

MAINTAINING A CENTRAL BELIEF SYSTEM

A Central Belief System does not, of course, simply have a life of its own without nurturing. In outstanding organizations you find top managers going about preaching the "gospel" and celebrating the pursuit of the "truth" whenever they see it. This is done much as a dynamic evangelist or priest. When it happens, well it is spiritual management at its best. The Central Belief System is taught. Its merits are extolled. Stories, epigrams, and myths are used to create enthusiasm, to encourage exuberance, and to make work an exciting place. High priests of management become not sad purveyors of cold liturgy, but harbingers of hope, joy and cooperation.

A Central Belief System seems at first glance to be somewhat intangible. It's not tightly quantifiable. The temptation is to not give it much attention. Yet, if you don't, the important qualities and elements will probably fail to be used much. On the other hand, if they are described, they are likely to be understood and used in very subtle ways, and to be springboards for revolutionary productivity.

The ultimate test of your Central Belief System will be how well it will promote service to customers, self-fulfillment of employees through creativity and accomplishment, technical efficiency, and responsibility to the total society it serves. Herein lies the paradox. Although your belief system will have somewhat soft and ambiguous principles, it should have hard and ambitious results.

PARTICIPATORY MANAGEMENT (PM)

Participatory management (PM) is an idea whose time has come in America. "Society's centralized institutions whose very existence relied upon hierarchies [are] crumbling everywhere."[37] Rigid hierarchies, which were once consonant with the industrial economy, are badly out of tune in today's information economy. Employees at all levels of the organization are changing. They are younger, better educated, need to be convinced rather than commanded, want to be heard, are pressing for job security, and demand shared decision making. These workers have been raised to take seriously the idea of participatory democracy. New management structures are being based on informality and equality. In addition, we are in face to face competition with Japanese workers who are clustered into decentralized, participatory decision making work groups, and we're not faring well in this competition.

P M describes the process of people who are a part of decision making, in one way or another. Whatever the form used, P M provides for broad dissemination and sharing of information and values, as well as to symbolize the cooperative intent of an organization. It is also important to realize that in American workplaces, although the decision making may be collective, the ultimate responsibility for decisions usually resides in one person.

Although the concept of P M is frustrating to some American managers, it **can** be extremely helpful in increasing employee satisfaction and productivity, lowering absence rates, and in promoting receptivity to changes. The problem is how to get it to work for you

rather than to be merely another fad. First, analyze
the present state of your workplace. Second, look at
critical attributes of P M. Third, consider why P M
doesn't work. Fourth, internalize some principles for
making it work. Fifth, read about two forms of
practice--quality circles and management teams.

HOW MUCH P M DO YOU ALREADY HAVE?

P M has been bewildering to many American
managers. Some have conscientiously tried it,
following specific guidelines, and found that it didn't
work. Other managers have never tried to follow
specific guides for P M, but they nevertheless have
always practiced it. What is the difference? Place
your workplace on the following continuum to get an
idea.

Low P M   High P M

1. If we let employees   Employees can always   Our company is
   change that deci-   make suggestions,   structured so that a
   sion, we might as   but we have to be   review of all
   well never try to   careful not to waste   policies is invited.
   enforce anything   a lot of time   We always listen
   again!   listening to many   carefully to what
                            ideas.   employees say, even
                                                      when it comes to
                                                      criticizing existing
                                                      policy, for we might
                                                      be able to improve
                                                      in this way. Change
                                                      is not necessarily
                                                      vacillation.

1   2   3   4   5   6   7   8   9   10

2. Employees will misuse information, so it's counterproductive to try to get much indepth agreement on goals.

We'd like for people to understand, but after all, this is a workplace, not a school. We expect agreement on quotas, but not necessarily on goals.

There is constantly an indepth emphasis on people understanding each other and the reasons for decisions. A consensus on goals is considered paramount.

1   2   3   4   5   6   7   8   9   10

3. We have aggressive competition, and naturally, employees and managers are very cautious about whom they tell what.

We expect managers to fight hard for their own decisions even if it means not always leveling with other managers, for the top executives can pull in the reigns when needed.

Employees feel free to be themselves, because our company is structured in such a way as to reduce to a minimum the potential for employees to harm each other, even in competition.

1   2   3   4   5   6   7   8   9   10

4. Some employees seem to sabotage decisions.

Most employees support company decisions.

All employees support decisions regardless of whether or not they prefer them, because the decisions have been arrived at in open and fair ways.

1   2   3   4   5   6   7   8   9   10

Low P M   High P M

5. Top managers make   There are various   There is always a
   the decisions,   opportunities for   genuine attempt to
   because they're   people to be   get people who will
   responsible for   involved in P M.   be the recipients
   them.   If they don't take   of decisions
                          the opportunity   involved in the
                          that's tough.   process.

   1   2   3   4   5   6   7   8   9   10

6. We promote a strict   Employees should   We promote a feeling
   hierarchy of manage-   have a feeling that   of egalitarianism,
   ment, for this is   they count, but they   reinforcing that
   the only way that   should also know   very few managers
   things can get done.   their place.   are totally superior
                                                    to their employees,
                                                    but that each
                                                    employee and manager
                                                    has some superior
                                                    ability.

   1   2   3   4   5   6   7   8   9   10

7. There is a feeling   There is more   There is a feeling
   of short-term   emphasis on short-   of collective, long-
   individualism.   term action than on   term responsibility,
                          long-term ramifica-   as well as of
                          tions of the action.   independence and
                                                    energetic activity.

   1   2   3   4   5   6   7   8   9   10

Now that you've assessed how much P M you already have, look at three reasons for why P M has a difficult time in America.

First, when trust, high similarity of goals, and egalitarianism do not exist, genuine P M cannot work. In the last decade, as P M has become popular, many managers have installed it, most often by the name of team management, and then see it fail. Time and time again, managers have been disillusioned, saying something like, "I followed the check list." "I did everything it said." "It's just another fad that doesn't work." The problem is that the critical ingredients were missing. Once again, a pervasive problem of American managers was probably illustrated-- the preoccupation with technical aspects of management to the relegation of the really important spiritual aspects.

Another reason that P M has been difficult to install in Western society involves a paradox. Although we Americans say we're committed to democracy, our workplaces tend to be very undemocratic. "There is a fundamental mismatch between the traditional love of personal liberty and the top-down, authoritarian manner in which the American workplace has operated. Employees habitually surrender the most basic rights to free speech and due process at work each day."[38]

Still another reason for P M's difficulty has to do with the American manager's idealized image of a Type A Manager who jumps off jets, marches into meetings and demands fast action. The Japanese manager, on the other hand, tends to idealize the decision maker as a man who can resist the drive for closure until he really sees what's required. The Japanese image permits deeper perception.

What to do? There are four critical attributes and at least eleven important principles for effective P M.

Four Critical Attributes

1. Trust

If P M is to work, participants have to feel that others are not out to harm them. When we replace excessive selfishness, exploitation and hostility with synergistic cooperation and trust building, participative decision making has a good chance to follow. Until then, it will only be a mechanical exercise. The first prerequisite for P M is for the manager to convey a conviction of trust in employees.

2. Consensus of Goals

Everyone knows that the main objective in the workplace is work and productivity, and that there are two basic approaches to productivity. One is to monitor and produce. The other is to get employees themselves to be autonomous, to work hard and to cooperate. When employees are autonomous, however, with explicit forms of supervision minimal, the problem is how to ensure high self-discipline. The main danger is, of course, that self interest will result in off task, selfish behavior, rather than energetic and cooperative behavior. One critical answer to this problem lies in developing a **consensus of goals**, for as people genuinely buy into common goals, they are also likely to buy into a commitment to cooperate with one another to reach those goals. The major mechanism for getting this unity of goals is P M.

3. Egalitarianism

This is the third critical part of P M. While traditional hierarchical management promotes elitism, segmented relationships and distrust, P M promotes holistic relationships, which encourage egalitarianism. Very few managers are totally superior to their employees, and we all know this. What hierarchical management does, however, is to make believe that this is so. That in itself causes distrust and disdain. On the other hand, with P M, the implications are that each participant has some superior abilities and that workers are to be trusted to pursue the goals of the organization without close supervision. Critical to these implications is Argyris' argument that the individual and organization must be integrated.

4. COLLECTIVE RESPONSIBILITY AND ACCOUNTABILITY

One of the past aspects of the workplace has been that of a dichotomy between those who wielded the power and those who acquiesced. This meant that executives took responsibility for production and people, and workers let others control their lives. No longer is this division so clear. Employees are increasingly less willing to give up power to someone else, and many are desirous of accepting more responsibility themselves. But regardless of the willingness to accept responsibility, if P M is to work, collective responsibility has to be a critical part of the process.

ELEVEN PRINCIPLES FOR P M

1. While P M may take many forms, from simply touching base with employees to elaborate systems of structural input and decision making, the bottom line is that employees who will be affected by a decision must have some way to give real input into the decision before it is made.

2. Managers should model personal traits such as unselfishness, cooperation and empathy.

3. Restrictions on the use of P M should be minimal, for they have a dampening effect.

4. P M won't usually work very well for the manager who seems to be weak, for P M then appears to be a cop-out from making decisions or accepting responsibility. P M is likely to make indecisive "democratic" managers seem even weaker than they might actually be.

5. P M is likely to become an empty gesture for the manager who uses it superficially, or to manipulate.

6. Managers can enhance the chances of P M by giving freedom for various and sundry items such as:

allowing workers to choose with whom they will work; reinforcing openness in channels of communication and employees' discussion of problems with their supervisors; allowing group discussions, and giving as much local autonomy as possible according to how "mature" the employees are.

7.   It is best to stay away from votes in trying to get consensus, for votes can be decisive and curiously unrepresentative. In place of votes, try getting consensus by means such as the Quaker or Delphi Techniques. In the Quaker method, disagreements are shelved without a present decision; later, consensus is attempted. With Delphi, issues are handled by questionnaire and collation of responses through three or four attempts to get a forced consensus. In the Delphi technique, people do not have much opportunity to get egos involved in defensive stances, for responses are anonymous. The emphasis is on creative and cooperative problem solving in both methods.

8.   Simple rules for P M should be known and agreed upon.

9.   Sensitivity for participants is, of course, a must.

10.   The limitations of team management should be recognized.

For example, try to get understandings that, even with the best democratic team management, there will still be quite a bit of evaluation and decision making by the leaders, but that managers will do their best to live by the spirit of team management summed up in the fundamental principles above.

11.   In the final analysis, democratic participative management is a matter of degree, not of something clear-cut vs. autocratic or laissez-faire management. It is a deep commitment to the principle of the thing.

QUALITY CIRCLES AND MANAGEMENT TEAMS

Management teams have been popular for the last

decade. Quality circles are just beginning to be considered widely. Whereas quality circles tend to be made up of on-the-spot workers, management teams tend to include managers and representatives of employee groups. Quality circles generally focus on the micro while keeping the macro in mind; management teams usually concern themselves with the macro while keeping the micro in mind. Both Quality Circles and Management Teams **should** make decisions that improve the quality of their lives on the job as well as to improve the quality of their products.

Regarding the general concept of teams, there is a sort of American ambivalence. On the one hand, we enthusiastically embrace the concept of teams. We glue ourselves to the T.V. screen when our favorite baseball or football teams are playing. We also join clubs, churches and unions in droves, indicating our need to be a part of a group or team. On the other hand, we prize rugged individualism. This ambivalence may help to explain some of the problems with management teams. While we proudly proclaim that so and so is a good team player, we also tend to think of membership in any group as somewhat confining, and constricting of individual freedom.

Maybe one of the problems is that we need to understand more clearly what management teams or groups can do for us. They can help us to get high quality decisions on complex problems by getting several frames of reference. Morale and commitment can be raised. Productivity can be improved. People can feel "in" on things, and feelings of isolation can be reduced. Employees can be coordinated rather subtly and wastage of energy from going off in different directions can be reduced.

Perhaps most important of all, teams and groups can allow subtle intimacy among people which permits deep emotions without embarrassing expression of these complex thoughts and feelings. It all depends on how the manager in charge handles things. If, for example, the manager in charge has a sort of "cheerleader mentality," both thoughts and feelings can easily be rather surprisingly stifled, as members of the team are likely to engage in surface level bantering and barbing, while sub-surface fears inhibit all-out constructive energies. On the other hand, if the manager has deep insight, is unafraid of deep feelings and intimacy, and is dedicated to high synergy, the stage is set for employees to release the highest kinds of individual creative energies as well as group participation. Far from constricting individual talents, personal contributions of the greatest kind are likely to be given.

QUALITY CIRCLES

One of the emerging forms of P M is called a quality circle (QC), famous because of its success in Japan. Ironically, American management consultants have tried to get U.S. managers to accept this idea for about 30 years. But American managers have failed to adopt it because it seemed to waste time and not to go directly to the heart of simply working and getting on with the job in precisely measurable ways.

A quality circle is generally considered to be a small group of about 10 workers who do similar work and meet to discuss and solve work-related problems. According to the Japanese Productivity Center, there are 6 million Japanese participating in more than 600,000 quality circles. Although the idea has been slow to catch on in America, it is beginning to become more widespread than it has been in the past.

The basic principle behind Q.C.'s is that the person performing a particular job is the one most expert in that job. What Q.C.'s are not, Honeywell managers point out, is a quick fix for problems. "Teams are a long-term commitment to a change in management style, not a short-term program."[39]

MANAGEMENT TEAMS

Management teams, in one form or another, have existed for a long time. In the past, they often promoted fear or elitism, as they were driven relentlessly by intense competitive pressures from a blood and guts type of chief executive officer. In the last decade, however, a different concept of management team has become popular as many CEO's have tried to bring in a "people" orientation. This included attempting to make it seem like there was a humanistic orientation, when what was really happening was a rather gross manipulation of one kind or another.

The kind of management team we are proposing includes decentralizing power and decision making, consulting subordinates on decisions even when they are centrally finalized, and striving to get unshakable information in humanistic ways. It includes emphasizing mutual support among managers and informal management team huddles when the need arises, in addition to regularly scheduled meetings. It stresses management styles which promote respect and agreeable disagreement rather than belittling conflict. It focuses on trusting peoples' motives, information and actions. And, even though the bottom line is results, the personal satisfaction and development of team members is equally important. Although checks and balances are constantly sought among team members, this is done in such a way as to give the feeling that everyone is searching for "truth," and what is right, rather than digging for the gossip and how someone is wrong.

An example of who should be on a school district management team, and what they should do, follows:

MODEL FOR A SCHOOL DISTRICT MANAGEMENT TEAM

WHO SHOULD BE ON THE MANAGEMENT TEAM

Superintendent

Selected other central office administrators

Selected principals and assistant principals

Selected classified supervisors (if not in a negotiating supervisory unit)

Selected confidential employees

WHAT THE MANAGEMENT TEAM SHOULD DO

Give input to the superintendent for district

goals, policy and decision making

Help to establish priorities and organize tasks to accomplish Board goals

Plan management inservice

Sharpen management skills through informal contacts and discussion as well as through more formal inservice activities

Take turns attending and observing Board meetings (non-cabinet level managers)

STEPS IN ESTABLISHING P.M., Q.C., OR OTHER FORMS OF TEAM MANAGEMENT

1. Look at your own style of management to determine if you can be comfortable with the Critical Attributes as well as the Eleven Principles of P M. Are you able to turn over responsibility to others? Are you willing openly to accept that some subordinates are superior to you in certain ways? Are you ready to form a true partnership with your employees? Are you committed to openness and trust? If you answer no, or if you have less that total commitment to any of these questions, failure is likely.

2. Learn all you can about P M, Q.C.'s, or other team management forms. Read at least 2 books which explain the theory behind team management--books such as **The Art of Japanese Management**, and **Theory Z**, in search of excellence and a passion for excellence.

3. Consider hiring a consultant who would:

   -- Give advice on planning and establishment.

   -- Train you and your staff in data gathering, setting priorities and problem solving methods.

   -- Objectively assess the quality of your commitment as well as time, energy and resources necessary.

4. Involve your staff in planning team or Q.C. activities.

5. Form voluntary Q.C. teams.

6. Train Q.C. or team members.

7. Establish a Q.C. or team committee to guide the Q.C.'s; one member should be from the union.

8. Implement with established meeting times and places.

9. Keep the following pitfalls especially in mind:

   -- Too little planning and training.

   -- Excessively high expectation.

   -- Too little time allocated for meetings.

   -- Making meetings on an "as needed" basis, (they must be regular).

   -- Seldom use team or Q.C. recommendations.

   -- Unclear role of team or Q.C. to you, your staff, or team members.

   -- Trying to use Q.C. or teams to manipulate.

FINALLY: SPIRITUAL MANAGEMENT IS FUNDAMENTAL TO PRODUCTIVITY

We believe that reaching a breakthrough productivity requires pervasive trust, real participatory management, and a strongly practiced Central Belief System. These are the backbone of spiritual management. We also believe, however, that spiritual management should be an important part of everything that a manager does in dealing with people. For that reason, this whole book is devoted to spiritual management; this chapter simply describes three of its fundamental features.

II

COMMUNICATION

"Communication is the lifeblood of every organization. When the communication flow through the various channels of the organization is smooth and effective, the organization "health" is usually good. When the channels are faulty, and the flow is inadequate, or interrupted, however, the organization suffers in a variety of ways."[1]

Norman Sigband

Introduction

John Naisbitt, author of **Megatrends**, points out that important trends of the 1980's include movements toward more information, more interdependence, more technology, more multiple options, more participatory democracy, and self-help networking. All of these trends embody a need for increased and caring communication.[2] That's what this chapter is all about.

Although we live in an information society, flooded by messages, media and talking machines, we often fail miserably to really communicate. Real communication is perceiving what others are trying to say and conveying our own messages clearly. It involves actions and reactions as people talk and listen to each other. It is not just the technical sending and receiving of messages through writing, reading, speaking and hearing; but it also means interpreting words, voice inflections and non-verbal expressions of the speaker, as well as listening to our own internal emotions and experiences which cause us to perceive things as we do. Communication is immensely complex, involving all our senses as they center in our perceptions, expectations and expressions.

While it is not our intent in this book comprehensively to cover the total field of organizational communication, we do not want to emphasize how to communicate with others in your workplace so that mutual understanding and mutual benefits are likely to result. These "how to's" will focus on perceptions, expectations, speech and listening.

Perception is included because being skilled in how and what people perceive is critical to communication and getting things done through others. Expectations are included because one of the more important aspects of the modern work force is its diversity of expectations, and until this heterogeneity is understood, the dilemma between the needs for individuality and commonality cannot be solved. Speech is added because it always has a central place in communication. Listening is a part of this chapter because it is crucial to modern management, and because even though it comprises about 65% of the average manager's total work time,[3] it has been given very little attention in most management training.

PERCEPTIONS ARE NOT JUST PASSIVE: THEY ARE FUNDAMENTAL TO ACTION

If there is to be a science of interpersonal behavior, it will rest on the cornerstone of discovering . . . how people come to perceive others as they do.[4]

Bruner and Taguiri

As a manager, you either make things happen (or you don't)) through the efforts of other people. You have to be skilled in dealing with their perceptions. This means talking, listening, and even laughing together. The psychologists call this interpersonal behavior. Two psychologists, Bruner and Taguiri, who have studied interpersonal behavior extensively, say in their **Handbook on Social Psychology**, that "if there is to be a science of interpersonal behavior, it will rest on the cornerstone of discovering . . . how people come to perceive others as they do." Part and parcel of perceptions are expectations. If this is true, it would seem that the place to begin predicting, changing and channeling others' behavior is with their perceptions.

How Do You Comprehend?

Begin your study of perceptions by looking first at how you yourself apprehend things. Count the F's in this passage:

> FINISHED FILES ARE THE RESULT
> OF YEARS OF SCIENTIFIC STUDY
> COMBINED WITH THE EXPERIENCE
> OF MANY YEARS[5]

Most people find only three F's when there are actually six. This is because we tend to read phonetically, and the F's at the ends of words are not pronounced. The problem is that all of us have scotomas. This is a sensory exclusion of certain aspects of our environment, based on conditioning and prior experience. You've learned to read phonetically, and you therefore tend to exclude some F's in this exercise.

Continue looking at how you perceive. Think about your watch, but don't look at it. Take half a minute to write down everything about your watch underneath the crystal that you can remember. Write words, numbers, colors and symbols. Now, look at your watch and see how you've done. Are you beginning to smile? Be honest. Did you forget the name of your watch? You may have had your watch for 20 years and forgotten the name or words on your watch. How about colors? Did you write down that you had twelve numbers and found that you had none?

Mistakes in this simple illustration can happen to anyone. What this illustrates is that you pay considerable attention to certain things and very little to others. This process is actually governed by a group of cells at the base of your brain called the reticular activating system. Based on what your past experience, values and goals are, you either screen in, or block out, the information you receive. You literally see what you're looking for, you lock on, then lock out.

Wayne Dyer, in **Your Erroneous Zones**, wrote about the speaker who set out to show a group of alcoholics that drink was harmful. She put a worm in a jar of water and promptly it writhed its way to the top. She then put a worm in a jar of undiluted alcohol and it died at once. With satisfaction, the crusader said, "See, what does that tell you?" An alcoholic quickly replied, "You don't get worms if you drink."[6] To varying degrees, we all sift out that which we don't want to perceive. We expect what we perceive and perceive what we expect; and in the process, we simply give meaning, even if false, to puzzling facts. But inaccurate perceptions are not simply academic, they are fundamental to action, and are therefore of utmost importance to managers, be they in business or public service.

In New York, black residents began the Harlem riots ostensibly because there was an incorrect assumption that a black cab driver had been killed by a white policeman. In another city, a high school was closed for extensive repairs as a result of a riot begun by white students. This riot was sparked by a false rumor that a white girl had been raped by a black student. Many of us also make perceptual errors by focusing objective facts to fit our existing beliefs. The result can, at the least, hinder effective problem solving, and at the most, plunge people into chaos, and lives into injury or death.

Yet another illustration of how we filter our perceptions occurred in a large school district in California where the teachers' union went out on strike because at the height of salary negotiations, the superintendent was mistakenly reported to have said, "Let the teachers clean the toilets if they want as much salary raise as the custodians."

HOW DO YOU DISTORT INFORMATION?

The first point of these illustrations is that we

screen what we perceive on the basis of our experiences, values and goals. The second point is that at the very best distorted perceptions can cause interesting arguments, and at the worst, wreak havoc. Most of us cannot have conflicting beliefs on the subconscious level, so we filter information so as to resolve the conflict. If we are to get better data, we need to know something about the ways we distort information through four kinds of thought filters.[7] These are:

1. **Forcing meaning, even if false, on puzzling facts.** This is illustrated by teachers who were about to strike finding it easy to believe the utterly erroneous report that the superintendent had said, "Let the teachers clean the toilets."

2. **Forcing facts to fit existing beliefs.** This happened when the drunk said, "You don't get worms if you drink."

3. **Playing down threatening information, and making the complex simple, often with either/or fallacies.** When the riot began from a false rumor that a white girl had been raped by a black student, this filter was operating.

4. **Emphasizing or exaggerating data which supports our own beliefs.** All of the above examples illustrate the operation of this filter.

You have no doubt thought to yourself while reading about these filters that all four often operate at the same time. You can also see that when even one filter is "locked in", you may be locking out profitable data. As part of beginning to understand these filters, look at how your subconscious accepts, stores and acts on information.

Your subconscious is a data storage bank. It stores your filtered information as "truth" and "reality." It stores your habits--all of your over-learned skills--such as the way you manage employees, relate to your spouse, play tennis, or close a sale.

Your subconscious is like a robot which has information, and then carries out tasks according to your beliefs, values and goals. Everything that your senses pick up is run through a feedback loop that is your subconscious data base. You then associate data that you accept with "truth" and "reality."

We are all creatures of habit. We tend to shop at the same stores and to listen to people with similar views. There is, of course, nothing wrong with this, except that there is a tendency to lock on to old viewpoints and to lock out accurate perceptions and new opportunities. If we are really to make things happen through other people, we do it by understanding how they perceive. This requires the ability to constantly look at the world openly, freely and differently.

Merely understanding this theory that you've just read can help to reduce perceptual errors. But perceptual distortions cling so tightly to most people that managers need to do even more. So next, we will look at strategies which can help further to reduce perceptual errors.

WHAT CAN YOU DO TO REDUCE PERCEPTUAL ERRORS?

Most managers spend many hours each day dealing, sometimes unsuccessfully, with problems of distorted and conflicting perceptions. The superintendent who said, "when the teachers' union calls a strike, it shows that they don't really care about kids," fell easily into the trap of distorting data with all four perceptual filters. He gave false meaning to puzzling facts. He forced objective facts to fit his existing beliefs. He tried to make very complex feelings of teachers into something overly simple. And he exaggerated the feelings of teachers against administrators. By falling into these distorting traps, he contributed to the problem rather than a solution.

You can help to eliminate distortions by (1) freeing tensions in interaction and communication; and (2) developing bases of common information.

Free Interaction In These Eight Ways

Tension usually complicates communication and perception. See if any of the following eight techniques can help to decrease tension and increase free-flowing interaction and communication.

1. **Respect.** There is usually a circle in which feelings, tensions, and inaccurate perceptions are connected. The more inferior one feels, the more tension there is, and the more distorted are the perceptions. This cycle of tension to poor perception and back around to tension again is often made worse by managers who fall into the traps either (1) of trying to convince people of their errors, or (2) of avoiding the problem of error altogether. Both traps tend to result in employee frustration.

To break the cycle and start building better perceptions, try focusing intently on inaccurate perceivers, building their self-respect, and **then** working subtly on their perceptual and communication problems.

2. **Being "Democratic."** A classic study from Frankel-Brunswick revealed that "democratic-prone" children were more accurate in perceiving and in relating stories to newcomers in a community than were "autocratic-prone" children. Youths whose home lives were characterized by authoritarian attitudes were relatively prejudiced and inaccurate in their perceptions. When they remembered a story, they tended to describe qualities of all the newcomers as undesirable even when they were not. The authoritarian children remembered only one side of a story and they tended to emphasize the parts of the story which conformed with preconceived attitudes.[8]

The point of the story for managers is that if you do not create a climate among your employees of freedom to speak easily, if you do not dignify even their "dumb" statements with understanding, you will not get the information and cooperation you need. Many employees are kept from communicating with you if you communicate to them somehow that you are "autocratic prone," and you will lose valuable input as a result.

Be a "democratic" manager who gives license to question and to be free from fear.

3. **Well Informed People.** "Feeling in" on things is ordinarily more important to employees than wages or good working conditions. People are down on what they're not up on. Keeping people informed can do much to take the defensiveness or hostility (arising from rejection) out of people, and indirectly to free them for more accurate perceptions.

4. **Span of Control.** A modern researcher named Mazor found that perceptions were more likely to be accurate in organizations where bosses had smaller spans of control than where spans of control were larger.[9] The critical factor seems to be that mutual interaction is freer, more open, and less complicated in the "smaller span" organizations. In "large span" workplaces you can, of course, either compensate by attention to dialogue, or you can reduce "spans" through organizational devices such as a department head system. In either case, communication which is warm and non-manipulative is obviously easier to achieve in smaller spans.

5. **Judgment, Complexity and Action.** An old Indian adage says, "Grant that I may not judge another until I have walked six moons in his moccasins." Even when situations demand immediate action, they do not necessarily require premature judgments. Former Secretary of State Dean Rusk once observed, "The beginning of wisdom is a respect for complexity." As you develop the ability to convey to your subordinates that you understand many of the complexities behind what they're saying and doing, as well as what they are in actual fact saying and doing, you increase your chances of getting input from them, for people like to talk to someone who deeply understands them (unless they're trying to fool you).

6. **Self-Knowledge and Acceptance.** This is important in developing accurate perceptions because it helps you to transcend prejudices. Among many techniques and systems now available for increased self-knowledge is some form of meditation. Allowing the entire mind and body to relax, not to analyze, not

to worry, and not to control but simply **to be**, is an important aspect of self-knowledge and openness to improved perspective.

Another important ingredient in self-knowledge is the checking of your self-perceptions with other people, trying to get at not only unshakable facts, but also multifaceted subjective opinions. Using meditation or introspection **only** can easily result in insularity and inaccurate perceptions of yourself, but the interaction and exchange of ideas can help you keep introspection and external perceptions in balance.

7. **Laughter.** One of the best ways to free interaction is through humor, as long as the laughter is unhostile. The problem is, however, that much humor contributes to tense rather than free communication, because it is aggressive and pokes fun at others in ways which hurt communication more than to help it. Humane managers, on the other hand, are often like Abraham Lincoln, who is said never to have laughed at jokes that hurt other people, but rather to have had a thoughtful, philosophical sense of humor. His humor probably elicited a smile more often than a laugh, was intrinsic to a situation rather than added to it, and was spontaneous rather than planned.

One of the authors subscribes to Orben's Current Comedy. About once a month, a four page bulletin of up-to-date one liners is received. This is a great help to freeing minds for communication. One example is, "What is one of the best signs of a recession?" "It's when you see a plumber's truck in your driveway and hope that your wife is having an affair."[10]

8. **Using Status for Better Perception and Cooperation.** Certain differences in status tend to result in different perceptions. High-status persons are likely to be thought of as **having** to cooperate. Thus, you might help low-status persons to overcome defensiveness by being warm and involving them in tasks at which they can succeed. At the same time, take care to develop perceptions of you as being cooperative.

There is often a critical choice between confrontation or cooperation. Cooperation will usually give more solutions than problems, and more accuracy in perceptions, whereas confrontation often causes the kind of emotional involvement which reduces accurate perceptions.

THREE WAYS TO DEVELOP COMMON BASES OF INFORMATION BY FOCUSING ATTENTION, BEING SPECIFIC & BEING CONGENIAL.

With thousands of messages from hundreds of different sources pounding our psyches, it is particularly vital for managers to ensure that our employees have a body of **common** information. Consider the board member who began his tenure absolutely convinced that the board was favoring various schemes to retard integration. After serving with the board for awhile, he found that the board was, in fact, committed to integration.

Here are some techniques you can use to maximize the probability that common information will help to overcome distorted perceptions. The first thing to do if you are to give common information among people is to focus attention. Can any of the following techniques help you to improve your focus of attention?

Eleven Techniques to Focus Attention.

1. <u>Ready to Listen</u>. Make sure your listener is ready to listen. Ask him or her if the time is convenient, especially if you are talking on the phone.

2. <u>The Subject</u>. Usually state your basic subject conclusion or purpose right away, but realize that there are times when you will want to lead into it.

3. <u>Easy Does It</u>. Demonstrate that you are not attacking.

4. <u>Feedback</u>. Stop often for feedback and discussion--possibly after 2 or 3 sentences.

5. <u>Speech and Voice</u>. Get your voice to help focus attention. Pronounce the listener's name clearly. Adjust your volume to the situation. Be sure

that the sound of your voice is pleasant; listen to it on a tape recorder, and make changes if needed.

6. __Multiple Meanings__. Watch for words that have different meanings, or which the listener may not know.

7. __Reaction__. Observe your listener's reaction. Is the topic something your listener can relate to? Listen to what he or she talks about. Is the listener asking questions? If not, try to prompt them.

8. __Interruptions__. Observe interruptions. They can indicate many things such as misunderstanding, impatience, inability to hear clearly, need for more information. Does your listener talk over you? That may indicate less interest in your topic than in the listener's.

9. __Personality__. Be aware of your listener's general personality type and the whole listening environment. Observe if your listener likes serious, meaty ideas, or small talk. Is your listener easily drawn into a discussion, or hesitant to speak? Is he or she an active listener?

10. __Stories and Fables__. Just as a picture is worth a thousand words, so can a fable or story be worth as much, in focusing attention on common messages. For example, if you want to emphasize the benefits of charm and persuasion, consider using Aesop's fable about the wind and the sun rather than a facts-only lecture. In Aesop's fable, the wind and the sun argued about which could be best in getting a man to take off his overcoat. While the wind huffed and puffed, the man simply held tighter to his coat. Then the sun said, "Watch this." The sun shone brightly and became warm. Soon the man simply took off his coat. The moral: try charm and leadership rather than fear and pushership.[11]

11. __"Outside" Experts__. The adage about prophets being without honor in their own country is well known. In terms of people's perceptions, this means that groups may be influenced more by unfamiliar people than by those who are familiar.

Be Specific. One effective manager often makes it a practice to open meetings by stating precisely what his objectives are for that meeting. Thus, he might say, "Today we have three objectives. They are; (1) To understand due process, (2) to find out how each school is punishing students for the following rule infraction, and (3) to get consensus on punishments for the future." These kinds of statements give common information regarding expectations, and they can help free interaction and improve the efficiency of meetings.

This same manager also speaks directly in terms which unmistakably provide the same meaning to all those who hear. For example, he might say, "I don't understand your description of that employee's behavior. "Please give me an example," rather than "I think you're being abstract." Or, "I want **you** to write that letter," rather than "I would like that letter written." Do not express yourself covertly when you want people to have common information. It leaves listeners unsure and with varying perceptions.

Be Congenial. In congenial situations employees are likely to perceive accurately the goal-directed behavior of others, even though personal behavior is perceived less accurately. Since goal-directed behavior is the thing you're most interested in, foster congeniality.

People seem to be ready to gloss over personal behavior which is not congruent with their own, simply because friendliness tends to produce a desire for them to see others' personal behavior as similar to their own. Thus, the administrator who has hopes of producing a dynamic work atmosphere would be well advised to heed the value of a friendly cup of coffee or even a dinner now and then.

EXPECTATIONS CAN BE FORMATIVE, FICKLE AND FATAL

"I am not what I think I am. I'm not even what you think I am, but I am what I think you think I am."

Diversity is a major characteristic of the new breed of employee. This results in many different expectations for roles of employees, managers and the organization and means that one of the hardest jobs of managers today is to work for compromise.

A crisis of identity has even developed for some managers. You have been called upon to deal with conflicting demands in such areas as collective bargaining and participative management. This poses a three-fold requirement. For you must: (1) be sensitive to all employees' needs as well as accountable to the organization, (2) delay decisions in order to get consensus and yet get things done, and (3) be sensitive to heterogenous lifestyles while still trying to get homogenous employee discipline. In fact, if the problem was not so serious, the role for many bosses would seem comic--like Pooh-Bah in the operetta "The Mikado," who was Lord High Everything Else, First Lord of the Admiralty, Second Groom to the Backstairs, etc. In the following section, you will read about several strategies for identifying varied expectations, reducing their differences and coping effectively with different expectations you cannot change.

A BALANCE OF HARMONY IN EXPECTATIONS -SEVEN TECHNIQUES

Japanese companies seem to be successful in defining roles subtly and implicitly so that almost all employees have an understanding of tasks and relationships. In these companies, American practices such as organizational charts, explicit job definitions, and formal reporting relationships don't seem to be necessary. Widespread attention to socializing employees in acceptance of similar goals and values helps to build similar expectations. This is dealing with expectations in a **pro**active way.

In America, however, we are often **re**active regarding expectations. Therefore, we are including seven techniques for guiding employees toward a balance of harmony in expectations.

1. IDENTIFY AND CLARIFY EXPECTATIONS

There is a certain similarity between pilots with cloudy skies and managers with foggy expectations. Many pilots love to "fly by the seat of their pants" when the weather is clear, there is little traffic, and the aircraft is functioning properly. For piloting an organization nowadays, however, when the expectational skies are fogged, the perceptual lanes are mixed, and the workplace is buffeted by winds of dissent, more sophisticated instruments are needed to reach the proper destination. One such instrument is a "people's expectation-measurer."

Writing your own "people's expectation-measurer" form is not difficult. First, write down the important aspects of your job. Second, ask your employees to mark how important they believe each aspect of your job is to the company, and then how important **they** think it is to them personally. Last, ask open-ended questions such as, "What other tasks do you think Mr. Y should perform?" An abbreviated model follows.

Please circle one of the numbers 1,2,3,4 and 5 for each of the blocks listed below. The first column of numbers will indicate how important you believe that item is for your organization. The second column of numbers will indicate how important **you** believe that item to be for **you** personally.

Sample	How important is this job of Mr. Y to the organization?		How important is this job of Mr. Y to you personally?	
	Not very important	Very important	Not very important	Very important
1. Mr. Y's job is to involve all employees in decisions about what to do for production problems which affect them. (Other statements or questions of this type)	1 2 3 4 5		1 2 3 4 5	
Please list any tasks you would like to see Mr. Y do which are not listed above. Also, circle appropriate number in the column at the right.	1 2 3 4 5		1 2 3 4 5	

This kind of questionnaire can also help you to clarify and organize expectations for your job in order of priority. Remember that research shows that in the average organization, about 30% of the jobs of most managers seem to be irrelevant to most of their colleagues and subordinates.[12]

2. PRIORITIES

One way to help clarify expectations is to put functions in priority order. From the data you get in the questionnaire to identify and measure expectations, you can begin to write a composite statement of the manager's future. You can use this statement to establish working priorities, and as a beginning point for discussion to resolve conflicting opinions.

3. OPEN DIFFERENCES

Once, while the late Senator Everett Dirksen was campaigning, a man came up to the senator, saying he would not work for him even if he were St. Peter! After a slight pause, Senator Dirksen told the man that it would be technically impossible for him to vote for Dirksen because the man wouldn't be in Dirksen's district.

While we're not always advocating a reply like this which might create more problems, it is often wise to deal with differences openly. You will often find, though not always, that if differences in values and expectations are **not** openly known, they cause more difficulties than do recognized differences. We recommend that you usually try to define differences openly. Then state whether there will be a "live and let live" existence or, coexistence with open persuasion to change expectations. Budget decisions in public service organizations, particularly those pertaining to cutbacks for example, should be made openly in this way, if participative management is to work.

Ambiguity in dealing with expectations, or even outright duplicity, is always tempting to the manager who has differing expectations from employees, because it is sometimes difficult to deal with these differences and still maintain an atmosphere of harmony. However, both ambiguity and duplicity are very likely to backfire, for it doesn't take long for notes to be compared.

4. CONFLICTING DEMANDS IN EXPECTATIONS

Try to make clear to others what the conflicts are. People may press their contradictory demands out of sheer ignorance; knowledge of the conflicts may be enough to provide a resolution of the conflict.

5. DELINEATION OF DUTIES AND AUTHORITY

A clear definition of duties and authority can help to reduce expectational conflict and increase productivity. On the other hand, poorly defined duties, ambiguity in expectations and values, and unclear delineations of authority for decision making tend to make American employees feel insecure, tense and confused.

6. RE-CLARIFICATION

Periodic re-clarification of expectations is important because (1) people's expectations and perceptions change; (2) perceptions are often inaccurate; and (3) there is seldom an easy consensus in expectations that vary. You cannot simply clarify expectations once and for all.

7. GROUP RIGHTS AND RESPONSIBILITIES

One way to minimize the cross currents of multiple expectations from different groups is to articulate expectations into a pattern of rights and responsibilities. In cases where reduction of conflict is needed, small groups can help to describe the conflict and to compose realistic rights and responsibilities to use as criteria in resolving the conflicts. This technique would prove especially helpful in emotional situations such as plant or school closures, or with racial integration problems. Sometimes it is helpful to publish (perhaps in handbooks) the rights and responsibilities so that they will be readily available to both managers and employees at all times.

Cope With Conflict in Expectations - Eight Techniques

Some managers, such as school principals and superintendents, are confronted daily with many potentially conflicting forces. Few, if any, large workplaces have naturally harmonious populations. Differences, instead, are often the order of the day. The temptation is to resort to duplicity. Some of the following eight techniques may help you to cope with expectational conflict without resorting to duplicity.

1. Getting a "Dynamic Homeostasis

Conflict in expectations is not necessarily dysfunctional; nor is it necessarily true that when conflict goes up, effectiveness goes down. Instead, the relationship should be curvilinear. While strongly clashing expectations can be destructive, differing expectations can constructively rearrange thinking and programs. Therefore, try to get a balance between no agreement and complete disagreement--in short, a kind of "dynamic homeostasis." Maintain a balance between the dynamic and homeostasis.

2. Finding Overlap

We all know that when a supervisor and a subordinate agree on expectations, they both think that the consultation is favorable, but when they disagree on expectations, they are likely to have doubts about each other. The critical variable is the belief that they have **similar expectations.** The evaluation of success or failure often does not depend on the actual behavior during the conversation, nor even on the specific expectations objectively defined together, but rather on the subjective perceptions (right or wrong) of similarity. Therefore, try to make perceptions for expectations similar among superiors and subordinates, and you will likely find both feelings of higher confidence and satisfaction among employees and higher ratings for managers.

3. ALLOWING MULTIPLE EXPECTATIONS

One of the keys of management and unions sitting on the same ruling board is to acknowledge that it's O.K. to have different expectations. Unions and cultural pluralism are not necessarily obdurate terms, though they may be used that way by some. They can also be the result of genuine and legitimate differences in initial assumptions. When managers and employees learn to respect each other and acknowledge that disagreement can actually lead to cooperation and productivity, we will all be better off.

4. PUBLISHING GUIDES

Job descriptions, written contracts and handbooks containing rights and responsibilities, and lists of duties, can help in taking the guesswork out of expectations.

5. ADJUSTING EXPECTATIONS

The executive has three options, all of them difficult: change the expectations of the group, change his or her own expectations, or try to modify both.

A certain priest modified the expectations of his congregation. He was in the middle of his Sunday service when suddenly the heavens erupted with unbelievable thunder and rain. Although he was in the middle of the liturgy, the priest stopped, turned around to his flock and commented on the marvels of a God who would wash the parishioners' cars while they were worshiping in comfort without even a sprinkle to spot their clothes.

In attempting to get groups to modify their expectations, expert leadership is usually called for. When you adjust your own behavior or expectations, you have to walk the fine line of being flexible without compromising basic convictions of your own. These changes are extremely complex in that they involve a deep understanding of the groups' concepts of reality and an integration of "multiple realities."

6. VARYING IMPORTANCES

Clarification of the varied importances of different groups which have role relationships with one another may help to cope with conflicts in expectations. For example, if you are in a school situation, parent groups which have children in school are more important than a taxpayer group which has no children in school. Expectations may conflict, but one group should be known as central, others as peripheral.

7. MANAGING COALITIONS

One means of coping with conflicting expectations is to manage coalitions of power within and among groups. The purpose, of course, is to keep any group or individual from imposing expectations at will upon other individuals or groups, and to get a balance of harmony for overall goals of the organization.

8. NOT EXPECTING AUTOMATIC AGREEMENT

There is a tendency to perceive expectations of others as being closer to yours than they are.

One hot day, when a certain minister in a small town was out for his morning stroll, he saw a mischievous looking boy at the front door of a house. The boy was so small that he could only barely reach the doorbell by jumping. He wasn't having much luck. The minister, being a spiritual humanist, walked up, smiled at the short boy, and rang the bell with enthusiasm. Whereupon, the minister said, "And now what?" "Run like hell," said the boy.

Finally, expectations can be formative; they can be fickle and even fatal. They can be helpful or harmful. The question is, how can managers not be immobilized by trying to meet all expectations nor handicapped by disregarding too many of them. Shakespeare wrote in "Henry VII," that Cardinal Wolesey found in Henry's court, "How wretched is that poor man that hangs on people's favors! . . . when he falls, he falls like Lucifer." Equally, Richard Nixon's coterie found how failed is he who disdains the expectations of people.

SPEAKING AND WRITING: ONE DOZEN WAYS TO HELP IN COMMUNICATING FOR MUTUAL UNDERSTANDING

The essence of communication for humanistic leadership is a dialogue, not just a monologue. In order to do this, are you clear and concise? Do you listen for feeling as well as content, find the right mixture of talking and listening, and ensure that you have ample two-way communication? Do you sent straight messages? Do you avoid power struggles? Do you own your own feelings and know how to express them? Always ask yourself three questions: (1) What is the best possible way to get my message across? (2) Can it be given back to me accurately? (3) What are others saying and feeling? A dialogue is highly demanding in either speaking or writing, but the following guides can help you meet these demands. There is a natural overlap between this section and "Developing Common Base for Information," in the "Perception" part of this chapter, because the basic purpose is the same, to communicate and perceive for mutual understanding.

1. CLARITY

Fight being fuzzy, convoluted, evasive, petty, irrelevant and jargonistic. Ambiguity in talk is not usually the result of ignorance; it is more likely to be caused by caution or courtesy. If you clearly state your request to a worker, or your position at a board meeting, people have three response options: (1) to agree, (2) not to agree, or (3) to agree partially. This puts you in an exposed position. On the other hand, if you are cautious, and not clear, people have other options, and you may not be seen as disagreeing or being wrong on policy.

When you need to be clear and specific, don't say, "You don't get a raise this year because your work wasn't good enough." Instead say, "I won't recommend you for a raise this year because (1) you allowed your employees to make the following crucial errors in the bookkeeping accounts; (2) you had the following grievances in which these should have been done in these ways (be specific), and (3) you have not volunteered as much time to company endeavors as those who will get raises did. Now, for next year, I'd like to work closely with you to help you do the things necessary to get a raise.

2. DIRECTNESS WITHOUT ALIENATION

Instead of saying in a group meeting. "I wonder what Jim thinks about this," say, "Jim, what do you think?" For reasons similar to those for not being specific, people are often indirect. Indirect approaches invite indirect responses, which invite ambiguous communication, which invites misunderstandings, unless enough time is spent in communication to allow clear understanding while being somewhat indirect. The Japanese seem to be adept in this kind of communication, even to the extent of being able to set goals and objectives this way. But while it is successful in Japan even for getting energetic action, it is doubtful that Americans are ready for this indirectness.

3. QUESTIONS OR STATEMENTS

When questions are made as statements, they usually avoid directness and promote feelings of weakness. If you want to say something, say it, and don't cloak what you want to say in an amorphous question such as: "Don't you think we should have more involvement in sales?" Either state clearly, "I want to be active in sales plans and actions all year." Or, ask directly, "Do you want to be involved. . . ?"

4. WHO, WHAT, WHEN, WHERE & WHY QUESTIONS

The journalistic five W's, **Who, What, When, Where, Why**, often help to focus even the most ambiguous communication.

5. ALTERNATIVES TO TALKING

Try communicating in silence. Most managers find talking easier than silence, yet sometimes silence, or near silence, is more effective. Next time you want to say something, try conveying your message silently-- with body language, with thought. For example, if you like someone, you almost always get the message across. When an employee does something noteworthy, try eye contact, a gentle nod, and a warm smile.

6. SAYING ENOUGH, BUT NOT TOO MUCH

Such a simple saying, but so hard to practice. Sometimes you have to be redundant to get the message across, but it's always wise to watch eyes and not to continue too long. Quite a bit of talk is merely masturbatory. Don't let yourself get trapped into telling your "war stories" to your employees. Don't talk unless there is some purpose for it; otherwise, listen!

7. SAYING SOAPBOXES

Don't use them. Preaching about your pet crusade is risky. If you don't alienate people who should not be alienated, you risk giving the impression of not being able to be objective when you should be.

8. CONTINUOUS TWO-WAY COMMUNICATION

As the manager, you become catalyst for keeping information flowing throughout your bailiwick. If you are a school principal for example, you must inform pupils, parents, teachers and your superordinates about new policies and practices before they are put into effect. You also need to give them all a chance for input and questions before finalizing the policies. You must be sure that leaders in the school groups are personally contacted and not just given policy publications of changes. People who are integral parts of policy decisions have vested interests in ensuring success, whereas those who are merely told of changes are likely to become disgruntled.

In order to keep informed yourself, at the very least the principal and other managers should:

-- Use suggestion boxes.

-- Eat lunch with different staff and student members (or other employees) and follow-up soon on suggestions.

-- Have staff and student (or other employee)
   advisory committees.

-- Use questionnaires so that discussions can take
   place with more face-saving.

9. EXTRA TOUCHES IN WRITTEN COMMUNICATION

The following are "extra" touches in written
communications for schools. They can also easily be
adapted to other organizations.

-- Be sure that teachers get the first copies of
   all publications going to parents and students.

-- Encourage staff members to try new curriculum
   ideas through a curriculum idea exchange letter
   both with and among schools.

-- Have an easy-to-follow guide to paychecks for
   each employee.

-- Write one page summaries of board meetings
   which pertain to your staff the morning after
   each meeting and hand out to staff.

-- Give information to parents at the beginning of
   the year and be sure to send home a calendar of
   school events. Also, be sure to include a list
   of staff members and room numbers, as well as
   assembly programs.

10. FEEDBACK

The only way you can be sure that you've been
understood is through feedback. Feedback can include
talking, writing, and non-verbal communication. Often
your best feedback will come in non-verbal
communication.

11. STRUCTURING COMMUNICATION AROUND LEADERS OR FOLLOWERS

When you use a "leader" pattern of communication,
the leader can communicate easily with members of the

group, but group members cannot communicate easily with each other. When you structure communication around the followers, there is a chance for democratic participation in decision making by all members of the group. The following two principles will help you decide which you want to use.

(1) If you want speed and accuracy for **routine** jobs and are **not** concerned about group feelings, use the leader structure.

(2) If you want speed and accuracy in more creative kinds of work and want good group feelings of responsibility, independence and security, use the circle or follower structure.

12. BODY LANGUAGE

Probably about 75% of what people say and comprehend comes through body language.[13] This includes tone of voice, face, posture, movement of hands and feet, and most importantly of all, the eyes. Therefore, every good listener is just as concerned about these things as about words.

As for the eyes, pupils usually enlarge with pleasant things and contract with the unpleasant. For example, men's pupils generally become enlarged at the sight of beautiful women. A cardplayer's eyes usually reveal good or poor cards similarly. When lies are told, the eyes tend to move more rapidly than when the truth is told. To keep from betraying his feelings, in fact, was one of the reasons Aristotle Onassis wore "wrap-around" sunglasses.

Other non-verbal expressions. Some people, though not all, lean forward for topics that interest them. Probably even more important is the intensity of concentration that comes through the eyes and certain body movements. Also, the tone of voice and its timbre are usually important.

Make a mental note whenever you see a physical reaction. Notice whether it is repeated or habitual. Check verbally to see whether you are correct.

Non-verbal messages sometimes seem to contradict verbal messages; when they do, we usually believe the non-verbal. When, for example, your boss enthusiastically and loudly proclaims that he is glad to see you and wants to hear about your new proposal, but then cuts you off with a wave of the hand before you've finished, you doubt his sincerity.

There are four basic assumptions which can be made about non-verbal behavior:[14]

-- You cannot **not** communicate.

-- Non-verbal channels are especially effective in communicating feelings, attitudes and relationships.

-- Check your observations verbally when it's important to be sure about your interpretation, for no non-verbal expression always means the same thing, and no non-verbal cue can be counted on as completely reliable.

Finally, communication is hard work. And when it seems really hard, think of the poor train conductor in Wales who has to call out this station everyday on his train:

Llanfairgwelgwyngllgogeychwyrndrobwelantysiliogogoch!

LISTENING FOR FACTS WITH EMPATHY

Two bums were sitting in a gutter one day. "The reason I'm here," said one, "is that I refused to listen to anyone."

"The reason I'm here," said the other, "is because I listened to everyone."

For years, people have been aware of the importance of speaking, writing and reading as part of communication. But until recently, the fourth area of communication--listening--has been almost totally ignored. For example, ask yourself how many courses you have had in speaking, writing or reading? How many courses have you taken in listening?

When you listen do you listen actively? Are you a reflective listener? Do you let people know what you've heard? Do you listen with feeling, and empathetically let the person know that you respect and love them? Do you listen with understanding which comprehends the other person's points of view and ideas; and on an even deeper level, what he or she is thinking beyond the words spoken? Do you somehow convey the message that one of the greatest things any of us can do is to care enough about our colleagues and subordinates to really know and understand them--to see things from their point of view?

WHY CAREFUL LISTENING IS IMPORTANT[15]

Why is listening important as something to study? Isn't it more or less automatic? There are at least six reasons for studying and practicing listening. These are:

1. Managers are notoriously poor listeners; we have conditioned ourselves to do the talking.

2. "There is no such thing as a vacuum in communication."[16] If employees feel their supervisor won't listen, they'll go to another employee, the union rep, or a higher supervisor who will.

3. Poor listening frequently results in significant losses, both monetary and psychological.

4. Listening is the most used of communication skills, even though it is the least taught. Of the 60-70% of time that most managers spend in communication, about 65% of that time is spent in listening. During this time, if you listen carefully, you can get many ideas and much information which will help you in your work and personal relationships.

5. Appropriate listening is good positive reinforcement, and it promotes humaneness, sensitivity and cooperation.

6. Careful listening can help managers to solve conflicts.

How Good a Listener Are You?[17]

How well do you listen? Did you know that the average American adult hears only about 25% of what is directed at him? Take this two minute test to assess your listening habits. Put down the number of points you give yourself for each answer according to the following list headed "Assigned Points."

Assigned Points

Scoring	Points
Always guilty	0
Almost always	2
Usually	4
Infrequently	6
Almost never	8
Never	10

1. When your employee talks about something remote, boring or uninteresting, do you tune out?

   Points_____

2. Do you smile, nod or say "uh huh" to fake attention?

   Points_____

3. Do you let your employee's physical appearance, facial expression, or accent interfere with your listening?

   Points_____

4. Do you conclude before you are through listening?

   Points_____

5. Do you interrupt or take over the conversation

   Points_____

6. Do you let personal prejudices, biases or subjective pre-judgements jam your listening?

   Points_____

7. Do you prepare your responses while your employee talks?

    Points_____

8. Do you let commonplace distractions interfere?

    Points_____

9. Do you make excuses instead of dealing directly with the issues?

    Points_____

10. Do you daydream, doodle, or fiddle with things while your employee talks?

    Points_____

Scoring Key

    80-100.........................Excellent
    70-79..........................Average
    69 and below.............Clean Your Ears Out

NINE LISTENING INHIBITORS

If you're not already an excellent listener, you can improve. First, know what factors tend to inhibit good listening, and then what to do about them.

1. Thinking vs. Talking Speed. While most people talk at 125-150 words per minute, they can listen at about 500-800 words per minute. It is only natural that distractions take place during the gaps as your mind wanders.[18]

2. Time. Time is one of the most precious aspects that a manager has, and therefore, is a built-in inhibitor. Even so, one of the best uses of time is to listen to your employees. One example of time being put to best use by managers is in the microelectronics firm, Tandem. Here, the top executives supposedly spend 100% of their time dealing with people-projects for which a lot of time is spent listening. They can do this because they have successfully computerized production and quality control, cost standards and reporting systems.[19]

Naturally, there are a few employees who will monopolize your time if you let them, and for them, a diplomatic cut-off is necessary. But for those who will not waste your time, listening to them patiently may pay huge dividends.

3. **Premature Judgment**. It is very easy to pass judgment immediately upon hearing something, and then either to embrace or reject it without much depth of understanding. Granted, it's very difficult not to judge. It may even be impossible. The trick is to keep listening with an open mind, and to hold judgments tentative.

4. **Excessive Emotional Involvement**. One of the most inhibiting aspects of listening is excessive emotional involvement. Regardless of whether it is anger or elation, too much emotion disturbs listening.

5. **Apathy**. Good listening often takes even more focus of energy than talking, and yet so many of us treat it as a passive activity.

6. **Past Experience**. Predispositions, or past experiences, were covered under "perceptions" in this chapter. Suffice it to say that most of us have conditioned ourselves either not to listen very well to things with which we disagree, or to attack them rather aggressively. Neither approach promotes open listening.

7. **Hidden Motives.** The agenda here is to manipulate others, to use "tricks" to make others believe they are speaking their own minds and making their own decisions. With hidden motives in listening, there is usually a strong desire to dictate a change in anything with which we disagree.

8. **Facts vs. Empathy**. Often, people listen for facts when what is needed is empathetic listening. Knowing which to listen for and how to do so can be a tremendous listening facilitator. Empathetic listening involves listening for feelings, hopes, perceptions, values, etc. Agreement is not necessary, but understanding is. An example: You've had a particularly rough time at work. It's not that you've

done a poor job; it's just the external problems. You tell your boss about it. He responds with a "cheerleader" type of answer or he simply says, rather matter of factly, "Well, that's too bad, see you tomorrow." You believe that he doesn't understand, or doesn't care. Result: You're discouraged.

9. **Reducing Speakers' Self Worth**. You **may** reduce your ability to listen effectively if you send responses which cause a dampening of self respect, but you will almost certainly reduce your ability to develop power **with** people by doing this. Some of the best known reducers of self value are: (1) ignoring, (2) interrupting, (3) lecturing, (in response), (4) being impersonal and (5) being irrelevant (in response).

You've just read about nine inhibitors to listening. Now, look at ways to improve your listening habits through **listening** and **responding** techniques, and through an **Action Plan**.

NINE LISTENING FACILITATORS

1. **Listen With Empathy**. Here are five suggestions for improving empathetic listening.[20]

-- Express respect for the worth of the speaker.

-- Share the speaker's feelings and accept his emotions at face value.

-- Listen for what is not said, and respond to that.

-- Recognize any negative prejudices you may have and don't let them interfere with your empathy.

-- Be sensitive to the way the other person is speaking and moving, and try to match that style. For example, if the speaker is subdued, try being subdued and extra polite yourself.

2. **Summarize in "Wholes"**. Remember key words; paraphrase main ideas and understand the "Gestalt" of what's being said.

3. **Judge Carefully**. Evaluate what has been said in the conversation or speech only after you've checked your own biases; don't make premature judgments.

4. **Associate** the speaker's ideas to your own experiences without limiting what the speaker is saying to what you already know.

5. **Look for non-verbal congruence**. Do non-verbal expressions confirm the words? Pay attention to how things are said: voice inflection, rate of speech and non-verbal communication.

6. **Clarify**. Ask questions when possible to amplify and clarify.

7. **Usable**. Try to find something from all speakers that you can use.

8. **The Speaker's Shoes**. Put yourself in them.

9. **Respond for Others' Self Worth**. Your responses to people and situations are just as important as your sending of messages. You can confirm the other person's worth, or you can reduce it. You can make peoples' self respect better or worse by (a) acknowledging content verbally or non-verbally, (b) giving reassurances or expressing understanding, or (c) by showing positive feelings.

LISTENING ACTION PLAN

It is so easy to do nothing about improving your listening, yet it is so important. Here is a standard action plan for improvement which can help you. Use it, or even design your own.

ASSESSMENT AND GOALS

Take a moment to reflect on what type of listener you are and would like to be.

1. I listen effectively when:

2. I do not listen effectively when:

3. I am best in the following three areas:

4. I want to improve in the following three areas:

5. I will practice my three "to improve" listening guides with the following people:

    A.

    B.

    C.

    in these three specific situations:

    A.

    B.

    C.

6. I will know I have become a better listener when:

TIME LINES

My time lines for the goals I want to meet in improving my listening are:

-- Today

-- This Week

-- This Month

-- The Next Three Months

SUMMARY THOUGHTS

This chapter is in no way meant to be a comprehensive treatment of communication. Rather, it is
designed to focus on some critical aspects of communication for mutual understanding and benefits to the
manager who wants to practice humanistic management.
Many techniques have been given for doing this within
the areas of perceptions, expectations, speaking and
listening. For a thorough consideration of all aspects
of communication, particularly speaking, writing and
listening, Norman Sigband's book, **Communication for
Management and Business** is recommended.

CONFLICT MANAGEMENT

Blessed are the peacemakers, for they shall save the fractionated earth.

INTRODUCTION

Even though most of this book is about conflict resolution in one way or another, a special section is now devoted specifically to this topic because of its relevance in a world where selfishness, exploitation and hostility are excessive. On any given day, some part of the world is bound to seem to be like a seething volcano. The hot lava of conflict pulsates, ready to erupt. You know that if it does, it will harden into grotesque ruts of ill-will which will be difficult, if not impossible, to remove. You know that unless intelligent forces can stop these volcanic rumbles and belches, vast wastelands of personal relationships will be destroyed, energy decimated, and productivity decreased. It's as though the elements which produce potential conflict are building up more and more pressure. When a volcano's ecological elements create too much pressure, devastating destruction occurs. So is it with conflict.

Not all conflict is harmful; a certain amount is stimulating and helpful. Maximum assets from conflict usually occur when there is some but not too much. If you look closely at the core elements which produce conflict, you will see that the potential for conflict increases as the following three factors increase: (1) interdependence, (2) pressures for change, and (3) multiple sources of the pressures for change. As long as these factors, which are forerunners of conflict, are neither too low nor too high, neither stagnation nor dysfunction occurs. But when these pressures arrive at high enough levels, either singly or in convergence, there are rumbles, or even explosions of conflict.

This is the situation in the world today. During the past 30 years, the pressures of interdependence, of change, and of pluralistic demands for change, have all increased substantially. The simple increase in any one of these pressures would have increased conflict; the convergence of all three of them has created some large dislocations.

Most people seem to have a sort of love/hate relationship with interdependence, change and pluralism. They want the increased comforts which technology has made possible largely by interdependent creativity and change. They also want to right the wrongs of society--to change things so that down-trodden races and sub-culture groups have dignity and become part of the mainstream. The rub occurs, however, with the problems of conflict: conflict from living too closely together, conflict from change that is too fast, conflict from differences in pluralistic cultures' beliefs and lifestyles.

The vast majority of people also seem to want to resolve conflict easily and peacefully. The problem is that millions and millions of people are unskilled in resolving conflicts, and they fumble badly when they try. Because they are inept, they make the problems worse instead of better.

One scorching summer day in ancient Greece, a young man hired a donkey to take him from Athens to Megara. At high noon, the youth, feeling very weak from the hot sun, got off the ass and started to rest in its shadow. The driver began to argue with the young man, saying that he had an equal right to the shade.

The young man exclaimed that he had hired the ass for the entire trip. "Yes, indeed," said the driver, "You hired the ass, but you did not hire the ass's shadow." And while they were arguing, the ass bolted and ran away.[1]

Although many conflicts have nothing but a shadow for a basis, the failure to cope well with conflicts is often followed by rage, feelings of inferiority, and hostility. Often when problems are not solved, conflicts continue, allies turn into enemies, and enemies become bitter and violent, all because many people lack conflict resolution skills.

What can we do? Although conflicts are inevitable, mutually satisfying resolutions to them are almost always possible. To resolve conflict on a widespread basis, however, requires right thinking and skills in resolving conflict.

THINKING RIGHT

Thinking right is imperative if you accept that thoughts control actions. You may say, "But I did that without thinking." In other words, you were on some kind of "automatic pilot." That may be true. Still, the "computer" which directs your automatic pilot can be traced to beliefs and attitudes which you accepted some place along the line of living. In other words, attitudes which result from your beliefs, which have grown out of all kinds of family and society programming. These attitudes then dictate your approach to, or avoidance of, conflict. This is true whether the conflict is one in which you are personally involved, or one you are arbitrating. The thing to do then, is first to eradicate those attitudes which make conflict resolution difficult, if not impossible, and to replace them with attitudes which improve your chances of resolving conflicts.

RECOGNIZE AND REDUCE COUNTER-PRODUCTIVE ATTITUDES

First, recognize and then simply discard counter-productive attitudes which keep you from being powerful and effective in resolving conflicts. In our society, there are certain widespread beliefs which lead to attitudes and behaviors that greatly inhibit conflict resolution. These are related in one way or another to the authoritarian personality. Some of the most important ones are:

PERFECTIONISM

Perfectionists are intolerant of ambiguity. They have much conflict because things **have** to go their way. They are superorganized, and when imperfections show up in their employees or their children, these people are easily upset. Conflicts then set in. On the job, they tend to be adamant in their "advice" to subordinates, gossipy, and narrow in their demands of co-workers-- their plans and actions. They are reluctant to entertain any new ideas that conflict with their own entrenched thoughts.

Perfectionists often have a kind of frightening integrity; they tend to think that they are perfectly righteous, or at least perfectly honest in admitting when unrighteous or mistaken. The problem with this kind of integrity is that it's often an illusion--life in a fool's paradise. These people are often mentally sick without the slightest realization of this illness. The Ayatollah Kohmeini may be this type of person.

INTRANSIGENCE

This is a state of mind showing unwillingness to compromise. People who are intransigent often believe that to change is to be weak. Since change and compromise are important in conflict resolution, intransigence makes conflict resolution almost impossible.

OVERSIMPLICITY

Oversimplifiers do not take into account shades of gray. They compartmentalize. They tend to be anti-intellectual and anti-introspective. As conflicts to them are not complex, they are practically never resolved, because in actual fact, conflict resolution takes a deep understanding of what the complex issues are.

WINNERS OR LOSERS

Many people believe that they have to be winners or losers in conflicts. This appeals to the "fighter", but it generates more problems than it solves. This belief can result in eternal cycles of conflict as the current loser has to become the winner next time, and so on ad infinitum. Northern Ireland and certain Mid-Eastern countries are examples of the futility of the win/lose attitudes.

IRRATIONAL FEARS

People with irrational fears find Bengal tigers and python snakes behind every bush. Out of irrational (but deeply felt) fear, these people drip with hostility and revenge and cannot really solve conflicts until they change. Conflict resolution requires the ability to be relaxed and to see things realistically.

AVOIDANCE

The people who avoid trying to resolve conflicts believe that most conflict resolutions are impossible anyway. They say, "People are just made the way they are; they won't change." To these people, compromise is dirty and weak. They think, "If the other person won't do what I believe in, they can rot in hell."

MINIMAL THINKING

Some people believe life is easier if you don't try to resolve conflicts. You don't have to think very much that way. Of course, thinking requires self-discipline, searching, reading and judgment; it's often downright painful. Minimal thinkers believe it's easier just to let things happen and then just muddle through. They don't want to pay the price of growing, and changing and compromising. They are the rigid Archie Bunkers.

THE SAME YESTERDAY, TODAY AND FOREVER

Some people believe there is a certain sacredness about things remaining the same. They may say, "God's word doesn't change nor compromise," and if you go around being open to compromise, you're in danger of violating eternal truth. Therefore, as this scenario goes, Moslems should not seriously entertain trying to resolve peacefully the conflicts with Jews. God is right; he is on my side. God doesn't change and neither should I."

BLAME

If you don't get deeply involved in conflict resolution, you can blame others. Like Archie Bunker, you can blame all those people who are different from you--commies, Jews, Blacks, Italians, artists/fairies, etc., for messing up your world with conflict. You're a member of the human race; they're not.

DICHOTOMIES BETWEEN GOOD AND BAD

People dichotomize when they believe that you need to draw lines clearly between good and bad, love and hate, work and play, and us or them. They forget that we are all bundles of contradictions. Dichotomists find conflict resolution difficult because it involves recognizing that we are all made up of opposites with shades of gray in between.

These ten beliefs and attitudes approach conflict from a negative, standoff point of view; they create unhappiness, revenge, and more conflict. You can easily see that these attitudes, which make conflict resolution almost impossible, are those of the authoritarian personality. They are diseased with infectious authoritarianitis, a destructive plague which spreads through families, companies and nations.

If pervasive and lasting conflict resolution is to take place, these attitudes need to be discarded, for they retard conflict resolution. If you believe that conflict resolution is important, develop a helpful set of attitudes and an effective group of skills. First the attitudes.

THE BEATITUDES OF ATTITUDES

Allow yourself a sort of ideal vision of what can be. One name for attitudes which result in ideal happiness is beatitudes. Use a set of beatitudes which can help to promote effective and happy resolution of conflict. Internalize some paraphrasing from one of the great lessons on positive attitudes.

And seeing the vast multitude of conflicts, he opened his mouth and taught them saying:

-- Blessed are the peacemakers for they shall save the fractioned earth.

-- Blessed are those who worship not power over people, but power with them, for such is the Principality of Eupsychia.

-- Blessed are those who deeply empathize with those in conflict, for mere objectivity is not enough.

-- Blessed are those who forge trust even when there is much suspicion, for there can be no real cooperation without trust.

-- Blessed are those who can tolerate ambiguity, for that is the beginning of empathy.

-- Blessed are they who respect complexity, for that is the beginning of wisdom.

-- Blessed are those who are not afraid to search for their own idiosyncrasies, for this is the beginning of understanding others.

-- Blessed are those who realize that the vast majority of people they come in contact with do not try to take advantage of them, for they have begun to escape from the State of Paranoia.

-- Blessed are those who deeply respect all people, for only then can a foundation for conflict resolution be laid.

-- Blessed are those who are not intransigent, for people cannot resolve many conflicts when their egos are stubbornly on the line.

These are some attitudes which can help to resolve conflicts. Now, look at some skills.

CONFLICT RESOLUTION SKILLS

The first skills you need to develop are probably those for combat survival. If you are shoved into combat before you are a seasoned veteran, it helps to have a few easy-to-remember skills for the tanks, snipers, exploders-complainers and know-it-alls.

SURVIVAL SKILLS

The following are adapted from management consultant Robert Bremsen.[2]

WHAT TO DO WHEN THE CONFLICTOR IS A HOSTILE AGGRESSIVE

There are three subspecies of hostile aggressives. They are "Sherman Tanks," "Snipers," and "Exploders." The basic strategy for dealing with each one is **not** to rise to the bait.

Tanks. Substrategies for the "tanks" who have jabbing fingers, stentorian voices, and overall omniscience, are simply: eyeball Mr. Sherman, call him by name, and state your disagreement with disarming phrases such as "In my opinion . . ." or, "Another possibility, which has proved successful, might be. . escalate; Sherman tanks are expert fighters.

Snipers. Substrategies for the "snipers," who shoot with sarcasm or irony are to draw them out; ask them to expand; smoke them out so that they either have to be direct or retreat. Don't push, for hostile people lose face easily, and then they are terrors, for they have nothing else to lose. Let them save face.

Exploders. Substrategies are also needed for "exploders," the sudden yellers--or they may curse or cry. Give them no action at all. Simply let the hurricane spend itself and end in an apology. If that doesn't work, try putting some distance between the two of you by saying something such as: "This is very serious, but we can't deal with it this way." If that doesn't stop the bellowing, leave the room, saying that you will return in five minutes.

Conflict Management   95   The Employee

COMPLAINERS

Talk by complainers is full of "always" and "never." Complainers who want action may stand up. Sitting complainers may only want to complain without action. They want to be comfortable. Neither agree nor disagree with complainers, but instead paraphrase the whiner's complaints back to them. Let them know you understand, and give a few sympathetic "ums" and "ahs."

KNOW-IT-ALLS

There are two types of "know-it-alls." They are the "real experts," who are right about three-fourths of the time, and the "phony experts" who are usually wrong. Real experts are valuable, but stubborn, and often so arrogant that they stiffen others with conflict. For "real experts," do your homework and don't argue; but ask questions which lend themselves to logic and complex analysis such as: "Will this method work with all five kinds of employees which B.F. Snickersdorfer described?"

After learning how to survive initial combat, look at strategies which will give you base for greater depth in conflict resolution: first, Phases of Conflict Resolution; second, Seven Cardinal Healers; and third, Miscellaneous Strategies.

The foundation of your skills should be the three principles in Phases of Conflict Resolution. You'll see them in almost all conflicts, whether in large groups, small groups, or individuals. People tend to move from phase one to two to three, or they tend to get stuck at one point or another. But if conflicts are to be resolved, people almost invariably need to move developmentally through these phases.

PHASES OF CONFLICT RESOLUTION

POWER PHASE

The power phase is where individual differences tend to be on the basis of subtle-to-overt confrontations and personal power struggles. In this phase, runaway talking can easily result in increased conflict rather than reduced conflict. Letting it all hang out in this phase can result in irreparable damage, for in spite of how much antagonists apologize, the words they say can never actually be withdrawn. The main job of the leader/arbitrator in this phase is to save everyone's face, calm the atmosphere, keep the problem from getting worse, and to set the stage for resolution.

TREATY-NEGOTIATION PHASE -- TRANSITION PHASE

If the first phase has been handled correctly, the antagonists will begin progressively to commit themselves little by little to ideas and actions which will resolve the conflict. The leader must help steer the "conflictors" to seeing the mutual benefits of resolving the conflict.

SYNERGY PHASE

This is where the leader helps to negotiate and synergize, where "group" generated issues take precedence, and where objective information can best be utilized. Aggression, anxiety, and suspicion change to cooperation, relaxation, and generosity as people realize that the advantages of mutually beneficial actions are superior to competitive actions in which some lose and others win.

While the lengths of any of these phases can be a few seconds to many generations, there seems to be a developmental progression through them which is necessary for successful and lasting conflict resolution. No doubt you have already recognized the principles as ones suggested all along in the book: (1) calm interest and respect for each employee's input, (2) promotion of mutual interest toward achieving goals, and (3) patient "hammering out" of solutions in an atmosphere of cooperation, relaxation, and openness. With these principles in mind, we invite you to employ strategies of conflict resolution such as the following.

SEVEN CARDINAL HEALERS OF CONFLICT

1. THIRTEEN WAYS TO CONTROL YOUR EMOTIONAL INVOLVEMENT

Even though you communicate acceptance of all people involved in the conflict with which you are dealing, you need also to show your objectivity. Naturally this is sometimes difficult. Charged vibrations of lightening and thunder may be streaking the atmosphere all around you, for people with conflicts are often like thunderstorms. To keep these electric pulsations from shaking your own psyche requires either immense self-discipline or gross insensitivity (the latter is certainly <u>not</u> being advocated). Thirteen short rules to help you control your emotions and to dissipate these storms are listed below. You will also find additional suggestions for this in other sections of the book, particularly in "Combat Survival Skills."

a. Never rise to bait.

b. Be more concerned with results than insults.

c. Think gnats, not hippos. (Don't let a gnat grow in size to a hippo.)

d. Raise respect levels in order to keep people from getting trapped in cycles of feeling inferior, then becoming hostile, then doing something foolish, feeling inferior... ad infinitum.

e. Eyeball the person, call by name and use disarming phrases such as "In my opinion."

f. Give no action at all, let the hurricane spend itself, or if that doesn't work, say, "We can't deal with that in this way . . ." or, "Excuse me, I must see so-and-so before he leaves. Help yourself to coffee and I'll be back in five minutes."

g. Without pushing, draw the person's sarcasm and anger out, so that the person must either retreat or admit error and anger. However, don't push the person to lose face.

h. Neither agree nor disagree, but paraphrase complaints.

i. Do your homework, know where the antagonists are coming from, and be able to use correcting information when appropriate.

j. React with kindness when the conflictor expects some less benevolent action or response. For example, your opponent has been mean and nasty to you. Look him in the eye, shake his hand, and say, "Bob, I'm sorry I've made you angry."

k. Don't preach.

l. Be Clear. A person in a fit of pique hears only a few words that are said and latches onto every third or fourth word. Thus, more confusion is created.

m. **Never** forget the power of food and refreshments. Hungry people tend to be harder to deal with.

2. DISCOVER THE CORE NEEDS - OFTEN UNSTATED

Find out the unstated hopes, needs, fears and dreams of both sides. This determination does not have to be an actual part of your conversation with the antagonists, but somehow discover where the parties are coming from.

Similarly, determine what the stock of potential satisfiers might be. For example, in one heated metropolitan conflict, one side demanded that the police chief be fired. Potential satisfiers were for minorities to be treated with dignity, and to be given minority representation on the Board which supervised the police. Find satisfiers which will promote well-being of all parties in any conflict.

Conflict Management   99   The Employee

Most often some form of esteem needs are at the core of conflict--feelings of being put down, held down, or trodden on. Therefore, if you don't know for sure what the core needs are, it is usually safe to assume the some form of esteem is the problem.

3. HAVE CLEAR GOALS

Persons with clear goals ordinarily solve more conflicts than those without. To pursue these goals in a humane and effective way, try asking yourself the following five questions:

What decisions do I want them to make?

How can I make it easy for them to make these decisions?

What are they hearing?

What do I think I'm saying?

What goals will be beneficial to all parties?

4. DE-ELECTRIFY COMMUNICATION. OPEN IT. SLOW IT DOWN. DEFLATE IT.

Slow down communication. Deflate the puffing which goes along with intense involvement. This can be done by an almost hypnotic personal demeanor, or by saying you're going to write down what is said, and you don't know any shorthand. But whatever you do, don't allow communication to run at the pace of high emotional involvement. Try saying, "I'm sorry, I can't write that fast, and I do want to write that point down."

Take issues point by point. If one antagonist or another is hotly blaming another for something, don't allow first one person to tell his side and then another to do the same, for this usually only does what a fire accelerant does to flames. Rather, control the situation with strength and empathy. Say something like, "I want to understand exactly how the problem occurred, and what each point is now." Then, try a

"Columbo" approach. Don't be afraid to bumble a bit. It puts others at ease and helps to slow things down. And sometimes it also makes the antagonists want to help you. This can also help you to get more accuracy from the antagonists. A great majority of all conflicts occur because of misunderstandings, and a point-by-point approach together with reminders of how easy it is to misunderstand, helps to reduce these inaccuracies (or distortions) of perceptions.

5. BUILD CONSENSUS--SMALL TO LARGE

In almost all conflicts there are small agreements you can ferret out. As you begin to build small consensus, also begin to articulate the core of the problem. Do not let the petty side-issues, which may well have caused the problem in the first place, increase the heat of the problem again.

6. DEVELOP WIN/WIN

Find out what solutions will bring the most self-actualization of all parties. Do not just solve conflicts with some sort of no-fault morality. Don't work for some kind of lowest common denominator compromise. Instead, be like the architect who talks with the husband and wife who want a house. He discovers their desires, their needs, their traits, and their differences. He then designs a house to meet those needs. He does not ask if one could sacrifice this, another that, but rather he discovers how to fulfill the needs of both.

An important part of win/win involves **saving face.** In saving face, it is usually best merely to maintain opponents' "social faces" rather than to affirm them extremely. For example, if Helen, who is subordinate to J.R., exaggerates the saving of J.R.'s face in conflict, J.R. is likely to perceive Helen as weak. On the other hand, of course, anyone in conflict with J.R. who affronts him is likely to get strong resistance. In the case of an arbitrator, either to talk down or to talk up to those in conflict is usually less effective than matter-of-factly saving their social faces.

Maximize **power with** and minimize **power over** people
in order to get lasting conflict resolution.

To use power over people almost always results in
continued conflict. Look at nations, races, and
families that have chosen to live by the concept of
power over people. Conflicts keep erupting.

Instead of approaching conflict resolution with
attitudes of "take it or leave it," or, "Let's sew it
all up now and forever," emphasize open-endedness.
Nothing is ever settled once and for all anyway. Only
as long as individuals, organizations, or nations find
it in their interests to live up to agreements do they
do so. Much needless bitter conflict occurs because
one group or another involved in a formal, closed
agreement becomes dissatisfied with it. Open-endedness
actually makes it easier to reach agreements. It also
can help to replace unilateral violations of agreements
with orderly and cooperative resolutions as problems
arise.

Whenever one person or organization perceives a
conflict, the conflict exists, and the problem becomes
a concern of the whole. So conflicts are always
potentially there. And the "open-endedness" can result
in potential conflictors concentrating their efforts on
discovering optimal solutions to immediate problems,
rather than worrying about every future contingency.

Win/win also includes a close focus on problems in
terms of **human concerns.** Get behind abstractions and
analyze each conflict according to human frustrations
and fear. As common human concerns are considered in a
climate of increasing trust, "conflictors" can begin to
deal with each other as allies with disagreements for
which solutions can be found, rather than as eternal
enemies.

7. LOVE

"And now abideth faith, hope, love, these three, but the
greatest of these is love."

"Love is patient, love is kind, and is not jealous; love
does not brag and is not arrogant,

does not act unbecomingly; it does not seek its own, is not provoked, does not take into account a wrong suffered,

does not rejoice in unrighteousness, but rejoices with the truth;

bears all things, believes all things, hopes all things, endures all things."

There is no doubt but that the great conflict resolvers are those who are able to convey the spirit of the 13th Chapter of 1st Corithians, regardless of whether or not they agree with your actions, they have some universal loving acceptance of your humanity. Look at Christ, Ghandi, Lincoln, Eleanor Roosevelt, and countless others.

FOURTEEN OTHER MISCELLANEOUS STRATEGIES

If you've had experience with conflict resolution, you know there are no simple formulas which always work. But the more you know about principles and strategies of conflict resolution, the better off you are. Therefore, here are fourteen more simple-to-use, miscellaneous strategies you can have at your fingertips.

1. Reduce incorrect perceptions and dissimilar expectations. A large percentage of conflicts result from these. (See Chapter II).

2. Suggest certain phrases such as the following that "conflictors" can use to make conflict resolution easier:

"I believe. . . ." rather than "You did that. . . ."

"In my opinion. . . ." rather than   "The fact is that. . . ."

"It would help me if. . . ." rather than "He'd better. . . ."

3. Do not be a hostage to your own ideals; you may find that everyone will be better off with slightly changed ideals.

4. Remember that even in the thick of the conflict there is life **after** the conflict. No matter how high the feelings of difference, try to get the conflictors never to say anything which might result in long-term hard feelings. People do forgive, but they don't often forget.

5. Be rooted and grounded in a knowledge of potential unspoken values and areas of conflict among the "conflictors," and prevent increased conflict by carefully steering through these shoals.

6. Know your own conflict tolerance level, and excuse yourself before you reach it.

7. Listen to, and communicate on, **all** points of view. Don't let yourself make the easy mistake of considering only fragments of information.

8. Sometimes you may want conflicting sides to express their views in writing. This can slow things down and be calming to a point.

9. If the conflict involves a group or a mob, have the group designate its major spokesperson. Further, choose carefully the place to talk. Never try to resolve conflict where group or mob reinforcement or heckling can be given to those doing the talking or negotiating.

10. Know your own role and act accordingly. Are you a protagonist, antagonist, mediator, or do you have the power of arbitration?

11. Identify whether or not the conflict is due to conflicts in expectations for roles. (See Chapter IV).

12. Identify the possible and probable outcomes of the conflict and act accordingly, asking the following questions to guide you:

Is avoidance of the issue the best resolution?

Is compromise the best resolution?

Is an agreement to disagree agreeably (peaceful coexistence) appropriate?

Is a win/lose pursuit really going to benefit almost all people?

Is win/win possible?

13. Ask yourself if you're being both optimistic and realistic. Be sure that you are honest with yourself, and that you always pursue optimism and realism.

14. Often you can use location in a room and physical proximity advantageously. Generally, the rule to follow first is to keep the antagonists a substantial distance apart at the beginning phase of the conflict, since this can help to reduce the heat of the conflict. Then, as the conflict cools, you might consider moving the conflicting parties closer together and re-establishing relationships.

FINALLY: "THINK RIGHT"

In resolving conflicts for the long-term as well as for the short, get rid of counter-productive attitudes. Build right thinking. Know how to work through the inevitable Phases of Conflict Resolution. Practice the Seven Cardinal Healers. And have at your fingertips many other miscellaneous strategies for use in all kinds of conflict.

UNDERSTANDING

ELEVEN MISUNDERSTOOD MOTIVATORS

Managing is about 85% people and 15% technical knowledge.

INTRODUCTION

Employees, as well as managers, are fascinated by the emergence of their own human powers, and they enjoy engaging in processes at work which develop these powers. Without proper motivation, however, a tremendous amount of human potential is stunted rather than nurtured.

Undoubtedly, you would not have come as far as you already have as a manager if you did not already know quite a bit about motivating, for getting people to do what needs to be done is essential to the success of any manager. However, if you are like most managers nowadays, you are somewhat confused about motivation. You would like to know how to be tough but not too tough; helpful but not too helpful; and oriented to people yet not blind to their foibles.

You know that the "old way" for the boss to motivate employees was to control ultimate rewards and punishments so that in cases of ultimate disagreement, the employee had to leave--fired usually. You're also keenly aware that times have greatly changed, and that persuasion, teaching and communicating are now ordinarily much more effective than force of crass manipulation. The question is, how can you affect attitudes, beliefs, and actions of some of the best educated, most secure and independent, and most demanding employees that have ever existed in the world without resorting to coercion, chicanery, or low cunning? In answering

this question,   first read a NIBS definition of   humane
motivation.

Next,   look   at   eleven   commonly   misunderstood
motivators.

DEFINING MOTIVATION IN THE CONTEXT OF HUMANE MANAGEMENT

*Reduced to its simplest terms, motivation is a need
and the belief that the need can be satisfied.*

In a selfish and cynical context, motivating
people through their needs means cheating and exploiting. The selfish, though appealing, Doolittle in
Shaw's "Pygmalion" exemplified this graphically in
these words: "My need is as great as the most
deserving widow's that ever got money out of six
different charities in one week for the death of six
husbands." In humane motivation, however, it is
essential to use means which are neither dishonest nor
exploitative. These other means will be described by
the acronym NIBS. "Nib," itself, is a word used in
England which stands for point. Here, the point is
that motivation involves need, incentive, bridge and
synthesis. One of the main points of humane motivation
is to use individuals' needs which, when synthesized
into those of their work organization, will be beneficial to themselves, the organization and hopefully,
also to others.

NEED

This need factor seems so elementary that you may
doubt if it is necessary to mention.   But the fact
remains that many managers still try to motivate others
from their own personal needs, rather than from the
needs of the person they want to motivate.

The central theme of this entire book is that
managers must concern themselves with individual
employee needs as well as organizational needs. In his
essay "On Liberty," John Stuart Mill wrote what
Confucius said in essence many hundreds of years
before: "The worth of the State, in the long run, is

the worth of the individuals composing it." Bringing out the worth of individuals means, at the very least, working with the following needs:

1. Love.

2. Cooperation.

3. Esteem.

4. Wholeness. This means to make order out of chaos; to feel integration with your world.

5. Self-fulfillment. This means to grow toward meeting higher order needs as lower order needs are met.

Regarding the last need, it is important to remember that there is a very important fundamental difference between "lower" and "higher" order needs. Satisfaction of lower order needs (physiological and security) tends to reduce drives toward satisfying them. On the other hand, the higher order needs of personal growth, worthy achievement, and self-fulfillment needs do not seem to work this way. Once activated, "higher" growth needs seem insatiable, unless there is a threat to lower level needs.

INCENTIVE

"I am giddy; expectation whirls me around;
the imaginary relish is so sweet
that it enchants my sense."

This is how incentive is described by Troilus in Shakespeare's "Troilus and Cressida," when he anticipates the joy of love's nectar. This is the incentive aspect of motivation most people think of when they want to motivate others. This is the element of T.V. advertising, showing beautiful ladies and handsome men relishing the nectar of this joy or that one. It is the expectancy upon which inspiration can be built. It may involve showing people what will satisfy their needs, helping them to believe that there is a good chance of this satisfaction actually coming about.

BRIDGE

You can have bold needs and incentives, and still have difficulty motivating when the bridge across the gap between need and satisfaction is not readily seen as being easily crossed. **Seen** is the key word here, and the key turns when you <u>visualize</u> clearly how to be satisfied.

This step's importance cannot be exaggerated nor stressed too often. It is the practical mechanism which vitalizes this whole motivation effort. Alan Monroe, the noted Purdue speech professor, almost literally cornered the textbook market for years because of his motivated sequence--the ANSVA formula. ANSVA is simple Attention, Need, Satisfaction, Visualization, and Action. If the visualization step is valid and appealing enough, the last step (action) is almost sure to follow. Remember, however, that the bridge (or visualization) won't be valid and credible unless it is practical, low-risk, and accessible. Even so, you must be ready to help some of your motivatees across, especially the first few times. People are afraid to trust the visualization easily in this television advertisement world.

SYNTHESIS

Now that your subordinate has recognized the need, been inspired with an incentive, and made a choice, and then even crossed the bridge into the "promised land," can you stop? No! If change is to be lasting, you must go beyond mere motivation to get work done. You must help integration of the changes into your employee's value schemes. When you integrate these, motivation is likely to result in a more holistic transformation, and not just superficial adjustments.

You can get small, incremental changes by motivation that the person is not aware of. You may also get large pendulum-like changes such as sudden

religious conversion by motivation. But if recipients
do not understand and synthesize these changes
harmoniously into their perceptual and value systems,
the change is unlikely to last very long. Also, in all
that you do, try to motivate toward goals which will
benefit the individual as well as the organization (any
other goals are short sighted). A simple diagram of
NIBS looks something like this:

Satisfaction Visualized

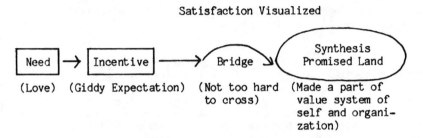

Need → Incentive ⟶ Bridge ↘ Synthesis Promised Land

(Love) (Giddy Expectation) (Not too hard to cross) (Made a part of value system of self and organization)

ELEVEN COMMONLY MISUNDERSTOOD MOTIVATORS

UNDERSTANDING MONEY

Money has variously been called the root of all
evil and the source of most satisfaction. Few people
fully understand money as a motivator, yet it is
frequently considered to be the panacea for
motivational problems. While it is true that money
used to be one of the fundamental motivators, as
pursuits of self-satisfaction have increased, the
relative power of money has decreased. You are left
now with a need to re-position money in its new and
proper perspective--neither overestimating nor
underestimating its importance. In doing this, use the
following principles.

MONEY IS ALMOST ALWAYS A MEANS TO AN END, BUT NOT AN END IN ITSELF.

Money is a means to **esteem** by providing symbols
which result in prestige. For example, houses, cars,
fur coats, exotic holidays, etc., are frequently
purchased as much for their status as for their
personal benefit.

Money is also important as a motivator to provide what any individual considers to be an appropriate standard of living--food, clothing, shelter and recreation. But beyond individual expectations of these basics, which are, of course, quite different for different people, cash has less and less importance. For example, a manager who makes $45,000 is offered $2,500 more to take a much more demanding job which will not really advance his career. This means that for about $20.00 more take-home pay per week, the boss would have increased tension. Not many individuals would accept the offer of money.

MONEY IS OFTEN NOT A BIG MOTIVATOR

The trappings of power and prestige are often greater motivators than money. Witness, for example, the effects on the average manager of the possibility of a more prestigious office or a limo, the executive washroom key, or a more elaborate desk; many will choose prestigious symbols over a raise in salary (which is ordinarily far cheaper for the company).

Peers are often more important than money. While most people would like more money, probably only about 10% of the ordinary work force will brave the disfavor of peers to make more money in a management incentive scheme which engenders the probability of peers' censorships; the other 90% favor more the opinion of colleagues, their own comfort, enjoyment on the job, and long-range security.

For the person who is self-actualizing on intrinsic goals, money is much less important than for the person dedicated to acquiring materialistic symbols.

WAGES MUST BE CONSIDERED FAIR BY EMPLOYEES

If employees do not perceive they are being paid fairly, nothing you do (including small raises) will motivate them. This will be true unless the national economy is in a shambles and many people are starving.

MERIT PAY SCHEMES CAN BE BENEFICIAL, BUT ARE FRAUGHT WITH DIFFICULTIES

Where pay is tied directly to production, as in piecework, your chances of getting reasonably high motivation and low transiency are rather good.

When merit pay is given in situations which have less **clear** indications of high or low production, your chances for rather universally low motivation are strong. In fact, you may even find that **de**motivation will set in.

While most people say they want their pay to be determined by their performance, most people also rate themselves well above average. If they don't get merit pay, "demoralization" sets in. **If merit pay is used**, however, it should be applied under five principles.

    a. Develop overlapping perceptions and expectations between superior and subordinate with dialogue and written guides.

    b. Ensure that a merit pay scheme doesn't result in "playing it safe," thus reducing creativity and appropriate risks.

    c. Ensure that dialogue between superior and subordinate increases trust, respect, assistance and help.

    d. Ensure that merit pay doesn't result in superior people thinking it is unfair.

    e. Ensure a mutual and holistic kind of accountability.

EMPLOYEES HAVE NEEDS OTHER THAN "WAGES WHICH ARE SOMETIMES FORGOTTEN

Ensure that there is consistency and that each employee understands the basis for pay.

Try to ensure orderliness and predictability. Minimize layoffs as they tend to cause extreme disruption and psychological damage (despite broad-based welfare). Many Japanese industries and businesses have thrived in spite of the fact that they seldom lay off employees; in return they have gotten loyalty, esprit de corps, and high productivity.

Finally, regardless of the multifaceted attraction of money, almost never is money an easy answer to motivational problems. In the final analysis, you, the manager, personally must understand your people and your work situation in order to choose the proper motivators. People are interested in moving beyond money to "meaning" and "being" dimensions. These dimensions make up the improved quality of life which people are looking for; a quality based on respect, mutually agreed-upon goals, interesting work, and attention to the heart as well as the mind.

MEANINGFUL WORK

There may be nothing under the sun except love that has more varied reviews and opinions than work. Hammerstein, in "Showboat," described the scourge of work (as well as of race), with his line: "Colored folk work on the Mississippi while white folks play." Carlyle, in "Past & Present" deified work with:

> *"All work, even cotton spinning, is noble; work alone is noble. . . . A life of ease is not for any man, nor for any God."*

Samuel Butler in "The Way of All Flesh," actually was probably closest to the truth when he said, "Every man's work, whether it be literature or music, or pictures, or architecture, or anything else, it always a portrait of himself." If this is true, when work seems dull, degrading or ugly, the employee sees a dissatisfying picture of self, and hostility and low productivity easily result. On the other hand, worthy work which is done well and which meets the employee's needs, gives the employee a satisfactory reflection of self, which is likely then to result in a feeling of exhileration and efficient work. Each person has a basic need for accomplishment which demands work with personal meaning.

One of your primary jobs as a boss is to arrange things so that work itself becomes intrinsically a good motivator. In order to do this, three elements of work and the worker must be present:

Desirability, do-ability, and allow-ability. Work must be desirable to employees in terms of helping them achieve personal goals; they must be capable of doing the work; and they must be allowed to do their work with as much freedom as possible.

In order to help make work as meaningful and rewarding as possible, begin with peoples' hopes and dreams, even when sometimes their dreams have been dimmed. For example, the dreams of inner-city school teachers have been at one time to help people (as well as to make enough money to buy the things they wanted). Put that dream back into perspective, and begin at that point.

Secondly, clarify employees' expectations and make sure that these are realistic. In the case of inner-city schools, make sure that teachers' expectations begin where the pupils are.

Third, constantly remind yourself of the importance of making work meaningful to employees, as well as to get employees to be meaningful to the organization.

SEVEN BASIC PRINCIPLES TO HELP DEVELOP HIGH MORALE

Napoleon said, "An army's effectiveness depends on its size, training, experience and morale. . .and morale is worth more than all the others combined." This is true, but morale's importance is sometimes exaggerated. In fact, many managers, and perhaps even more workers, believe that high morale is a magic mortar with which to build high motivation. While it is undoubtedly helpful; magic it is not. High morale and happiness do not always result in increased productivity, even though there is a much stronger probability of high productivity with high morale than without it.

There are at least seven basic principles which can help to bring about high morale.

1. GOOD FEELINGS AND REWARDS

While high morale does not **cause** high productivity, when people **believe** that their work will be satisfying, they are likely to be motivated to higher productivity. Giving people meaningful rewards and helping them to feel good about their performance is likely to motivate.

2. FRIENDLINESS

Most managers realize that good relations among people are conducive to good work. Yet many managers believe that because it's natural for some people to rub others the wrong way, there's nothing much that can be done. Nevertheless, by facing the problem rather than evading it, effective managers can often eliminate tensions and create cooperation.

There are lots of things you can do to reduce irritation and build friendliness. Some of them are:

-- Talk to the people until you discover the real causes.

-- Give people joint goals they must reach cooperatively.

-- If two people are hopelessly abrasive to each other, reorganize to minimize their contact.

-- If it's personal, explain in a kindly way why the person is irritating.

-- Point out that people are valuable not only for their productive talents, but also for their cooperation.

-- Seek a total atmosphere of understanding rather than one where irritating criticism is allowed.

3. FOCUS ON MATERIAL OR PSYCHOLOGICAL ASPECTS OF WORK

When workers are not **challenged, interested, responsible nor fairly recompensed**, dissatisfactions will then tend to cause workers to focus on such things as salaries, promotions, work conditions, and the gap between supervisor and subordinate.

4. NEEDS SENSING "KALEIDOSCOPE"[1]

Because an extremely wide range of factors contribute both to satisfaction and motivation, the effective manager has to be extremely sensitive to complex nuances in employee expectations and needs. Also, it is very important to remember that needs are never static. The state of anyone's needs is constantly changing and complex. Just think of them as kaleidoscopes. Look at these kaleidoscopes (figuratively) each week (or each day!) to see how the patterns keep changing--according to the movements which affect them.

5. NO SUB-STANDARD WORKING CONDITIONS

Job factors such as working conditions (including especially job security, wages, and mutual respect) almost certainly contribute to low morale and dissatisfaction if they seem to the employee to be sub-standard. On the other hand, these factors do not always appear to contribute much either to job satisfaction or motivation if they are higher than some optimum level. They may be taken for granted. This situation could remind you of the housewife's perennial dilemma over curtains: "Nobody appreciates me when I wash them, but they certainly notice when I don't!"

6. CONTINUAL PREVENTIVE THERAPY

The old adage "An ounce of prevention is worth a pound of cure" is one of the manager's most valuable principles. This can help you catch all kinds of reasons for low productivity.

7. ALERT BOTH TO POSITIVE AND NEGATIVE TENSIONS

Too much emphasis on high morale is likely to result in a certain self-satisfaction and eventually to lowered motivation. Try being like an orchestral conductor, helping one player to relax and another to be more taut, and at the same time, always listening to the whole effect. As manager you are always on stage, open and alert to whatever is happening, particularly the tensions of the individuals and the group--be they positive or negative tensions.

Finally, high morale is likely to contribute to high productivity because it provides: (a) a better climate for supervision where constructive criticism is more likely to be effective; (b) emotional support and comfort for the supervisor and worker; (c) a congenial climate where transiency and absenteeism are likely to be less; and (d) all in all, a continual preventive therapy which can retard, or stop, the potential for strikes and other work stoppages at an early stage.

SECURITY

*"Security is the mother of danger and
the grandmother of destruction."*

Thomas Fuller

Although many managers themselves thrive on risk, they make the mistake of believing that the need to feel secure is a dominant motive for most employees, when, in fact, it is often not. If you overrate the importance of security, you probably create more predictability than is necessary, thus lowering innovation and motivation. What are some of the basic principles to guide you for maximum motivation in this area of security?

RISK TAKERS

There are two fundamental kinds of desire for security; the first is the desire to be **free from accidents**, such as war, disease, poverty and accidents themselves; and the second is to be **free from fears**, such as fear of risk, conflict, disapproval, high expectations, and hardships of life.

People have confused the two types of needs. While most workers, as well as managers, desire freedom from accidents, many actually seek out the second kind of insecurity--insecurities such as risk, high expectations, and reasonable self-proving hardships. It is from some of these hardships and searches for ways to overcome them that some of our greatest innovations have come: for example, the cotton gin and electric lights.

SECURITY SEEKERS

On the other hand, there are some employees who prize security needs highly. They tend to be people who get their delights in faithful performance of routine work. They may have grown up with over-protective parents, or in poverty, and therefore, they feel greater than average security needs. In poverty communities where chances for improvement are poor, people are likely to feel incompetent to control and influence the world they live in. It is likely that they will have a low frustration threshold and distorted perceptions. They are also likely either to avoid conflict and to be likeable, **or** to be extremely aggressive. In either case, security needs are apt to be strong. In the best of all worlds, the manager would help them to feel secure, yet present them with challenges for growth which would inspire yet not frighten them.

SOCIAL RELATIONS AND GROUPS

Groups can be willful, contemptible, and petty. Then can render society helpless. They can transcend the finiteness of each individual member, and they can envelop members with greatness. To a large extent, what they will do is up to you. Facing this challenge as a manager, some of the following principles may help you.

1. "TOGETHER POWER"

Groups, if they have a feeling of togetherness,

have tremendous power to enforce standards of productivity (either high or low) among themselves.

2. INFORMALLY ARRIVED AT STANDARDS

Generally, the higher the standards of performance established informally by groups, the less that absenteeism, tardiness, and early leaving will occur.

3. SATISFACTION IS NOT NECESSARILY PRODUCTIVE

Employees in informal work groups may be quite satisfied in what they're doing because they have feelings of loyalty, generosity, and shared group values among themselves. On the other hand, they may not be very productive in attaining the organization's goals. This can easily happen either when there is a feeling of employees against the manager, or when the manager tries to keep everyone happy to the neglect of the organizational goals. A certain mild tension seems to be necessary.

4. NEEDS BEING MET

Negative behavior such as absenteeism, tardiness, and turnover tend to occur when individual and group needs are not met. This negative behavior is not necessarily aimed at management (unless there are clear reasons for anti-management behavior), but rather it usually results from a lack of group needs being met.

5. SOCIAL RELATIONS AND PRODUCTIVITY

Needs for employees' social relationships at work stem not only from desires for friendship, but also from the need to be with like-minded people. Being with persons who have similar beliefs seems to help satisfy needs for control, for order, and for being in the "same boat." If this is true, managers who help informal social groups to have goals which are similar to those of the organization are likely also to help build feelings of control, order and togetherness which will be advantageous to the organization.

There is not an inherent dislike of management by workers, as some managers feel, but rather a drive by workers for preservation of their identities. If these identities are threatened because management has dissimilar goals or operational methods, workers are likely to coalesce around certain tactics for work diminution.

6. Loners

Loners cam have a deleterious effect on productivity. Loners tend either to be defensively suspicious of their fellow workers, or so secure and competent that they are contemptuous and fend for themselves. In either case, loners can easily weaken other workers' feelings of dignity and significance, particularly if there is a dichotomy between workers and boss.

In trying to lessen the damage a loner can do, do not make the "loning " more pronounced by allowing pressure tactics for change, for they are likely to backfire. Loners are used to pressure, and they are well acquainted with the propensity both of leaders and followers either to seduce or to push them out of their isolation. Rather, first ferret out where the loner is coming from. Understand, and help the loner to be a self-actualizing individual. In so doing, you probably stand the best chance of reducing the strains which the loner causes, and you may even reduce divisions in the work force which the loner might otherwise increase.

Finally, no brief discussion of job-related social relations can clear up all their complexities. Still, practicing principles may help to increase motivation.

Threats and Punishments

There is no terror Cassius, in your threats;
For I am armed so strong (in education and security)
That they pass me by as idle wind.
Which I respect not.

If you allow the substitution of the words "in education and security," Brutus, from Shakespeare's **Julius Caesar**, fits for today's employees.

For centuries threat and punishment have been major motivators of human beings. Threats of wild animals, supernatural forces, and punishment from omnipotent bosses have cowed frightened people into desperate actions just for survival. The world, however, is changing. Aside from nuclear war, which many feel powerless to affect individually, actual survival is no longer often at stake. Employees increasingly respond to threat and punishment by filing a grievance, becoming an insidious influence, or quitting. The old negative devices of threat and punishment no longer work as they used to. You must now know when **not** to use threats and punishments, as well as how to use them deftly and sparingly when they are appropriate.

WHEN NOT TO USE PUNISHMENT OR THE THREAT OF PUNISHMENT

Ordinarily, do NOT use threat and punishment to increase productivity. When the threat of punishment is used as a motivator, the "threatee" often ends up hating the threatener (the boss), and productivity then usually declines. For example, Mr. Hardast, the principal of a school in Arkansas next to a military installation, was a tough, no nonsense principal. He punished students heavily for small infractions. Students who had previously been energetic became docile. Mr. Hardast thought this was great. What he had difficulty understanding was the decline in academic work. He resorted to explaining it on the basis of the transiency of "military" children--an explanation completely at odds with other "military" children. The truth actually seemed to be that productivity declined because inordinate threats and rules for punishment discouraged enjoyable learning and initiative.

Ordinarily, do NOT use threats and punishment when you want predictable results. For example, one employee, Jane, will look carefully at the supervisor's reprimand, figure out what to do, and improve. Geraldine, on the other hand, becomes even more careless, sarcastic and disruptive. Do not make the mistake of thinking you can easily get people in line in today's world with threats and punishments, for threats and punishment boomerang and knock out part of the production when they come back to where they started from.

Do NOT think that threats and punishment will get a person to do something right. Punishment shows what the boss does not want done, but it does not show what should be done. Many mistakes are by managers who assume that employees should be able to straighten out the problem now that they have been stopped from doing the wrong thing. If punishment is successful, the "bad" action is stopped. Then what is needed is to teach and coach the subordinate to the right action.

DIFFERENTIATE BETWEEN EXTINCTION AND PUNISHMENT

Some managers confuse punishment with extinction. **Extinction** is the disappearance of an act or response. **Punishment** tends to weaken or decrease a behavior or to cause a temporary suppression of an act or response, but it may **not** result in its disappearance. For example, an opera prima donna discovers that when she cancels a performance she receives significantly more attention from the world press that when she does not. The punishment by management of cancelling her fee plus making her pay a penalty does not equal the additional money she will make in the future because of the inflated fee she has begun to receive because of press attention. Far from being extinguished, the diva's immaturity has been reinforced by management's punishment.

How, then, do you punish to extinguish behavior and not to reinforce it? First, know **when** to punish; otherwise, consider merely ignoring.

WHEN THE THREAT OF PUNISHMENT, OR ACTUAL PUNISHMENT ITSELF IS LIKELY TO WORK

Try threatening when all else has failed. If you've done everything you could to try to help a person improve, and the improvement is insufficient, then use your ultimate weapon. "You've got to improve, or you will have to look for work elsewhere." Unless the employee is absolutely hopeless, this may work, for the fear of being fired still scares many people, particularly older workers more than younger ones, since they tend to have more financial commitments, more conscience for loyalty and duty, more memory of days when firing was a disaster, and more shame at being fired. But it can also help with young ones, primarily when there is a high jobless rate.

TRY "PUNISHING" ONCE IN A GREAT WHILE TO GIVE A SHOT OF ADRENALIN

When a short burst of energy is needed and the fear of punishment is not too overpowering, a threat will often work. Try saying, "George, you're going to have to explain to the president why this project isn't finished if it's not done by noon tomorrow."

GUIDES FOR GETTING AWAY FROM THE USE OF FEAR

1. Get used to the fact that fear, threats, and punishment are not what they used to be; they can actually be extremely counterproductive.

2. Develop ways to be an effective manager who relies primarily on **other tools** of motivation such as the Golden Rule, developing mutual goals, and attacking the problem not the person.

3. Let people know what is expected, and help them to fulfill these expectations rather than to try to keep them off balance with uncertainty, or threats and punishment. Give people their responsibilities in writing, and when practical, also include lists of do's and don'ts.

4. Emphasize feelings of understanding, cooperation and appreciation by discussing questions and problems in ways that are not put-downs nor humiliations. In all things, let people know that your number one rule for yourself and others is to show respect, compassion, and understanding, even when having to be tough. Make it plain that you do not tolerate fear tactics for fear's sake. You can do this in many ways such as by:

-- giving small correction to minor errors (not threatening unnecessarily);

-- not smiling when there is laughter at someone's fear in superior-subordinate situation;

-- saying things like, "We're in this boat together, and we can make it go fast or slowly," or "We can enjoy ourselves much more and get more done by mutual trust, comfort, and even nurturing each other";

-- Simply making it visible that you have discarded (or never picked up) that old dirty bag of threat tricks.

Finally, always keep basic control of general situations. Do not allow yourself to seem weak, for if you do, chaos is likely to reign, and chaos creates uncertainty, which employees do not want. Employees do want order that is tempered with fairness, compassion, and some degree of control themselves over their own destinies.

SEVEN INGREDIENTS THAT WORK FOR POSITIVE REINFORCEMENT

"In nature there are no rewards or punishments; there are consequences." -- Horace Annesley Vachell

Positive reinforcement, like nature, is built around rules and consequences more than simple subjective rewards or punishments. In its worst sense--when rules are not known, or when they are administered quixotically--positive reinforcement may be seen as capricious and destructive, just as nature is when we fail to understand her laws. But, when rules and consequences are carefully created, well known, and consistently administered, positive reinforcement can be a valuable tool for humane managers. It can help to give consistency in manager judgments and actions, and it can result in employee growth and satisfaction.

Positive reinforcement is an action technique which can increase the chances for lasting changes in your subordinates. It can be goal oriented, easily used to accomplish objectives through others, and in helping people to fulfill their own aspirations as well as those of the organization. It simply means recognizing the worth of something or someone. Practicing positive reinforcement depends greatly on the following seven elements:

1. THE RIGHT REINFORCER

First, find the reinforcer which is desired or needed by the individual whose behavior you are hoping to change. There is a certain uniqueness to reinforcers even though some can be used more or less universally. For example: Whereas a country and western record would positively motivate one customer, it would repulse another. Also, even though a country and western record might motivate a person at one time, it might have a negative effect at a later time due to the individual's lifestyle change. Thus, the manager must respect the uniqueness of people as well as their fluctuations, and use reinforcers appropriately.

2. RIGHT TIMING

The best time to reinforce is almost always immediately following a desirable behavior. If, however, an immediately contiguous reinforcement is impossible, try it anyway, as soon as you can, although it almost certainly will be less help than an immediate reinforcement. Then, say or write to the employee that this has just come to your attention; you're sorry that you didn't know about it when it happened, but you want to pass on how great it was.

3. BE SPECIFIC

Make the reinforcement fit one specific performance. Generalized compliments and vague, cheerleader type backslapping are often seen as phony. They can damage your credibility. Your employees may even think you're from Uranus.

4. KEEP IT PURE

If you mix your good news with bad news, the bad

news will take precedence. Also, if you add advice
with your encouragement, employees will tend to be
cynical about your compliment.

5. IGNORE POOR WHEN POSSIBLE

Use positive reinforcement for good performance,
and try to ignore poor performance. By focusing energy
on desirable acts, you will tend to crowd out the
undesirable acts.

6. REWARD THE SLIGHTEST GOOD

An example of this is Jim, a student who was below
average in his studies and who disturbed students who
were trying to study. All teachers had difficulty with
Jim; all but one even despaired of making progress with
him. This one teacher first stopped Jim's
inappropriate behavior by consistent punishment every
time inappropriate behavior occurred. He then followed
the punishment with rewards for the tiniest modicum of
desirable behavior, and with modeling the behavior he
sought. Soon, Jim was working hard for the reinforcers
and dropping the undesirable behavior. The same
technique also has been extremely successful with
employees.

7. RIGHT SPACING

Reinforce desirable behavior frequently at first.
Do this in order clearly and strongly to establish the
behavior. Once the behavior is established, begin
gradually to diminish the frequency.

In summary, behavior is often controlled by its
immediate consequences. Positive consequences tend to
result in an increase in the desirable behavior which
is lasting, while negative consequences tend to cause
disruption and suppression of behavior with neither
lasting nor sure results.

COMPETITION

Competition is highly volatile. Like nuclear
energy, it can be immensely destructive or extremely
helpful--it can blow the place apart or it can help to

build. Competition can create animosity, sharp criticism, caustic gossip, and reduced quality and quantity of work among employees. It can also produce high quality success in reaching quotas and goals, and give consumers and clients the best possible service. Further, competitive tests can be beneficial in selecting the best candidate for a particular job.

The problem of course, is to use competition so that it will build, rather than destroy both the organization and the individual. In order to do this, you need to know when competition is likely to be harmful and when helpful.

HARM AND HOSTILITY

Competition is harmful when it causes serious fears about one's ability to continue to thrive, or even to survive, for the maelstrom of negative emotions and actions which can be unleashed are likely to be detrimental both to one's own success and co-cooperation with others.

Competition is harmful when there are harsh critical evaluations and bitter jealousies among competing individuals within an organization. This is likely to happen when individuals are pitted against each other within the same organization, or when there are close emotional ties. Rumors and gossip feed on people's desires to make themselves look superior and others seem inferior. The end result is, of course, reduced quantity and quality as people hold back from invigorating and helpful cooperation. They may even be duplicating work needlessly in their fearful or angry isolation.

Without any doubt, competition can unleash primitive and destructive instincts for survival. On the other hand, competition can be used for cooperation and maturation when certain sportsmanlike rules are followed.

SEVEN BASIC RULES FOR MAXIMIZING BENEFITS FROM COMPETITION

The key for unlocking maximum benefits from competition is to get people to compete cooperatively. Here are seven basic rules for helping to bring out the best in people through competition.

1. Use **individual** competition only if you are sure that there is reasonably healthy morale in the first place. If not, you are more likely to preside at a disaster. When there is already strain, people are not likely to respond well to more tension and change in the form of having to prove themselves.

2. Choose an impersonal or inanimate object such as a quota or record to compete against, not another person directly. For example, the boss who goes to Lou and says, "I'd like to see if you can't make this design better than Bill, and if you do, you get a bonus," is almost sure to stir up harmful hostility. But if he says, "There's a bonus here for anyone who can overcome such and such a problem in this," he is more likely to get helpful competition. Fears and hostilities are often by-products of competition. Be sure they're directed at impersonal objects or, at least, at people outside your organization. Try to direct competition at a common problem-enemy, such as environmental waste.

3. Do everything possible to get winners to emerge from victory as humble, gracious and humane. Never cast aspersions on the loser, but on the contrary, give emotional face-saving reassurances to losers. For in competitive situations, there **are** losers, and their ego redemption is extremely important if they are not to become bitter drags on the organization, as well as psychologically lame themselves.

4. Be sure the competition is fair and not simply the result of capricious judgments. One way to do this is to keep close watch over what's going on. Prevent undercutting and insults. Discourage rumors, petty politics, and anything which tends to detract from objectives and meritorious winning according to

prescribed rules. Keep a watch on all parts of the competition. Eradicate foul play with the wings of justice.

Try to insure fairness of individual competition by objectively communicating progress through charts or symbols which show precisely how well the goals or objectives are being met. Ensure that competitors must know in advance how their progress will be measured.

5. Use groups which are reasonably independent of each other if you are using **group** competition. For example, army commanders of similar kinds of units can motivate group progress effectively by using certain objective-type goals (common problems for all the units).

6. Remind both individuals and groups that they are parts of the whole; that no matter which person or team wins, all will benefit.

7. Three basic kinds of competition are listed in their order of <u>danger</u> in use:

Individual vs. individual	-- Most dangerous
Group vs. group	-- Less dangerous
Individual vs. him/herself	-- Least dangerous and easiest to use

The competitive spirit of people is of vital interest to the manager. It is also a complex problem requiring deft management by you, for you must make competition become a part of an overall cooperation. If you don't achieve an overall cooperative feeling, then competition can wreck everything. Use it, but treat it with the utmost respect.

<u>MAXIMIZING AND NURTURING CREATIVITY</u>

The word "creativity" is surrounded by a certain aura of mystery. In getting beyond the mystery, it may be necessary to look first at what creativity is and why it is important to managers; next, at how to maximize your own creativity, and last, at how to nurture it in others.

Creativity is any kind of effective problem solving, and not just an idiosyncrasy of artists and musicians. If you think of creativity in this way, then of course, anyone who provides imaginative and successful solutions to problems--be he caretaker or chairman of the board--is very important. And creativity in this context is just as important as in business, industry and public service as it is in art, music, literature or architecture.

FOUR STEPS TO MAXIMIZE YOUR OWN CREATIVITY

You can do this by conscientiously practicing four basic steps: (1) Prime, (2) Ponder, (3) Perfect, and (4) Prove.

1. **Prime.** This is the tough stage of getting started, of "priming" the pump. You make yourself investigate, research, and write down possible scenarios, outlines, or approaches. You immerse yourself in the problem. As in writing this book, the start is, for most people, the hardest part--pushing yourself to begin, slogging through the underbrush of material, saturating yourself with research, and then writing outlines.

Creativity is not just a mysterious miracle. It is not just blinding flashes of light. It can also be laboriously searching for years for what would work as a filament for a dim electric light bulb--as Edison did. Tchaikowsky, the great Russian music composer, referred to the painstaking preparations for creation when he reminded people that the seeds of musical composition sprout forth into verdant growth only after the soil has been properly prepared.

2. **Ponder.** The first stage--priming creativity--merges into the second stage as you seriously study and re-study all sides of a problem in analyzing, reviewing, rearranging, and re-thinking. At times your mind may appear to be inactive, but in actual fact, it may be turning over possibilities without your conscious awareness. In fact, one of the best techniques for maintaining the pursuit of a problem

when you are stuck is to meditate. Let alpha brain waves become activated, and you almost certainly will find regenerated powers.

3. **Perfect.** In a sense, this is the illuminating stage, when insight opens up a great idea. This insight can be a sudden awakening, or it can be the gradual emergence of what you have been searching for. Whichever it is, solutions almost always require further development and perfecting by modifying the framework to fit your precise needs.

4. **Prove.** In this stage, you prove whether or not your solutions will work. You've refined the ideas; now is the moment of truth.

Some managers and employees are good at one or two of these stages but not at others. Some can generate ideas. Some are great at separating good from poor ideas, and some are purely action people--creative at putting ideas into action, but hopeless at coming up with ideas themselves. Therefore, don't be discouraged if you're not totally creative, but rather, choose the kind of creativity for which you have potential and maximize it. Commit. yourself to seeking fresh viewpoints, and allow yourself the luxury of serendipity (the gift of discovering the unexpected).

FOUR BASIC GUIDES TO NURTURE CREATIVITY IN OTHERS

People with much potential for creativity are never passive. They have burrs in their saddles. They sometimes thrive by working on the edge of hysteria. They let themselves be baffled by things. They don't fear being different. They often desire to excel, to be alone, and to be thorough. They are receptive to new ideas, to attempting difficult jobs, and they are very receptive even to disagreement. But they are not usually receptive to fear or pressure tactics. While they want to know the rules within which they are to work, to understand the exact nature of the problems they are to work on, and to see the real need for their services, almost universally they will not respond positively to threats and anxiety.

Good supervision of creativity is one of the most valuable assets to an organization, and a good relationship between the manager and the creative person is of paramount importance. Some strategies which you can use to nurture creativity in employees are listed under these following four basic strategies, and seven supplementary suggestions.

1. **Question customs and practices.** One day a young bride set out to cook a fish. She cut the fish into two pieces and placed them in a large pan. Her husband saw this and asked why the fish had been cut. She said she didn't know, but that her mother had always done it that way, so she always cut her fish into two pieces too. Her husband, being dissatisfied with this reply, checked with the girl's mother, who said that she didn't really know, it was simply that her mother had always done it that way. The husband then contacted the grandmother, who said, "Oh yes, that's simple; my old pan was too small!" One of the greatest barriers to creativity is "But we've always done it that way."

There are two basic reasons for holding onto old assumptions and practices without checking on their worth. One is laziness; the other is insecurity. Both of these reasons have many guises, some of which are the guises of politeness, or of good taste, of respect, of happiness, and of not getting too far ahead of the pack. For example, there is an art student who is gifted at drawing, but she's hopeless at generating ideas for design, using brilliant colors or drawing anything that is not a literal representation. The reason? Her parents consistently conveyed to her the impression that anyone who took risks in art did not have good taste. Whatever the guise, the fundamental reason is some form of passivity or insecurity.

An example of an insecure, high level manager holding onto old assumptions is Jay. He genuinely believes that he pushes creativity because he says things like, "I want you to throw out lots of ideas. I want you to use your initiative and be creative." But then, as ideas are thrown out, if Jay doesn't instantly see their merit, he is prone to discard them, and sometimes with a manner which makes the originator feel small and awful.

If you are to foster creativity, you have to have enough security yourself to strongly reinforce ideas you have not thought of and may not even at first understand. You have to get your people to ask questions such as: "Why is it this way?" "Does it have to be?" "Wouldn't it be better if. . . .?" "How can we do it more efficiently?" "Is that really important?" "Is it actually trivial and petty?"

Learn how to use different perspectives. Turn the customs and the problems inside out, upside down, and change the order of component elements. Free the mind to think in all the possible ways about possible problems or improvements without fear of what the manager will think.

2. **Dare to be different, and reward differences**. Brainstorming, a rather common group practice used to generate ideas and to find solutions, needs an atmosphere of acceptance if the participants are to think differently or a little wildly. Being different is something which most managers find a little difficult. You need to be urged at appropriate times to let your thinking jump in all directions. Brainstorming is just such a time. When you are "brainstorming," be sure to: (a) be permissive, wholly open to any ideas, and don't be critical; (b) allow "wild" ideas; (c) encourage "piggy-backing" on others' ideas; and (d) get many ideas--don't try to rush the thinkers with too rigid a time limit on the session.

Another way to dare to be different is occasionally to pose unusual and even impractical problems such as: What if Columbus had been Chinese? How would our country have developed? Dare to be unconventional yourself as long as the unconventionality does not deter progress from your goals.

3. **Discipline**. Being "different" without any discipline guideposts is likely to result in little creativity. Discipline, however, that is insensitive to the creative person is also unlikely to produce many

results that you want. Instead, try these three guides.

(a) Guide the creative person by keeping just enough pressure on to maintain commitment to the job. The objective must be constantly in sight, but pressures should never be too great. Ask yourself how gentle you can be in guidance. This will generally pay dividends with the creative person.

(b) Differentiate pressures for long or short periods of time. If you want to motivate to the maximum for a short period of time, create moderate positive pressures. If it's long-term motivation you're working for, do not create too much pressure--it is likely to bring about only immobilizing anxiety.

(c) Ensure familiarity with rules and policies within which creative persons must work, for ambiguity and unclear boundaries are also frustrating.

4. **Reinforce analogies**. Help to relate problems to the old and familiar. See similarities, don't just see differences. Managers who are defensive, or have limited perspectives, are prone to see why things are not analogies, even though they are similar, and they are likely to reject analogies on the bases of insignificant differences. This tends to stymie employees who are creative. To encourage the use of analogies, ask questions such as: "What is this like?" "What else do I know that is similar to this problem?" "What is like this, but better?" "What ideas can I borrow from some other solution to a similar problem?"

SEVEN SUPPLEMENTARY SUGGESTIONS FOR PRODUCING AND MAINTAINING AN ATMOSPHERE CONDUCIVE TO CREATIVITY

Some of the most important means for getting and keeping this kind of atmosphere follow:

(1) Place creative people in an environment which is conducive to creative thought. You might even consider relieving creative people of some routine chores which could be filled by persons who are neither creative nor expensive.

(2) Recognize creative work by salary structure, publicity, and time off for convention/conference achievements and reports as well as through sincere, specific and sensitive compliments. Maintain frequent communication, listen empathetically, and never lose contact. Watch for any signs of brooding or resentment. Creative people are sometimes victimized by others who are jealous. Further, they are sometimes prone to temperament by pushing themselves deeper into the sensitivity their creative impulses seek. Meet these problems with sincere appreciation of their achievements and whatever other aid you can give.

(3) Evaluate. Most creative people have a strong need for evaluation of their work. Exercise special concern in this, and do it as quickly as possible. Don't do as is done in one government bureau where the evaluation of new ideas takes an average time of six months to process. Needless to say, this effectively kills almost all creativity. Evaluate at once and get the results of the evaluation back to your employee immediately.

(4) Respect failures as well as successes. Failures have been necessary steps to success for most inventors, and for many other creative people as well.

(5) Reinforce, rather than reduce, the creative person's refreshing contacts with people, ideas, and developments outside those of the organization. The creative person needs contacts which are outside the subject scope of his or her work. There is something about rubbing elbows with creative people in totally different spheres which stimulates the mind and "the creative juices" to new and often more diversified achievements.

(6) Allow creative people their harmless idiosyncrasies. Don't dismiss these creators' differences and "security blankets" as mere trifles. Allow them when you can.

(7) Reduce habits and attitudes which cause barriers to creative work. For example, don't allow a talented person to be kept from bonuses or promotions

on the basis of not knowing a few insignificant technical details about a job. Reward on the basis of overall and important contributions.

Finally, when creativity is discussed, there is a certain sense of the individual set apart from society. In this context, Thoreau, who was dedicated to the individual, wrote in **Walden**:

> If a man does not keep pace with his companions,
> perhaps it is because he hears a different drummer.
> Let him step to the music which he hears,
> However measured or far away.

Non-Interference in Employees' Deeply Personal Affairs

Should the manager ever get involved in a subordinate's affairs? Not usually. In spite of the emphasis of this book for the manager to be very concerned about employees and to try to help them with those problems which cause them to be less effective than they could be, we recommend that you seldom, if ever, get caught in problems such as extramarital sex, financial disorders, or deep, personal or family dysfunctions.

If, however, a problem interferes significantly with the person's job, and the matter is no longer just personal, but one which must be dealt with in fairness to other employees, be candid and careful about what should and should not be done at work. As long as the employee is doing what should be done at work, however, don't get involved. Many a well meaning boss has contributed to a subordinate's demise by interfering, even with the best intentions in deep-seated personal affairs. If the employee asks you for help, try advising the person to go to a professional counselor who deals with those kinds of problems.

Dealing With People Who Overrate Themselves

When you have employees you believe to be overrating themselves, first be sure that you are right. Get an independent opinion. Also, be sure to use that tool that is all too seldom used--**evidence.** This can be hard data such as complaints, production quotas met or not met, profit and loss, and relevant test scores. If there is no evidence, don't waste your time. Certainly it is true that you can discourage a man by treating him poorly, but don't think on the other hand that you can "make a silk purse out of a sow's ear." This is not the time to act through intuition. To encourage or promote on the naive basis of wanting to give the person a chance when it is not merited, simply paves the way to that employee's eventual failure. Continued success has to rest on a sound foundation.

When you are sure that employees actually are overrating themselves for promotion, and the time is ripe to break the news to them, do it! But do so ever so gently. Present evidence, and if at all possible, help to counsel these persons into the kinds of jobs for which they are suited. Often, the man who would have been a failure as a manager will be a whiz at teaching piano, or with his own bicycle repair shop. Help people to fulfill themselves, not to be miserable failures. Help them to see themselves as they are, but positively.

CONCLUSION

You have looked at a definition of humanistic motivation which involves Need, Incentive, Bridge, and Synthesis. These involve satisfying individual needs in ways which will be beneficial both to the employee and the organization, incentives, low risk bridges, and thorough synthesis of changes into the individual's lifestyle. Principles were given to help you understand eleven commonly misunderstood aspects of motivation: money, meaningful work, morale, security, social relations and groups, threats and punishments, positive reinforcement, competition, creativity, employees' personal affairs, and people who overrate themselves.

TEN MASTER MOTIVATION STRATEGIES

(Love, Persuade, and Expect)

INTRODUCTION

Robert Shook has studied what he says are the **Ten Greatest Salespersons**.[1] There is no doubt whatsoever that these are super sellers. One of them, Joe Gandolfo, for example, sold over one <u>billion</u> dollars worth of insurance in 1975. This figure takes on astonishing significance when one realizes that any insurance salesperson who sells one million dollars a year is considered worthy of some of insurances' most important sales awards. But for one person to do what 1,000 superb salespersons did, is mind boggling. With that setting for the extraordinary accomplishments of these people, look at what Shook's ten super sellers consider to be most important aspects of selling.

- Sell yourself
- Use a soft sell
- Give service, service, service
- Love each client
- Establish a special relationship with each client
- Understand human beings; that's 90% of selling
- Have a strong conviction for what is best for each client
- Think positively
- Find a need and respond to it
- Strive for excellence--it's a matter of price
- Be highly self-disciplined

All of these aspects of successful selling are also characteristics of today's successful manager, for the effective manager today is first and foremost a person who understands and persuades people.

In translating this into "how to" techniques for this book, we have chosen the following action subjects. Learn to:

Esteem	Teach
De-Rut the Rut-Packers	Help Defensive People
Call Irresponsibilities	Use Emotion as well as Intellect
Set and Use Goals	Serve, Praise and Reward
Practice Openness	

MOTIVATION STRATEGY ONE: ESTEEM

"I can live for two months on a good compliment."

Mark Twain

Most employees don't mind working hard. What really gets them is when others think that their efforts are not worth much. Low esteem, probably more than any other factor, lowers productivity. All people cry out to be esteemed at work; if they are not, they become discouraged, and passive or aggressive, and slacking off usually follows. Some managers have the attitude, "They're getting paid. What more should they expect?" Where these managers exist, the effect is depressing.

Other managers think that their employees are out there always primed for receiving esteem, so that if they (the managers) walk through the workplace, dispensing esteem remotely and impersonally, sort of like a cheerleader chanting a "Rah, Rah" slogan, saying something like, "Good job, yeah, good job!" that the employees will be fulfilled and be motivated. Not so. Esteem must be deeply felt, intimately and subtly conveyed, and pervasively given. If it's not, the employees will think that their best efforts are not being noticed and understood. They will eventually feel that they're being "used." They will become resentful, and often even cantankerous. What has really happened is simply that the employee feels exploited.

Frederick William I, the mean and greatly over-weight ruler of Prussia in the 18th Century, thought he could force his citizens to esteem him. He would go on foot through Berlin using his big cane as a club on anyone who happened to rub him the wrong way. Because of this, Berliners counted themselves lucky if they could see him soon enough to be able to duck into a house or sidestreet before he got to where they were.

Once, as Frederick was bearing heavily down a street, a subject saw him and attempted to slip into a doorway, but he was too late. The imperious emperor asked if the man was going into his house. When Frederick discovered that the man was going into the house of someone he didn't even know, he asked why. The distraught subject didn't want to be thought a robber, so he tried the truth. While trembling, he said that he was simply trying to get out of the King's way because he was afraid. The mad Frederick, with eyes and neck veins bulging, hurled invective at the faltering man; then he shouted that Berliners were supposed to **love** and appreciate their King, not be fearful.

This rather extreme story illustrates three problems of some bosses: (1) exploitation, (2) insensitivity and (3) the belief that managers, on the basis of their position, are to be esteemed.

If you want to be an effective manager today, one of the best ways is to **give** esteem generously and deeply to employees. One simple way to do this is to deliberately look each day for genuine good in at least three employees, and then tell them about what you see. What you tell them, however, must be meaningful and usually specific, and not just superficial.

At first, this job will be difficult. But as you train yourself to look for worthwhile acts of kindness,

trust, generosity and work effectiveness, you'll find
that it becomes easier and easier. After a time, when
people realize that you're for real, your esteem will
be returned tenfold. When you can then get subordinate
managers to do this, the "ripple in the pond" effect
has started, and breakthrough productivity is probably
not far behind.

Another way to build esteem is by remembering at
least three things that each of your main employees is
good at and prides his or herself on. Then, each time
you meet that person, convey in some way a positive
message about one of those things.

In addition to these simple strategies which can
pay huge dividends, there are three important elements
of esteem to keep in mind: these are prestige, power
and competence. Use these in unleashing the power of
esteem.

PRESTIGE

Prestige indicates admiration and respect; it is
shown in the way that people treat others. It is
integral to overall esteem. If, for example, an
individual is disdained, he has little prestige; if he
is venerated, he has much prestige. Try the following
basic prestige principles in raising esteem.

1. The level of prestige which people need
changes at any given time according to such variables
as age, idealized image, background, and one's success
and failure record.

2. The desire for a higher level of prestige is
generally higher in youth than in older people.

3. Most people tend to seek prestige only to a
certain level, to become resigned to that level, and
then to want to maintain their prestige at that level.

4. When you give prestige to your subordinate,
through such acts as deference, appreciation or
valuation, there are often mutual benefits. The status
and esteem of the receiver are also usually raised.

5. As manager, you can largely train others to treat you with the prestige you desire as you help your subordinates to receive the prestige level they desire and need in order to thrive. In order to do this, keep in mind first that the way others treat you stems from two sources: (a) their on-the-spot judgments about you, and (b) their own habitual reactions to what they perceive as your "category," or class of people. People make these judgments and assign these categories also on the basis of the personal traits you convey and the symbols you display. Thus, by controlling personal traits and symbols, you can help both others and yourself to get the prestige desired. This is largely true both for external material symbols or internal personal traits. You can help to have importances clarified and maintained at the level each feels is deserved.

COMPETENCE

Personal competence is also an important part of esteem. Competence is simple mastery, or at least adequacy, in the performance of tasks that pertain either to a specific job or to life in general. As you help to increase competence in employees, you give them an esteem that is difficult for anyone to take away.

POWER

In order for individuals to acquire esteem, they need to feel that they can make a difference, that they can then exert influence over their own destinies. You may have an Einstein under you who does not have the power to harness his genius to productivity, and so he cops out. Each day, for many years, Einstein worked in a patent office--but not for very long. He simply finished his work quickly and then took the rest of the time to satisfy his curiosity by figuring out how space and time and other such things worked in the universe. His manager never did see the potential in this man.

There is no greater motivator than esteem. As you increase the esteem of your subordinates in loving and caring ways, you can begin to tap the greatest sources of human power that exists. As you make it a point of honor yourself that employees go away from your place a little more fulfilled in prestige, competence, and power than when they arrived there, you will almost certainly be honored in turn with more productivity.

MOTIVATION STRATEGY TWO: HELPING PEOPLE OUT OF RUTS

A typical frustration for managers is the employee who has been on the job for several years, long since mastered the necessary skills, and is now "just sort of going through the paces." This person (we'll call him Homer) is capable but stale. Homer avoids risks by staying in areas he knows. Not for him are the wanderings into the unknown or the excitement of new discoveries. In short, Homer has homed-in on just Homer, and even though he is sometimes bored, he's comfortable. Even though Homer's rut prevents personal fulfillment and happiness, he just stays there--it somehow seems easier that way.

True, there are payoffs in being in the rut. One is that Homer never has to use his wits, nor to "ad lib" nor "think on his feet." He simply plays old tapes. Staying in the rut pays off for Homer because he doesn't have to overcome his fears of trying new things. The rut is also comfortable because Homer doesn't have to really get involved with new people anymore. Paradoxically, even though the plans no longer really suit the new customers, Homer feels he's doing the right thing because these plans are tried and true and that makes Homer feel important. Yet another payoff for being in a rut is that it's stable, and because it is so static, the rut-packer feels that he shows dignity and mature behavior--none of that spontaneous childish stuff for mature adults. Homer and all like him are slowly dying on the vine as the organization's momentum dies with them. What can you do?

THREE STEPS OF "DE-RUTTING"

With all those typical payoffs for being in a rut, you have a tough job ahead. There are three steps that will help you de-rut people in your organization.

First, know the most common reasons for being in a rut. They are fatigue, burn-out, procrastination, fear of failure, laziness, compulsive planning, and turn-offs from managers, or a failure to self-actualize themselves in their workplace.

Second, determine which of these reasons fit Homer, and then tailor your strategies to Homer in helping him to get out and stay out of his ruts.

Third, make Homer aware of the liabilities of being in a rut. Sameness, and a kind of death are almost inevitable, as is a lack of job progress which will stifle promotions. What is also likely is that Homer's work actually will continue to deteriorate; it will not just level off. There is no such thing as standing still. We must either go forward or backwards. Problems will get worse and solutions less workable; this will actually result in rut discomfort in the future, rather than rut comfort. For as old solutions fail to work, Homer's wits will be taxed even more than they would be by making new plans; mere survival will demand this, and the payoffs of comfort from sameness will turn into discomfort, increasingly forcing a loss of respect from his co-workers and from himself.

ELEVEN "DE-RUTTING" STRATEGIES

Sell the Homers on the idea that, as nice and warm as a rut is, real happiness comes in getting out of it--in ceasing to be a rut-packer. Some strategies which will help to accomplish this are:

1. Help Homer to get involved in a new project which will require him to meet with employees he doesn't know. Do a little pushing, if necessary. You might put him on an action committee.

2. Bring new ideas to Homer, write him notes on these, and follow up on what he's doing about them.

3. Give him extra responsibilities which will force him to get out of the rut.

4. Let a problem develop without stepping in to solve it--the kind of problem which will help to emphasize to Homer that "rut-packing" isn't really as comfortable as making some new plans which will stave off this kind of problem in the future.

5. Get Homer to try new things when he is away from work. These things should get him outside his present environment. They might include a new kind of restaurant, a new (unplanned) place to go for the weekend, or different clothes.

6. Get Homer to experiment without an adult reason for it, rather like brainstorming is to problem solving--just to try some new ideas.

7. Help Homer to attempt some of the things he always wanted to do, but never tried; maybe some painting, leatherwork, or otherwise. Encourage him to do it just for fun, even though it may not be expertly done.

8. Subtly, help Homer to be aware of the reasons for his being in a rut and of its liabilities. "Awareness" is often the beginning of change. Be sure to include face-saving here, perhaps even a little ego building.

9. If cooperative methods don't work, try creating some tension for Homer.

10. Stop stifling Homer into submissive conformity, and allow him to fulfill himself in ways that are important both to him as well as his workplace. One of the great pleasures in life is involving oneself in work which the person himself recognizes as mighty.

11. Last, but most important, get Homer to realize that a life withdrawn from involved service loses its meaning. The great 19th Century violinist Paganini gave his incomparable violin to the City of Genoa, Italy, where he had been born. He did this with the stipulation that the violin never be played again. This was an awful mistake, for one of the immutable

laws of wood is that as long as it is used it can last for long periods of time without decaying. However, as soon as it remains unused, it begins to deteriorate.

Paganini's superb violin has now become worm-eaten and without value. This instrument, ravaged by disuse, is a reminder that life also loses its meaning if withdrawn from involved service.

MOTIVATION STRATEGY THREE: CALLING IRRESPONSIBLES TO TASK

The bane of the boss' existence is the feckless, unreliable, or untrustworthy person. There are two basic kinds of irresponsibles. One is the active irresponsible, the other the passive irresponsible.

ACTIVE IRRESPONSIBLES

The active can be either hostile and seeking revenge, or playful and conniving at games of work evasion. Actives thrive on confusion, because confusion makes it easy to evade responsibility. Chief among the methods actives employ are confusions of expectations, poor organization, excessive permissiveness, and even the manager's helpfulness. All of these confusions provide easy chances to evade responsibility. Also, they give great opportunities for blame. For example, on role confusion: "Oh, I haven't been told what to do." Or, on organization, "I tried, but due to poor organization, others kept getting in my way." Or, on permissiveness: "The boss is so nice and doesn't really seem to want us to do much work." Or, on helpfulness: "I really wanted to do that, but that what can you do when the boss does the job for you?" Actives will disrupt the entire organization if you let them change, set and generally flaunt the rules; so don't.

PASSIVE IRRESPONSIBLES

Passive irresponsibles are either lazy, limited in ability, fearful, or combinations of these traits.

"Lazies" tend to be quietly, overly involved in their own little world--they want to be left alone. "Limiteds" often smile and say, "Oh, I'll get right on that, " or "Thanks so much for your help, I'll do that." But they can never seem to go fast enough to get things done, nor do they take things seriously (or honestly) enough to tell you they're not getting things done! "Fearfuls" of course, are stifled by their fear, and do not get the job done.

CALLING IRRESPONSIBLES TO TASK

Whether active and calculating, or passive and happen-chance, irresponsibles must be called to task. You may want to consider using some of the following "don't and do" suggestions to help you meet this problem.

1.   Don't try to be a psychiatrist.

2.   Do look at your relationship to your subordinates. You may need to de-emphasize the warm relationship somewhat and increase job-related requirements.

3.   Do clarify job duties and performance standards, adding deadline times.

4.   Do take a closer look at how you are coming across to others. If you seem to be too permissive, toughen up a bit.

5.   Do be sure you have developed a practical and effective organizational structure.

6.   Do be ready to cautiously decrease the directness of your influence, and the amount of organizational structure, as responsibility increases.

ANOTHER THOUGHT ON RESPONSIBILITY

Personal responsibility is essential to the survival of democracy and freedom, as well as of productivity. Ultimately, the personal sense of responsibility (in its collective sense) by each leader and parent in America determines the character of our nation. The extent to which this individual sense of responsibility may have deteriorated may be a primary reason for our widespread disillusionment and feelings of powerlessness.

MOTIVATION STRATEGY: GOALS

GOALS! GOALS! GOALS! You know that you must constantly be goal-conscious. Without goals, all other motivators are practically useless. You must have clear goals yourself, and you must help others to sharpen the focus on their own goals.

Whatever you do with goals, you must not have a snowstorm of paperwork. You must help people to pick just a few really key results. Then get people to talk about these key results at every chance they get. Tell your employees that when they are asked what they do, they should not respond with an "I'm vice-president of such and such." But they should say, "I'm working on improving the tile shields for the space shuttle." Writing about things does not make them happen. At every opportunity, talk about your key results that you're trying to get.

Clear goals help to avoid wasted effort, and they provide the opportunity for efficient progress. If, for example, you are taking a trip, you usually decide first where you're going. You can then plot the best available route and means of getting there. This is generally considered superior to simply wandering around without a goal or route unless, of course, your goal is to wander.

Here is a sample of goal planning guide you might want to use in order to focus on key results.

GOAL PLANNING GUIDE

Name	Position			Date	

Number	Goal and Standard	Priority 1 low	5 high	Complexity Factor 1 low	5 high
1.	To coordinate with the installer of the data processing system. It will be completed by 1 Feb. 198_ according to design specifications on proposal #3		5	2	
2.	To increase customer service without hiring additional persons. There will be an increase of responses from 30 to 40 per day.		3	3	
3.	To reduce the percentage of customer complaints from 5% of all customers to 3% of all customers.		5	4.5	
4.	To provide staff development training for every employee which will result in: -- ability to cope effectively with customer complaints. -- ability to give information which is accurate and clear. -- ability to defuse anger, emotional involvement, and conflict with customers.	4		3	

SIX GOAL SETTING STEPS

After studying the needs of your people and your organization, you are ready to set goals. At this stage, don't muck about with the complexities of the situation, but sit down with paper and pencil.

1. **Main Function**. Write out the most important functions of your job. Be sure you think of planning as writing (don't just think, for thinking can easily be mere daydreaming).

2. **Things To Do**. Write the most important things you want to accomplish.

3. **Committed People**. Write the names of people from whom you can likely get deep commitment to carry out these tasks. Have exploratory talks about the tasks you have in mind with the people you've listed. Carefully assess their interests and advice.

4. **Resources**. List the resources which are needed and are likely to be available.

5. **Synthesis**. Put these three elements together: (a) goals to accomplish, (b) people to help do the work, and (c) resources.

6. **Realism**. Now, be realistic about what your final goals can be.

FIVE CRITERIA FOR SETTING GOALS

Whenever you set goals you need to answer the following five criteria questions with a "yes".

1. **Mutual agreement**? No matter how great the need, nor how valuable you think something is, success will be limited unless the other key persons buy into it.

2. **Specific**? Broadness is escapism! Specify single results to be accomplished. Global goals are good for broad directions. They are also nice for mellow late-evening world problem solving. But for daytime action results, be specific.

3. **Relevant**? All people have hobby horses they would like to ride. The danger in objective setting is that these will creep in and govern your action. Ask

yourself three questions:

(a) Will this objective help me to achieve my long-term desires?

(b) Will it help the organization significantly?

(c) Will there be visible short-term results?

4. **Reasonable, realistic, and reachable but challenging**? No further narrative is needed; this is crystal clear.

5. **Measurable and verifiable**? The objective "to find out more about school discipline" is pure folly, for you are embarking on a venture without knowing where you are going, or when you would get there. You need specificity.

ORGANIZATION FOR ACTION

Your job is only half done when you state your goals. The other half of your job is to organize them for action. This organization includes:

1. Target dates.

2. Responsibilities of the superior as well as of the subordinate.

3. Precise expectations.

4. Precise ways to measure results.

MANAGEMENT BY OBJECTIVES (MBO's) 5-4-2 RULE

M.B.O. is a well-known system designed to do just what it says. The problem, however, is that while top managers tend to think M.B.O. is a godsend, middle level managers know that it often doesn't work. Lower level managers tend to say, "O.K., I'll fill out the forms, but it's only getting in the way. It ain't really workin'."

M.B.O. is definitely tricky. But if you get the following "5-4-2" Guide under your belt (five main ingredients, four benefits, and three pitfalls), you can make it work.

Five Main Ingredients of M.B.O.

1. <u>System congruence</u>. The goals of the employees must fit with the goals of the organization.

2. <u>Measurable outcomes</u>. Goals must be precise. When accomplished, you will be able to say that you did it, and know it is done.

3. <u>Shared responsibility</u>. We recommend emphasizing a bond of reciprocal responsibility between you and your subordinates and not just a "one-way" subordinate-to-boss responsibility. Everyone knows that the subordinate is responsible to the manager, but too few managers emphasize their own responsibility for their subordinates.

If the worker fails to do well, the manager also fails and his record will show it. In ancient China, it was understood that the Emperor had the responsibility to meet the needs of his people. If he failed, it was also understood that he was to be deposed. And so it is in modern organizations. Attention to employee needs should be evident in every aspect of management.

One good way to get the best shared responsibility is for you to ask: "What is the highest standard you and I together can achieve, and how can we go about it?"

4. <u>Definition of job and performance standards</u>. When you give clear standards for performance to your employees at the very least you will reduce wasted energy. If you add fairness, clarity in expectations, consistency, and flexibility, you will very likely be well on your way to motivating your employees to maximum energy. If, on the other hand, you are not clear in your expected standards, you can easily disorient people and cause erratic and dispirited performance.

5. Minimum paperwork. Be sure about this!

Four Main Benefits of M.B.O..

1. Priorities set for action.

2. Monitoring so that aggregate systemwide changes can be made as needed.

3. Managing so that the mission of the organization as well as the tasks of the individual can be meshed with maximum ease in team and participative management.

4. Regular and organized looking at what the subordinate is doing.

Two Main Pitfalls of M.B.O.

Monologue and Manipulation . So what's new? MBO's can easily seem to put a respectable face on extremely authoritarian manipulations--by either the manager or subordinate.

Finally, you can be charismatic, brilliant and pleasing to be around, but if you don't have clear goals, all the personality characteristics in the world will profit you little in the world of action. You can't just "wing it!"

MOTIVATION STRATEGY FIVE: OPENNESS

While openness in management is an extremely important motivator, it is also dangerous. Some managers have most certainly failed because they were too open, and some have failed because they were not open enough. Why is this? Why is openness important? What kind of openness is effective? What pitfalls exist? And when and how should you be open? And, what are some phrases that universally indicate that you yourself have a closed mind?

IMPORTANCE

If you think about an organization that is open vs. one that is closed, it is a bit like comparing a brightly decorated Alpine chalet with a gray and forbidding European castle. The chalet has large windows and probably some flower boxes under them with bright red geraniums. People pass by, and feel free. The castle has narrow slits for weapons. People look up with awe and they wonder about the suspicion, anger and exploitation that made such a place necessary.

All things being equal, people appreciate the refreshing mountain-like air of openness and respond to it with thanks and commitment. In that hardy atmosphere, employees can stop wasting time and energy trying to find out where they stand, or gathering information to defend themselves.

In a sense, the bracing air of openness not only carries the message to employees that there is nothing to hide, but it also reinforces that employees are strong and important. They're not so fragile as to have to be sheltered from truth, nor so unimportant as to be ignored. In this work climate, both employees and managers are likely to cooperate in mutually beneficial endeavors.

On the other hand, when people sense that communication is somewhat closed, they tend to suspect dishonesty, manipulation, or incompetence. Employees then tend to withhold, waste or misdirect their own energies.

While there certainly are good reasons to be enthusiastic about openness, there are also deep pitfalls to avoid. Seven of these follow in the form of what **not** to do.

WHAT NOT TO DO IN BEING OPEN -- SIX DONT'S

The toughest leaders who have ever lived have had weaknesses which, if revealed to their followers at inopportune times, might have resulted in disaster.

For this reason, great leaders are careful not to reveal weaknesses, wounds, and fears in ways which would cause their followers to lose confidence in them.

The leader must be stronger and more resilient than his or her followers. A good analogy of this is a school of fish. As long as you are the front fish and are strong, the other fish will follow. But if you become visibly wounded, the followers may at best scatter, or at worst, devour you. Therefore:

1. **Don't easily reveal your fears and anxieties**: Consider for example, the worried principal in a multi-racial school, who, with nothing but rumor to go on, sent an open note to teachers asking them to be on the lookout for any KKK visitors on campus--even though no one but the principal had heard of the rumor before the note was sent. Soon the campus was seething in anxiety, even though there was no KKK and the chances were extremely slim that there would be.

2. **Don't let it all hang out**: The past decade has seen a wave of "sensitivity" sessions where in some cases it was popular to confront and "to let it all hang out." In fact, things have become so "sensitive" in some organizations that workshops have been needed just to learn how to talk to each other again. We recommend that even though you are intensely interested in others, do not be too open. Keep a bit of positive mystery about yourself.

3. **Don't confuse openness and vacillation in decision making**: One of the reasons that openness has gotten a bad name is because it has been used as an excuse to do whatever the group wanted to do. It has also been used as an excuse to abdicate responsibility for decision making and follow-up. When these things occur, openness is vacillation. It's swaying with the winds of short-term convenience. It's the kind of openness that is weak, and it should never be construed as the kind of openness that is being advocated in this book.

4. **Don't discard all your defenses**: People are not going to follow someone they believe to be weak.

ordinarily do not want to know about these faults. Therefore, don't discard all your defense mechanisms, just don't let them be compulsive or detrimental to your leadership.

5. **Don't always try to be loved**: Openness does not mean striving for love, even though it often results in people liking and respecting you. There are times when you must resort to fear, and even to "breaking the bastards."

6. **Don't be too open nor trusting, especially with neurotics or enemies**: One good rule of thumb for neurotics is that the more neurotic a person seems to be, the more likely you will need to be cautious in the use of openness. With enemies, it would of course be foolish to be completely open. The best you can do is to try to change enemies into friends through cautious openness.

SIXTY-ONE CLOSED MIND PHRASES

One of the easiest ways unwittingly to stifle openness and creativity is unthinkingly to use "closed mind" phrases. Therefore, we've included a section on some phrases of the "closed mind." You can say over and over again that you want an open operation, but as long as you communicate with a closed mind vocabulary, there won't be much openness.

Put a check beside each phrase that you tend not to use.

61 EXCUSES FOR A CLOSED MIND

1. We tried that before.
2. Our place is different.
3. It costs too much.
4. That's beyond our responsibility.
5. That's not my job.
6. We're all too busy to do that.
7. It's too radical a change.
8. We don't have the time.
9. Not enough help.
10. Let's hold it in abeyance.
11. Let's give it more thought.
12. Top Management would never go for it.
13. Let's put it in writing.
14. We'll be the laughing stock.
15. Not that again.
16. We'd lose money in the long run.
17. Where'd you dig that one up?

8. That will make other equipment obsolete.
9. Let's make a market research test of it first.
0. Our plant is too small for it.
1. Not practical for operating people.
2. The men will never buy it.
3. The union will scream.
4. We've never done it before.
5. It's against company policy.
6. Runs up our overhead.
7. We don't have the authority.
8. That's too ivory tower.
9. Let's get back to reality.
0. That's not our problem.
1. Why change it, it's still working O.K.
2. I don't like the idea.
3. You're right-but. . . .
4. You're two years ahead of your time.
5. We're not ready for that.
6. We don't have the money, equipment, room, personnel.
7. It isn't in the budget.
8. Can't teach an old dog new tricks.
9. Good thought, but impractical.

40. We did all right without it.
41. That's what we can expect from staff.
42. It's never been tried before.
43. Let's shelve it for the time being.
44. Let's form a committee.
45. Has anyone else ever tried it?
46. Customers won't like it.
47. I don't see the connection.
48. It won't work in our plant.
49. What you are really saying is. . . .
50. Maybe that will work in your department, but not in mine.
51. The Executive Committee will never go for it.
52. Don't you think we should look into it further before we act?
53. What do they do in our competitor's plant?
54. Let's all sleep on it.
55. It can't be done.
56. It's too much trouble to change.
57. It won't pay for itself.
58. I know a fellow who tried it.
59. It's impossible.
60. We've always done it this way.
61. May cause confusion.

ount the number of phrases you did **not** check.

core: If your score is 57-61, skip to the next section. If it's 50-57, you're pretty open, 30-50 above average, 15-30 about average.

Many people have been trained from birth to have a closed mind. This attitude comes out in phrases they use. You can change the way you think and speak, however, with conscious positive imaging, replacement of closed with open mind phrases, and with 20 other techniques listed next.

Twenty "Do's" for Developing Openness

1. **Going All Out**: When you decide to establish a reputation for openness, make sure that you go **all out** to let others know of your resolve. Tell people of your intentions, do what you said you're going to do, and then even repeat what you have done. Because employees often suspect their boss's intentions to be open, it is necessary to establish clearly by words, decisions, and actions what you're doing.

2. **Being Suggestible**: Always be open to any suggestion. Never turn employees off by belittling their advice in any manner. Even when your superior wisdom tells you not to heed it, treat their desire to help as pure gold.

The ancient Saducees and Pharisees of Israel epitomized the closed mind. They had studied and become experts, knew more than anyone else, and therefore thought that they had the right to discard new insights and suggestions from lesser mortals. This is one of the best ways to have a static and stagnant workplace.

3. **Freedom for Results**: Inspire and control results, not conduct (unless conduct definitely interferes with results). There are strong drives in most people to be both independent and competent. Capitalize on these through freedom for results.

4. **Flexibility**: Don't be dogmatic. Winston Churchill said, "To improve is to change, so to be perfect is to have changed often!"

5. **Hostility**: When you're "attacked" by others, be open enough to be able to listen, and to tolerate the attacker's emotions and criticism, without either compulsive counter-attack or repression.

6. **Ambiguity**: When there is complexity, be able to tolerate ambiguity until it can gradually evolve to clarity; don't feel that you have to "nail" everything down at once.

7. **Honestly Spontaneous**: Allow yourself enough openness to be spontaneous and unpredictable, but don't let spontaneity become compulsive.

8. **Reasoned Disagreement**: Thrive and grow with disagreement as your mind stretches to take it in. Don't require "yes-people."

9. **Self-Understanding and Helping Others**: Be open enough to accept and understand yourself; in so doing begin to reach out to others, empathize, and help them grow.

10. **Gracious Honesty**: Be open in letting others know where they stand, but in a constructive way.

11. **Awareness of Expectations**: Know your employees' expectations and meet them whenever you can. When you can't meet them, be open about why.

12. **Open Door**: Try to maintain an "open door," "drop by" policy unless pressures absolutely prohibit this. An open-door policy may require you to work a little faster, or longer hours, at times, but it is likely to be worth it. You might wish to do as one very busy superintendent did. Have one day a month open to employees dropping by to make any suggestions they wished. Appointments could also be made at other times, but they liked having "their" day.

13. **Helpful**: Always maintain an open and empathetic attitude, even when you are helping to channel an ineffective employee into another job.

14. **No Secrets**: Let it be known that you allow no secrets or secretive operations except those which are absolutely necessary to a person's need for confidence or your company's competition with another company.

15. **Hurtfulness**: Let it be known that your openness stops when hostile or hurtful humor about another individual begins.

16. **Meaningful Voice**: Devise ways to ensure that every single employee under you has the opportunity for meaningful input into the company's operation.

17. **No Favorites**: Ensure that you do not gain a reputation for favoritism. Everyone has certain likes and dislikes, and these are often rather transparent to others. Ensure, however, that your personal preferences do not result in special privileges to employees who share those preferences.

18. **Information Available to All**: Give information freely and completely unless it is truly confidential. Knowledge tends to cure ill-will and paranoia; it also helps the well person to feel relaxed and a part of things. Even evil gossip can usually do less damage when information flows freely.

19. **Being Practical**: Season your openness with discretion and common sense. An Irish friend calls this "Irish truth." What he means is: (a) do not debase nor destroy a person with the truth; and (b) always remember **who** you are, **where** you are, and **what** you are!

20. **Evaluate Yourself Frequently by the Above "Do's."**

MOTIVATION STRATEGY SIX: TEACH -- A SIX POINT FORMULA

To some managers this seems at first to be a mundane part of motivation; it doesn't seem to ring with the dramatic go-get-'em inspiration that they like. But the fact of the matter is that the teaching part of motivation can be one of the most rewarding and productive parts of being boss. In teaching, you don't just give orders, you help your employees learn what to do to bring productivity up, or to increase cooperation, or to resolve conflicts. And almost always they will respond not only with improved skills, but also with gratitude to you.

Although teaching is fundamentally understanding

and guiding people, you need a structure to follow. Try this six point formula: (1) explain, (2) demonstrate, (3) involve, (4) use variety, (5) be relevant, and (6) set deadlines.

1. EXPLAIN.

Explanation involves describing first the overview, next the specific view, and last, how to. Explain what you want people to do. Show people the relationship between what they will be doing and the total project--the "trees in relation to the forest." It is usually very important to show people how their particular work is integral to the whole. You will usually want to answer the journalistic W's at this stage--who, what, when, where and why. Show specifically, step by step, what you want done, and exactly how to do it--unless, of course, you are relying on their creativity for the specifics, in which case, of course, make this expectation clear.

2. DEMONSTRATION.

Demonstration, of course, means showing how to do something, as practically and graphically as possible. The way you demonstrate--all at one time, or only in part, with drawing, overhead projector, etc.--must naturally be contingent upon what you need to demonstrate. Whatever methodology you use, the key is to get your audience to hear, see and especially to feel what you're talking about. Never try to demonstrate something you don't understand well yourself.

3. INVOLVE.

Involvement is the actual practice and performance by the learner. This requires encouragement, understanding, and patience from the boss. Be sure you establish a climate in which the employee can feel comfortable making mistakes. Everyone does at this stage. Get a slow start, and then help people gradually to increase in facility. The important thing is that practice makes perfect, so you can't expect the first trial to yield perfection.

4. USE VARIETY.

In order to get and maintain interest, present your material in various ways. Make use of "outside" experts. Use supplementary audio and visual aides to intensify and motivate learners as well as to clarify. Change your methods as needed to reflect your particular learners' interests and needs, and be sure to use different teaching methods as needed because of the general style of learning that your audience has.

5. BE RELEVANT.

An old adage says: "Don't fire with a shotgun when you need a rifle." Much energy can be wasted, and much resentment can result by giving general directions or admonitions rather than precise ones. Focus also on what is relevant and important. In a certain Greek class there was a student, Arnold, who rambled. Dr. Zakinthos, the Greek professor, finally tired of Arnold's pointless verbosity and said, "Arnold, you express yourself beautifully, but you have nothing to say!" What profit is there to anyone if you say beautiful things to your employees but don't help them to move in the right direction? In short, focus with precision on the matter at hand and let your discussion help move the group toward its goals and objectives.

6. SET DEADLINES.

Remember always to set the dates by which certain objectives should be reached. There are three reasons for this: (1) all people have some inertia; (2) it provides the framework for the feedback needed for corrective action; and (3) progress reports according to time-lines provide the basis for cooperative action as problems are revealed. Use these to help your employees make improvements.

MOTIVATION STRATEGY SEVEN: HELPING DEFENSIVE PEOPLE

Defensive people need protection from their own self-images. Defensiveness is an automatic way of responding to self-threat. It usually involves strong needs for acceptance and for reassurance that one's world is not crumbling. Defensiveness often results in angry blaming and complaining in order to postpone confronting and solving problems.

While humane managers generally avoid challenging or uncovering defensive behaviors, they also try to understand them in order to bolster self-respect in the defensive persons, and to help find solutions to problems causing the defensiveness. While most of this section will be about helping defensive persons to develop competence and self-respect, the first things a manager must think about are paradoxically what **not** to do.

Avoid The Five Basic Don'ts

1. Don't destroy another person's mask.

Defensive people are likely to need their disguises. In fact, probably only about 5 to 10 percent of all people have the ability to see their own masks. If you tear off the other person's mask, you destroy the person. When the mask is ready to come off, it must release itself gently if the person who wears it is not to "lose face" destructively. People have need of their disguises for two reasons: (a) they need to like themselves (this sometimes means protecting a good picture of themselves); and (b) they strongly need to be liked by others. This means that they need to master whatever skills are needed to make them look good in their colleagues' eyes.

2. Don't be a therapist, but do reach out to help.

If you understand a person's real motives for doing something, you can reach out to help. A person who talks very fast and compulsively may do so because of fear that no one will listen. Your careful attention can help. One who boasts inordinately may need your praise. The person who lacks skills may profit from your detailed and factual descriptions of what needs to be done.

3. DON'T PUSH IN CRISIS

A friend who is a high state department official once said that in times of crisis, first consider doing nothing. Regardless of the cynical opinion of some that this is the modus operandi at the Department of State, and therefore to be disregarded, this is good advice for defensive disguises as well as for other selected crises, for people often instinctively hide behind masks or respond with some irrational reactions to crises. They do this both to get attention and also to save face. Doing nothing at the time may discourage both masks and irrational activity.

4. DON'T USE HACKNEYED PHRASES WHICH ONLY MAKE THE PERSON FEEL WORSE.

Such platitudes as "Heal thyself," or "Pull yourself up," or "Stop whining" routines won't help and they may harm. While these phrases may work for the person who needs a kick in the pants, the majority of defensive people need new skills and new attitudes, not a push which undermines their confidence even more.

5. DON'T COMMUNICATE ANY FEARS YOU MAY HAVE.

Instead, **encourage**. Do help that person to be rationally positive, to respect himself or herself, to build courage and to have realistic expectations and goals.

BUILD COURAGE THROUGH BELIEFS

Talk to your employee (we'll call him Joe) openly, but positively. Say that you have a personal interest in him and that you want to help him use the considerable talent that he has (if this is so). Emphasize that you don't have any magic powers, that you are not in any way a psychiatrist, but that you have been reading some of the psychologists, and you would like to try to help him use his own resources more effectively. If Joe agrees to this possibility, you are ready to use the following principles and strategies to help him.

Help Joe to understand that he can best generate

his inner courage by understanding that he, himself, determines what he thinks, and that his feelings and actions come from his thoughts. It is the way he **looks** at life that ultimately affects him most.

Personal Beliefs that destroy courage. There are three kinds of beliefs that inhibit the building of an inner courage which in turn will raise self-confidence. These are (1) belief in perfection, (2) belief in miracles, (3) blaming or complaining. Perfectionists believe that you're worthless unless you are perfect. Those who believe in miracles are sometimes prone to expect miracles or other supernatural sources to fall into their laps while they sit passively and wait for them. This way their goals are achieved without any work or effort on their part.

The blamers and complainers, on the other hand, blame fate, other people, or environmental factors for their discouragement. The result of all three beliefs is a certain rejection of one's own responsibility to get done what can be done. They are basically avoidance techniques.

Building courage. If you sense that Joe is lowering his self-esteem by irrational beliefs, help him to get his thoughts straight. The following affirmations by Joe can help:

1. I don't have to have approval from **all** people.

2. I don't have to be perfect to be worthwhile.

3. I give people power over me if I let them make

   me angry, upset, or cause me to act in unacceptable ways.

4. When people treat me badly, I will respond to the task at hand, but I will not respond emotionally to their hostility.

5. I can, to a large extent, control my feelings by my thoughts.

6. I will use my past to learn but **not** to feel

guilty and then to worry about the future.

7. I can be happier by actively confronting
   problems with positive action than by avoiding
   them.

One of the first steps in increasing self-
confidence is to help Joe energize an inner courage.
The first element of this process involves developing a
dynamic, complex, and growing self-identity rather than
one which is rigid, simplistic, and hard like granite.

Help Joe to move from a rigid to a dynamic
identity.

Rigid Identity	Dynamic Identity
I'm the kind of person who always fails. I'm just a loser.	In the past, I have had a tendency to be dis- couraged by failures rather than to use them to spur me on.

Help Joe to have some successful experiences and to
relate these to the strengthening of an inner courage.

Four Ways to Inventory And Restore Personal Resources

If you ask any Joe with low self-esteem to list his
personal assets and liabilities, the list he produces
probably will resemble that of a "disasterizer"--98
liabilities and 5 assets. Discouragement results to
anyone who focuses on personal weakness. Practically
every discouraged person you talk to says something
such as "But I'm only being realistic." The problem is
that this is "irrational surrealism"; it is distorted.
It is focusing on negative resources and neglecting
positive ones. Therefore, help Joe to focus on
positive resources as well:

1. Have Joe write the benefits of focusing on
liabilities.

2. Have Joe write the benefits of focusing on

assets as well as liabilities, "rationally and realistically." Be prepared to discuss this in terms of the debilitating effect of dwelling on one's failures, embarrassments, and physical "carbunkles." Say to Joe that he can open old wounds, keep them festering and inflamed, or he can put salve on them, to help reduce their effect to minor scars and give at least equal time to his good points. He can live life with re-energized enthusiasm by looking at the sun as well as the darkness.

3. Now have Joe write down an asset analysis of himself based on:

> Physical resources
> Mental resources
> Emotional resources
> Social resources
> Personality resources

4. Have Joe resist the benefits of allowing himself to mope about in a slump. Wallowing in misery is a form of self-indulgence too lethal to encourage.

Use Helpful Language

As a man speaks, so does he think. As he thinks, so does he act. A highly significant part of becoming more confident is to use words which indicate responsibility for thoughts and actions. Some examples are:

Instead of using these left hand column phrases	Use these right column phrases
You made me . . .	I choose . . .
I couldn't control myself . . .	I chose . . .
It shouldn't be that way.	It is that way. Now, do I want to expend the energy and change it?

| You ought not to treat me that way. | However you treat me is your business. However, I choose not to be disturbed by it. |
| I'll die if she goes away. | If she leaves me, I'll have some serious adjustments to make. |

FOUR EXERCISES FOR BUILDING SELF RESPECT

Another important element of increasing self-confidence is to build self-respect. Self-respect is truly courageous; it involves Joe's trusting himself and taking personal responsibility for his decisions and actions. It means that Joe faces problems and stands tall. He grows out of those childhood needs to be taken care of by others. He no longer retreats from the normal demands of life. When he truly respects himself, it means that he is one of the great people who have become fully accountable for their actions. If, however, Joe needs some help in getting to this point, you might ask him to try the following four strategies as exercises:

1. Change disrespect for self   to   Self-respect by using
                                        Right hand column phrases.

-- The devil made me do it.   -- I did it.

-- Everybody does it.   -- Even if everybody does
                                     it, it doesn't make sense
                                     to me. I will not do it.

2. Each day for the next two weeks, write down two things you can do to increase trust in yourself and your decisions. For example, you might think of people whom you have, in the past, asked for answers to problems. The next time there are problems, find the answers for yourself.

3. Challenge self-defeating assumptions. Think of ideas that have been passed to you about others, or work, or even yourself that didn't make sense. Now, challenge these ideas. Write down as many as you can

think of, and ask yourself if it's really to your
advantage to be talked into them.

4. Develop a comprehensive plan for overcoming
debilitating domination by others.

Eight Steps in Solving Problems Realistically

Give Joe a simple framework for analyzing
problems, for most lack of confidence stems from
insecurities about coping with various kinds of
problems. These steps can help Joe to analyze his
problems and to find solutions.

1. Try to remain calm.

2. Try to decide what exactly is the problem.

3. Try to think of at least three different
   solutions to the problems. If you can't think
   of enough solutions, ask someone else to help
   you.

4. Think of the results of each solution--what
   will happen if you use the solution? The
   results should consider: (a) how others will
   react; (b) the immediate good and bad
   results; and (c) the long-term good and bad
   results.

5. Decide on the most desirable results--the one
   with the most good and least bad.

6. Choose the solution that leads to this result.

7. Figure out the steps to do this solution.

8. If the solution does not work, go back to
   Step 4 and pick the second best result and go
   through the steps again.[3]

   (You may need to combine solutions to get the
   results that you want, so be ready to do
   this.)

Help Joe to set from one to three goals which he can reasonably meet within a set period of time. (Generally, the lower in self-confidence, the quicker you will want him to see successful results.) Be sure that the goals are mutually agreed upon, specifically relevant to an improved self-concept as well as to the organization, achievable, and success oriented. Also, be sure that the goals are a bit above what Joe knows he can do. Then, help Joe achieve his goals with just enough guidance to ensure success, but not enough to spoil Joe's feeling of success.

In helping Joe to set realistic goals, help him to remember that one of the most frequent errors people make causing low self-confidence is failing to accept the non-changeable realities. The first non-changeable reality is that there are certain aspects of your life that you cannot change. Know what these are. The second non-changeable reality is to accept those things in life to which you are not willing to devote enough resources to change. Accept these non-changeable realities early on in your life and then don't waste energy setting fruitless goals concerning them.

Finally, helping the unrealistically unconfident people to develop can be one of the most satisfying aspects of being a manager. Naturally, it also benefits both "Joe" and the organization.

MOTIVATION STRATEGY EIGHT: CONSIDER EMOTION AS WELL AS INTELLECT

There is no way to motivate well unless you involve the heart along with the mind. Although we all like to appear to be led by reason and logic, we are also strongly influenced by emotion. If, for example, your husband (or wife) goes to the department store and buys something, the chances are that she or he will attempt to justify the purchase with logic: "I saved a lot of money," "I needed it," "It's fine quality and rugged," etc. However, if you delve deeper, you almost certainly will find that the purchase was motivated at least partially on the basis of how it appealed to the emotions: "Did I look sexy?" "Did it make me look thinner, younger, etc?" In order to appeal to the heart as well as the mind, be emotionally involved yourself, and involve the heart as well as the minds of your people.

REACH HEARTS

If you're able to tap your employees' beliefs and enthusiasms, the sky will be the limit in both personal and organizational success. In order to tap heart-power, create a somewhat permissive atmosphere. Begin to stimulate positive and dynamic emotional vibes by drawing out personal feelings. Many people are eager to get these across to the boss, and the boss who either gives no chance for feelings, or who puts down peoples' expressions, loses great opportunities to tap heart-power. So draw out feelings. Allow work to be a place where spontaneity and humor take place, where emotions stir, and where ideas begin to unfold.

Practice the Golden Rule on all people, both hostile and friendly. Ask yourself, "How would I want to be treated in this situation?" By taking this approach, permanent solutions can almost always be found, and personal stress can be greatly minimized.

On the other hand, if you practice the tit-for-tat rule of, "I will be just as nasty and stubborn as you are," you will find almost permanent stress, usually only temporary solutions, and very little heart-power.

COMBINE EMOTION AND INTELLECT APPROPRIATELY

In trying to motivate people to certain action, there are times when you are uncertain about how "emotional" and how "intellectual" to be. Bill Georgiades, Dean of the College of Education at the University of Houston, has designed a guide for this in the form of a paradigm.[4] It centers on guiding what kind of influence you should use in trying to get action from followers. On one hand consider how complex the task or issues are; on the other, know how resistant your people are. Then use emotional and intellectual influence in appropriate combinations as the tasks are low to high in complexity, and as people are low to high in resistance.

LOW   LOW   HIGH

	RESISTANCE BY PEOPLE	
Give Information	Be Emotional
Stimulate Intellectually or Physically	Be Intellectual and Emotional

COMPLEXITY OF TASK

RESISTANCE BY PEOPLE

HIGH   LOW   HIGH

KEEP SOME DISTANCE.

Although it is important to be emotionally involved, it's also imperative to keep some distance. This closeness yet distance paradox helps to keep things in balance.

MOTIVATION STRATEGY NINE: SERVE

If you want to motivate, one of the best things you can do is to make it clear to subordinates that you will help them to solve their problems in a non-manipulative way. In other words, you're not just helping them in a "tit for tat" kind of way. You're not just helping them in order to get an "indentured" servant, but you're genuinely sincere. This is something that can't be faked, at least not for long. If you truly do care for your people, it will show in your actions time after time.

On the other hand, if you use and manipulate your

people, these motives also show through. No matter how glib you may be, nor how clever an amateur psychologist, you're bound to be unmasked sooner or later.

An extremely successful general stuns subordinates regularly by opening most conversations with something like, "How can I help you?" Needless to say, he has more power and loyalty than the average general. The power he chooses to use most of the time is emotional, personal, and helpful. By being a dedicated servant as well as commander, he does not need to use much raw power. His basic attitude, even as a military general, is how can I be the best servant/commander of my subordinates as well as my superiors? Effective leaders have always been those who were adept at serving the needs of their followers without letting the follower take advantage of them.

MOTIVATION STRATEGY TEN: PRAISE AND REWARD

"The greatest efforts of the human race have always been traceable to the love of praise."

Unknown 19th Century English Essayist

Praise and reward are sticky problems. People are **not** just standing out there waiting with open minds for your pearls of praise as you hurry by. In fact, people have been padded with layers of defense against accepting your compliments. In order to get through these defenses, you need pointed and appropriate rewards and praise which the recipient feels have been earned. Only then will your compliments really be appreciated.

While praise is widely recognized as necessary to motivation, the principles which make praise successful remain widely obscured. Nine principles and strategies to make praise and rewards work are described here.

Nine Guides for Giving Praise & Reward

1. Never underestimate praise needs:

The fact that many people have good crap-detectors for phony praise should remind you that praise should be sincerely given. But it **must** be given. Nearly all people seem to have a nearly insatiable desire for praise so long as it is palatable to their individual tastes and credible enough to accept. The secret is to zero-in on areas of real concern or need.

Everyone, no matter how successful, has some kind of inferiority complex. There are no completely superior people. Excepting a few mental cases, no one believes he or she is invulnerable. Praise can be used with everyone to enhance self-confidence. The problem is how to give it effectively.

With highly intelligent and perceptive people, be sure to recognize their brilliance. Indirect praise is often effective. For example, "Bob tells me that everyone in your department is enthusiastic about the way you're including them in your planning." Perhaps the most important element of praise for an intelligent person is that the "praiser" understand and appreciate what is important. A chief executive officer we know sends many notes of appreciation to his managers, and he always seems to perceive exactly what was really significant. As a result, people prize his appreciation, believe in his ability and work hard for him.

Referring to what someone said during a previous conversation is usually successful. When you say, "Jim, at that workshop five months ago you mentioned how important it was for a leader to use emotion with his employees, as well as objective analysis of problems," this is flattering to Jim.

2. Individualize praise.

Study the person you are going to compliment and know his or her strengths and weaknesses, so that for the sake of credibility you can praise a strength and not a weakness. If, for example, you extol the sensitivity and kindness of Anna, a person you hardly know, when it's common knowledge that she's a cow, you're in trouble.

Individualizing praise for the person you do not have time to study well is difficult at the best of times. However, you can at least try to determine if the person is shy. If shy, tone the praise down; if not, you might make the praise a bit more profuse. In trying to find the balance between spreading praise too thickly or thinly, err on the thin side, if you must err.

You can also be in trouble with people you think you know well. This was the case with Mr. Biz Zee. He criticized his secretary Renee for her generally slow speed of work and also complimented her at the same time on her intelligence. The secretary was offended because she thought the boss was being sarcastic. Renee herself was a complex combination of defensiveness (she knew she wasn't getting all her boss wanted done) and false self-confidence (but it couldn't be her fault). Mr. Biz Zee should have been more sensitive to Renee's defensiveness. He should have toned down the criticism by giving some specific ways to organize work for more speed, while emphasizing Renee's intelligence as a key factor in her being able to make the changes. He would also need to show diplomatically how the job was not an impossible one.

3. <u>PRAISE IN PUBLIC ONLY WHEN YOU WANT OTHERS TO KNOW OF YOUR ESTEEM</u>.

Public praise increases your difficulties. If you give too much praise, embarrassment is likely; if too little, then a lack of confidence by colleagues is likely. Also, the kind of praise which is effective in public depends on very complex factors such as the audience's collective sophistication, mood, and personality make-up. Naturally, the more homogeneous the audience, the easier the praise and vice versa, so that audiences composed either of engineers only or salespersons only are usually easier to use praise with than an audience of both engineers and salespersons together (providing, of course, that your generalizations about engineers and salespersons are valid).

4. TELL IT STRAIGHT.

People bitterly resent being manipulated. Praise easily can be thought of as a form of manipulation unless it appears to be straight. For best results, praise persons for things they already believe to be true about themselves, and give the praise plainly, free from contrived and manipulative slickness. Remember most people come equipped with pretty good crap-detectors.

5. DON'T MAKE ONE PERSON HAPPY AND 49 OTHERS UNHAPPY.

Certainly, it is counter-productive to give rewards or praise so that few gain. In overcoming this problem, learn what is important to the audience or group, as well as what is important to you. Also, consider giving one main reward and many lesser recognition awards, perhaps graduated ones.

6. BE PERSONAL.

Use terms such as: "I owe you . . ." "you really helped me. . . ." or "That's the best . . . I've ever seen." Also, use the person's name; this helps to give "heart and soul" impact. There is one rare exception to using names. I have met only one person who becomes a bit uncomfortable with the use of his name; he preferred a simple, "Sir."; but this is a rare exception.

7. COMPLIMENT FAIRLY OFTEN, BUT GIVE FORMAL AWARDS INFREQUENTLY.

8. RECEIVE COMPLIMENTS WELL YOURSELF:

Compliments are complex and perplexing. In addition to giving compliments yourself, deal well with the different kinds of compliments which come your way. They come in three varieties: **sincere**, **barbed**, and **puzzling**.

Receiving Sincere Compliments. Never belittle complimenters by giving them the feeling that an accomplishment really wasn't very important, or that anyone could have done the same thing as well. Rather, be gracious and say something simple like, "Thank you very much."

Receiving Barbed Compliments. The manager of ten either hears, or is the recipient of barbed compliments. The temptation is to give tit for tat. The best policy, however, is a simple "thank you," or a relaxed smile. Seldom, however, engage in the retaliatory zap for revenge.

Receiving Puzzling Compliments. Either when receiving or giving compliments, be aware of puzzling compliments, but don't let them affect you seriously. For example, when you suspect that someone is complimenting you primarily to get something in return, reply with a simple thank you, but don't let your suspiciousness override your relationship so that you become unpleasant in return.

Also, in giving a compliment, be aware how puzzling you, yourself, can be. By giving a non-job-related compliment such as, "What a pretty necklace," you can cause questions of, "Aren't all my necklaces usually nice?" "Dirty old man," or "What does he want?" So, with these kinds of compliments, be sure that the compliment is not misunderstood.

9. LISTEN WELL.

The need to be listened to is great in all of us, and you can praise the speaker simply by listening intently. Keep your hands still and watch the talker's face. Don't interrupt, and ordinarily, don't argue,

particularly if the other person is stubborn. Rapt attention can be high praise indeed.

FINALLY: LOVE, PERSUADE AND EXPECT

In public service jobs, as well as in profit-making companies, the first secret of humane management and motivation is to treat each individual as though he or she were an important client. Be the best salesperson you can, even if the "client" is your subordinate. This does not by any means imply a degrading role for the boss. Rather, it implies the superior role of service to the individual, the organization or the organization's constituency.

Master motivation strategies were described which, if used appropriately, will help you to be effective.

PART TWO

THE MANAGER

HUMANISTIC POWER TECHNIQUES
AND ERADICATION OF VICTORIAN BOSS HABITS

The guts of power is being a positive humanistic entrepreneur.
To do this, eradicate Victorian Boss Habits, maximize personal
fulfillment and persuasion and minimize force.

THE MANAGER

THE GUTS OF POWER

"It is the impotence of
force to establish anything.
In the end, the sword is
always conquered by the mind."

Napoleon Bonaparte

INTRODUCTION

As an effective manager today you have an alter ego whose name is "Personal Power." Regardless of how lowly or exalted your position is, and regardless of how often you change jobs or get promoted, you always take this companion with you. Although you may change your "Personal Power's" walk, talk, stance or demeanor at any time, it remains your most important asset, or liability. While old-time bosses got most of their power from their position, new-age managers get most of theirs from themselves, and the way they treat others. You can worry about this change in where power comes from, or you can use the change for the benefit of yourself and others. The choice is up to you.

You can use power for many reasons: you can use it to control and humiliate, to get security or fame, to help and protect, to compensate for paranoia or insecurity, and various mixtures of these. Power can produce a healthy glow of security and prosperity. It may even be, as Henry Kissinger once said, the "ultimate aphrodisiac." It can also result in worry, illness, insecurity and even bitterness. Even for those who may seem to be using power successfully, ill effects may result. Constipation can be the price of power. This is perhaps because people who strongly seek power tend to want to control everything. Erich

Erikson described Martin Luther as a man with an outsized need and drive for power who suffered perpetually from constipation. Power, and other factors surrounding the use of power, can also increase your anxiety and paranoia, as it appeared in Richard Nixon and some of his top aides.

You can struggle for power in a joyless way. You can pursue power so that deep internal conflicts develop if you want excessively to control and be in command as well as to be comforted. Some of us Americans have an additional problem in the use of power; we want it, but we're not supposed to like it. Therefore, we sometimes give the feeling that power has been thrust on us against our will and that it is an onerous burden, when in fact we actually relish it.

Regardless, however, of whether the exercise of power results in euphoria or frustration, the problem for all managers is how to use it effectively. You no doubt recognize that while in the past few years workers and society have changed dramatically, managers' habits and practices have remained nearly static. This is one of the reasons that approximately 85% of manager failures are due to ineptness in dealing with people, while only about 15% are due to technical inadequacies.[1] You know that today's employees are much more sophisticated, complex, and knowledgeable than workers were twenty years ago. Where money, or mere employment, used to do it all, neither of these suffice very often now. The vast majority of today's employees also demand esteem, meaning, and appreciation. They need to feel that the power you use is much more with them, than over them. Therefore, your greatest "Personal Power" is in fusing individual needs with those of the organization through persuasion, not through money or fear.

Pascale and Athos describe the "effective leader as one who adopts the style of a superfollower, who serves with his followers' blessing and consent, and who is able to inspire because he is first able to respond to their needs and concerns." They go on to say, ". . . people who use power best use it directly only as necessary to get the job done. They do not worry much about it as an end in itself."[2]

DIFFERENT USES OF POWER

As you ponder your "Personal Power," first ask yourself how you generally use power. To illustrate one of the most prevalent uses of power, try an experiment. Ask anyone to put his hand up in the air. Without saying anything, take hold of the person's hand, and push. What happens? Almost all people will push back. Ask yourself how much power is used in this way? It's natural in our society to think in terms of "You gotta kick a little to get good results," and, "You gotta control to be powerful." "You have to put 'em on the spot." Or, "Show 'em what's wrong and make 'em think about it." But, when you push, you get creative avoidance of all kinds.

When you stop kicking, pushing or controlling, work often decreases, and you may have to start pushing, kicking and controlling again. In order to get the work done, you have to give constant directions. This is not unusual; it's normal. But there are better ways.

Look at two different uses of power in a simple illustration about washing a van. First, ask your son simply to wash the family van because it needs washing. You have the power to get the job done. But what is your son likely to do? He may grumble and then do a quick and perfunctory job. If, however, when the van is dirty, you ask you son if he wants to use it this weekend, you may find you don't even have to ask him to wash it. Not only is the van voluntarily washed, it is also waxed, the sidewalls cleaned, the interior vacuumed, and the paint is even touched up. Why the difference? You know that the answer is demand vs. desire, "have to" vs. "want to," or raw power vs. mutual benefit. In most situations, we have a choice; we can use a form of raw power in force and fear, or we can employ power with people through incentives and positive attitudes. When confronted with this decision about how to use power, the first inclination of many of us, because of habit as well as frustration, is to show employees what raw power and muscle really are. We might actually be convinced that the best way to be effective today is to use power over people as Victorian bosses might have done.

Look at the situation carefully, however. Think about the logical consequences. Even if you do chose this approach, and win in the short run, you may still lose in the long run. For raw power used over people frequently results in those over whom it is used feeling powerless. When this happens, one of two things is likely to occur. Either the people who feel shut out are likely to turn to negative uses of power themselves to achieve a power balance, leading ultimately to a kind of madness, or, those who feel the desperation of powerlessness may hang a wreath of apathy around their necks and become passive. Neither alternative is desirable; each lessens the effectiveness of both employees and managers.

When you use raw power over employees, you take away accountability and responsibility. Even when raw power works, it takes away dignity. It may also create tremendous stress both for manager and employees. With fear and raw power, all of human life becomes an exercise to control one's existence and escape the degradation of submissiveness. When this happens, the losers are bound to feel powerless. Without power there is no pride, and without pride civility, community and self crumble.

Lord Acton once said, "Power tends to corrupt, and absolute power corrupts absolutely." But power**less**ness also tends to corrupt, and absolute powerlessness may corrupt absolutely. If it is true that both excessive power and excessive powerlessness corrupt both managers and workers, it would seem logical that a form of management is needed which would help both manager and employee to be appropriately powerful. This we call humanistic entrepreneurship, or power **with** people; it begins with attitudes and incentives.

INCENTIVE AND ATTITUDE POWER

Regardless of whether or not you are a humane manager, you succeed or fail as you do, or do not, get others to work effectively. There are two kinds of

positive power **with** people; they are incentive and
attitude power. Donkeys and carrots characterize
incentives, and incentives work as long as the carrot
is shaped and colored brightly, the donkey is hungry,
and the reach not too far. The problem is that the
donkey needs to eat only spasmodically, or the carrot
needs to get larger and tastier. For example, what
about those times when you used to get your little
brother to do your chores--such as taking out the
garbage. Remember how the first time was fair and
reasonable. "I'll take it out if I can use your car to
go to the movie." Before long, it may have developed
into, "O.K., I'll take out the garbage if I can have
your car and your girlfriend Didi for two dates."[3]

Or look at incentives in business. They tend to
become jaded unless changed or enlarged. The first
time, a weekend at the Sheraton Plaza 30 miles away
produces results. But before too long, two weeks in
Tahiti may be needed.

Attitude power is different. It is internal.
Attitudes grow and grow, and they develop into habits.
Whether you need power to get a company to be
productive, to heal yourself of an illness, or even to
keep yourself sick, nothing is as important as
attitudes. One of the most dramatic examples of
healing power is Norman Cousins, who in **Anatomy of an
Illness**, describes how he healed himself of the
degenerative and incurable Lou Gehrig's Disease through
attitude power.[4]

Attitudes are powerful destroyers as well as
healers. A former prisoner of McNeil Island
Penitentiary, who had spent 22 of his 45 years of life
there, decided that he wanted to go back to jail
immediately after being out eight weeks. He stated to
the judge that he was "terrified" at being out, and he
demanded that he be returned at once. The prisoner's
image of himself was that he had lost ten times.[5] His
attitude dictated that he was comfortable only in
prison. Non-prisoners often imprison themselves with
negative attitude power. If you look carefully at the
people around you, you will probably see that about 70%
of what they tell themselves is negative. Look first
at yourself, even on the days you receive 25 positive

or neutral comments and 2 negative ones--what do you dwell on when you go home? A similar thing tends to happen in the workplace unless positive attitude power is used to turn things around. Workplaces, as well as families, have self-talk. What kinds of self and workplace talk do you have? Do people say such things as:

-- Don't try to trust 'em.
-- Things are going too well; they can't last.
-- They just can't seem to do anything right.
-- I knew they'd screw things up.

If people are saying these things, you can be sure that they are helping to make losers of potential winners. You can see what you don't want and make it happen, or you can see what you do want and make it happen. What you and your workers say paints pictures; pictures trigger thoughts and actions. Thoughts and actions become habits. It all revolves around images-- what people think and how they think.

THE GUTS OF POWER

"You are more likely to act yourself into feeling than to feel yourself into action."

Jerome Bruner

PERSUASION THROUGH THOUGHT, EMOTION AND IMAGERY

The guts of power today is persuasion through thought and emotions. This involves imagery. As a manager, you can perpetuate habits you want to extinguish simply by criticizing or ignoring people in ways which produce lower and lower spirals of self-esteem images, which cause more and more negative self-talk, and which result in lower and lower productivity. Or, you can produce and maintain higher and higher spirals of self-talk, self-esteem and productivity. It all begins with the motif of peoples' self-talk, and imagery--what you and your employees think, feel and say.

Self-talk and imagery need to be based on getting employees to relax and try easier, not harder. This is efficiency. When you have higher output for less work, everyone is happier. When you push in certain ways, you lower efficiency, because people get uptight and can't work well. An awful myth that some managers genuinely believe is that if you're really calm, you don't care. They then push a frenetic Type A management which has long been popular in America. But Type A management is not always as efficient as its proponents would have you believe, because it tends to create tension. What you should do is to manage so that your employees try easier, not harder. When you do this, you will be likely to begin to improve perceptions, inspire cooperation, build energy and promote efficiency. One of the best ways to do this is through **self image psychology.*** First, be **aware** of the past and present images which strongly influence you; also be fully aware of the opportunities which can await you, and go beyond the "I am" to the "I can." Next, build power through positive thought and talk. Last, begin systematically to change and control actions through clarification, celebration and maximizing employees' self control. In short, awareness, affirmation and action; we'll call these the Triple A's of excellence.

*Several systems are currently available to help people maximize their potential through self-imagery. Three of these have been developed by Bob Moawad, Louis Tice and Dennis Waitley. Some of the illustrations, descriptions and exercises found in this section have been modified from these systems. The reader should note, however, that the references in this chapter are brief and do not adequately describe any of these three systems. For detailed work in this area, see sources in the bibliographical notes under the above names.

TRIPLE A's OF EXCELLENCE
AWARENESS, AFFIRMATION, ACTION

AWARENESS

Whereas traditional power has been wielded from the standpoint of, "Do it; don't question it," modern employees tend **not** to do it unless they can **understand** it, and even get a satisfactory answer. If work is to get done, "whys" must be answered, and if motivation is to work, positive images must be seen and used. This means that managers need to be aware of how people think and how they form attitudes and habits.

Begin by briefly analyzing what people and forces have influenced you most. Take just a few minutes to jot down five people or institutions who/which have had a strong influence on your life. (Parent, manager, teacher, church, club, nation, etc.) Also, answer why, and the main negative or positive part of the influence.

What People or Institutions Have Had a Strong Effect on Your Life?	Why	What Was Positive or Negative?
1.		
2.		
3.		
4.		
5.		

Look for commonalities; then try to draw conclusions. If, for example, you find that the common thread of main influence in your life is people who are rather arrogant and aloof, you may want to look closely at what you need to do to become a genuinely humanistic manager. With that background, it may be a bit more difficult, though certainly **not** impossible, to become a dynamically positive manager, than for the person whose main influences were warm and caring people.

In order for you to maximize the positive power you have with yourself and your workplace, you need first to understand a little theory about the forces presently influencing your more or less automatic actions as well as what goes on consciously.

Many psychologists believe that two basic parts of thought can be described as conscious and subconscious. The **conscious** part of our minds perceives data through our five senses and attempts to maintain contact with reality. It operates rationally and logically, associating our perceptions of objective reality with our subconscious "data bank" of accumulated experience. It then evaluates what the perceptions mean and decides what to do.

Our **subconscious** has two functions: one is to record and store information, like a data bank, and the other is to handle inherent, automatic functions such as breathing and digestion, and learned automatic functions such as walking, driving a car, etc. In the data bank functions, storage occurs by a chemical change in the protein structure of the nucleus of the brain's basic neuron cells. Most human brains probably contain more than 10 billion neuron cells. But that's not all; each of those neuron cells is capable of storing 1 to 2 million bits of information. All our experiences are recorded automatically. They are also modified by subjective, sensory and emotional colorings. What we think or imagine in relation to these experiences results in our distorting some of reality. In short, we program attitudes into our data bank about ourselves and our workplaces that we then become stuck with--right or wrong, helpful or harmful--until we consciously change them.

One of the main characteristics of the subconscious is to drive you to be what you believe yourself to be. What you see yourself to be may not coincide with objective reality, but for you, it becomes "truth." You may say to yourself:

"I'm a poor speaker," and become one.
"If I don't manage perfectly, I shouldn't manage,"
and immobilize yourself.
"I always foul things up," and do it.

Or, you may say to yourself:

"I usually do a good job of solving problems."
"I am dynamic, caring, and efficient," and be seen
with these traits.

In other words, if you think you can, you probably
can; if you think you can't, you probably can't.

This is where power with people begins to make
sense. If what employees perceive and believe has such
influence, why do managers frequently lower
productivity by lowering employees' images of
themselves and their work? One of the main reasons may
well be because we live in a country with a
predominantly negative management system. The vast
majority of managers seem to operate on the basis of
trouble shooting and maintenance. They find the
problems and then tell employees what they're doing
wrong. Most managers do not go out of the way every
day to tell their employees what they're doing right.
It's the same in families. Parents yell and tell their
children when they're unhappy. But how many parents
and managers literally spend much time celebrating the
daily acts they appreciate? Only in great companies
and in great families do you see this.

Four Reasons for Negative Management. We perpetuate our negative management systems out of inertia
and ignorance. Four of the main reasons for this are:
(1) role ambiguity, (2) meaningless work, (3) focus on
trouble-shooting, and (4) routine and exceptions.

1. Role Ambiguity. Many American managers allow
time wasting, ulcer-producing role ambiguity for two
main reasons. First, unlike the Japanese, we don't
spend a lot of time in being sure that all employees in
a company are attuned to a general philosophy regarding
the product and the society. Americans tend to think
this is a luxury, not a necessity. We tend to focus on
narrow, short-term and sometimes separate actions,

rather than to focus first on values and philosophies which will then result in the best kind of action.

Second, in the absence of a clear philosophy, we also often fail to clarify specifically what a person's role is in relation to the many variables he or she encounters. The result is uncertainty, inefficiency, and even premature deaths as the acid of ambiguity attacks the body below the waistline.

2. Meaningless Work. About 30% of the work of about 80% of managers is irrelevant to the goals of the organization.[6] This does not mean that managers are intentionally goofing off. On the contrary, many managers worry and fret about this 30% of their work at home; they wrestle with its problems. Still, it's irrelevant. They are confusing motion for action, and they don't even know it.

3. Focus on Trouble-Shooting. Many managers proudly consider themselves to be expert problem solvers. They may even believe in a way that they are indispensable to their organization. What they usually contribute to the company, however, is uptightness, non-creativity, and a closed and stable environment. They set themselves up to speak a negative language. They are the messengers of bad news. And in their departments or organizations, the best that can be hoped for is a tight reign on things, with little or no initiative.

4. Routine Management and Exceptions. One popular form of management which is also an important part of our negative management system, is that of management by exception. This is characterized by the person who sets up, or who works in, a system that works, only to believe that management's job is mainly to deal with the exceptional problems which come along. It is stifling and destructive.

In becoming a vibrant organization with a "feverish" breakout from stagnation, awareness is the first step. The next step is to affirm what you want to do in ways which will trigger action.

One Way to Overcome Negative Management - Pygmalion Power.
If you learn how to use Positive Pygmalion Power, your employees may even begin to attack hell with buckets of water. Everyone is a creative artist to a certain extent. You draw and mold your own life according to your own image. As a manager, you also carve, cast or chisel the lives of others. You have an influence on everyone around you. This has been called the Pygmalion effect.

Pygmalion was a sculptor in Greek mythology, who made a statue of a lovely maiden. So beautiful was his creation, that Pygmalion fell in love with the statue. So strong was Pygmalion's imagery of his love for the statue that Aphrodite, the goddess of love, gave the statue life and named her Galatea. The modern musical "My Fair Lady," adapted from "Pygmalion" by George Bernard Shaw, describes how Professor Higgins changes Eliza Dolittle from an uncouth flower girl into a cultured lady through the power of expectations, imagery and practice.

Bill Tice says that managers who are "positive Pygmalions" are usually the best managers. ". . . [They]:

-- Believe in themselves and have confidence in what they are doing,
-- Believe in their ability to develop the talents of their employees--to select, train and motivate them.
-- Communicate to workers [that] their expectations are realistic and achievable."

Bill Tice goes on to cite that Rosenthal believes that managers produce the Pygmalion effect in four main processes:

(1) Climate - develop a warm, social, emotional climate,
(2) Feedback - give lots of verbal feedback clues (both positive and negative) about workers' performance,
(3) Input - teach considerable, and sometimes difficult material to workers who have the potential, and

(4) <u>Output</u> - reinforce "chosen" workers to ask more questions, take more time, and have more benefit of the doubt than "ordinary" workers.

AFFIRMATIONS - MAKE A DIFFERENCE WITH POSITIVE POWER BUILDERS

One of the greatest potential aspects of power that a manager has is to guide and form attitudes. This can be done systematically through Positive Power Builders. Everything you do has some impact on the formation of attitudes. Words, as well as non-verbal messages, trigger pictures. Images and ideas then determine what we do. We all try to do what our images say we should. Our subconscious does this; it is a servant.

Our subconscious operates on the basis of what we picture. It holds these pictures and tries to make them come true. Physically, emotionally and psychologically, we all create activities which coincide with our images and opinions. Whether they're good for us or not, as long as we hold pictures in our minds, we steer ourselves toward those pictures.

We also have dynamite power with employees in the way we use imagery. One of the authors taught his wife to drive a car. (Yes, the marriage survived.) He discovered that if he said, "Look out for that curb," there was an almost imperceptible move toward the curb. He triggered a negative picture. On the other hand, if he said, "Good, now steer slightly to the left, stay exactly in the middle of the lane," that's what happened.

If you play golf or tennis, you may have noticed that you can be your own worst friend or enemy. You tell yourself, "I'm liable to hit the ball to the left." Or, you may say, "Damn, I wish I didn't do that," and you do! In golf, you may even have some "woods or water balls"; they're the balls you use when shooting near a particular woods or lake. You get tense, and there it goes again!

As managers, if we create negative imagery, we may

cause more problems than we solve. The school board member who says to a disturbed parent delegation, "We don't need you to tell us what to do," may invite needless problems. The superintendent is then left to handle an even greater problem than he had in the first place. Instead of dwelling excessively on what you don't want, use visualizations to help you to get what you want. Picture and describe the direction in which you want to lead, not the trap you want to avoid.

Traps are tricky; be aware of them. You may even want to analyze traps and problems, but then, as soon as possible, start imaging positive pictures of what you want. Throughout this book, you'll find descriptions of negative aspects of management such as the six despots in Chapter I and Victorian Boss Habits in Chapter IV. These are for awareness. The trick then is to replace them with positive practices and action.

Active, Systematic Imaging. Every statement you make to yourself has an effect on your subconscious; the same is true for all of your communications--verbal or non-verbal--to others. To illustrate the impact of this, list two or three attitudes that you consider "good" attitudes, and then describe how you got them. For example, you might write, "I really believe that almost all employees are basically energetic and want to do the right thing."

Good Attitudes	What Formed Them?
1.	1.
2.	2.
3.	3.

Now do the same thing for "bad" attitudes. You might write, for example, "I really believe my boss is only out for himself; he's extremely selfish."

Bad Attitudes	What Formed Them?
1.	1.
2.	2.
3.	3.

See how your attitudes have been formed from what you told yourself--what you perceived as objective reality. If, for example, you had a different frame of reference, you would have perceived the attitudes differently. If any of the above "bad" attitudes pertain to your manager, you might have gotten a totally different perspective if your manager had dealt with you in a different way. Attitudes are directions in which to lean. They are formed on the subconscious level as we interact with our environment. As managers observe and evaluate performances, subordinates record both spoken and unspoken opinions. Negative and positive thoughts act on our souls like rocks or balloons, weighing us down or lifting us up. One of the biggest balloons to increased performance is a feeling of self-worth. Conversely, one of the heaviest millstones of poor performance is low self-esteem.

The power of imagery! Who is the most accident prone? The person who worries about having an accident, of course.

What happens when the basketball coach shows his players films from the last game and then says, "Jack, don't you see where you were screwing up? I showed you this thing last week, and you're still doing the same things--you're still shooting too short. When we get to the gym, I want you to sit on the bench and think about it." What happens? Jack thinks about it; he pictures the problem, reminds himself of it, and then repeats the mistake again and again. We are destined to repeat the errors we continually remind ourselves of.[8]

If this is true, doesn't it also make sense that we can create **upward** spirals of esteem and productivity by the same process? This can be started by creating images through positive promises to ourselves. By affirming things to ourselves in a systematic way, we can use the rational and logical part of our brain to get our creative subconscious to work for us rather than against us. This is how it works.

We move toward what we picture. First, know what's wrong. Next, tell yourself or your employee to stop. Then build positive power and change by helping yourself and employees to picture what is needed. The problem is that so much management is built on what we don't want. You may say, "I focus a lot on trouble-shooting and problem solving." While this is helpful to a certain extent, it should never be the focus of management. There are few, if any, outstanding managers who focus on trouble-shooting. The great managers emphasize positive images. They focus on what they want, not on what they don't want. They create an excitement of being best. They get their employees to describe **what** they want to be best at, **how** best is defined objectively, and how to **become** best. And then they use Positive Power Builders to build clear goals, positive reinforcement and attitudes which then result in employees consistently "becoming" best.

Olympic class archers and pistol shooters almost invariably have powerful images of hitting the center of the target; they don't concentrate on thinking "What did I do wrong last time?" They visualize and shoot. Successful managers are similar. Although they learn from past errors, what they really focus on is the image for the present and future. Then, from these images, there is a natural flow of action to make the image come true. Instead of the literally impossible task of pulling yourself up by your own bootstraps, you're following your desires and pictures of what you can and should do. There are two main aspects of positive power promises. One is composing them; the other is making them work.

Six Guides for Composing Positive Power Builders.
1. Personal. The first thing to do in composing a Positive Power Builder is to make it personal. You can affirm a change in yourself that will make a difference in others, but you cannot affirm a change in

others. Therefore, you say that you will make **int**ernal changes in order to affect **ex**ternal results.

2. Positive.   The second thing to do is to make your affirmation **positive.**   Leave out the negative. For example, don't say, "I will no longer be a rascal." Rather, "I am loving, caring, and considerate." Instead of concentrating on **not** shooting the golf ball into the trap, remind yourself to shoot it onto the green.

3. Present Tense.   The third element of a Positive Power Builder is to make it in the present tense.   There is a subtle and significant difference between saying "I will" and "I am." If you use the present tense, the creative subconscious begins to put your affirmation into action more readily than if you use the future tense.   The degree to which your subconscious acts as though you were already doing what you want to do, is the degree to which you are likely to actually do it.

4. No Comparisons. Make no comparisons, for you are always better or worse than someone else.   Just commit yourself to the changes you want.

5. Active and Realistic. Use words which are active, exciting and realistic.

6. Private. Keep your positive commitments to yourself, for if you reveal your goals to others, it allows others to work against you. An exception can be made of course for close friends.

Examples:

-- I like and respect myself; I am worthy, capable and valuable.

-- I easily relax as deeply as I wish at any time; I use this ability to conserve energy, to think clearly and to make good decisions.

-- Everyone I talk to is a customer; I simply discover his or her needs.

-- My service and expertise allows me to compete with anyone.

-- I pride myself on being organized.

-- I enjoy delegating responsibility and seeing my employees feel the overwhelming satisfaction of success.

-- When I am speaking in public, I relax my stomach and throat muscles; I breathe deeply and enjoy speaking.

-- Pressure is exciting and stimulating to me; I do my best work under pressure as I relax, concentrate, and work fast.

Here you see a variety of Positive Power Builders which may help you write your own. Whatever you write for yourself, make them fit you, so that you are talking to you. Take some time now to begin by writing four or five affirmations. First, decide what your goal is, then your Positive Power Builder.

Using Positive Power Builders. As you concentrate on your own Positive Power Builders, remember that people stifle themselves more by a lack of positive image than by lack of potential or responsibility. Most of us are picture oriented, and our subconscious creativity works to accomplish what it sees as truth. Every time you or your employees try to do something that is not you, whether rightly or wrongly, there is an internal need to correct the "mistake." "Sanity", or congruence, is more important than winning. We all act as we see ourselves. Just as our subconscious sees what we've told it to see--distortions, defensiveness and all--we can also override its dumb perceptions by rational pictures of reality.

One of the best ways to begin rationally to control your actions, is to write your Positive Power Builders on 3 x 5 cards and carry them with you. Learn to repeat them so that you involve your emotions and imagery.

As you repeat your Power Builders, picture yourself accomplishing them. Displace old self-images through new positive power reminders. Vividly picture and experience what you want. If you need to go back in your memory to the fourth grade, when you were class president, or city elementary school queen to build self-confidence, do so. Remember and image when you have been powerful and successful in the area you are affirming. Ignore the failures. See yourself interviewing for the job you really want. Picture yourself as poised and secure. Then let the actions of preparing for that interview naturally follow, and don't worry about mistakes you might make. Give feelings of security and poise, rather than fear and doubt to your creative subconscious. Feel the emotions you want engulf you. Your creative subconscious will act on your Positive Power Builders in proportion to your strength of feeling and imagery. What you want to do is replace current negative images in yourself and your workplace with new images, which will then create new outcomes.

As a general rule, you will probably find that you can use your Positive Power Builders with varying impact. If you only read the remainder, there will be only part of the full potential impact of reading, picturing, and feeling them.

Therefore, look again at your commitments. Think of a picture for each of them. See the good accomplished and feel the joy of completion. Now jot down pictures for your Positive Power Builders.

1.

2.

3.

Timing is important too. Repeat your Positive Power Builders at least two or three times a day. Do this when you are relaxed. Good times are usually in the early morning before going to work, late at night before going to sleep, and any other time during the day when you have time and are relaxed.

The object of great management is to get people to be action oriented in ways that are free-flowing, trusting, and energetic. You don't want to be merely a maintainer; you want to be a transformer. You want to get people to practice these new strategies they image until they become habitual. You want to shape values, make meanings and impel purposes. You want to be a pathfinder, an artist and an implementer. You want to rise above daily affairs, and to coalesce employees around central values which are important both to the individual and the organization.

James McGregor Burns says that "Leadership, unlike naked power wielding is . . . inseparable from followers' needs and goals. [Transforming leadership] occurs when one or more persons engage with others in such a way that leaders and followers raise one another to higher levels of motivation and morality. Their purposes, which might have started out separate, but related, . . . become fused. Power bases are linked not as counterweights, but as mutual support for common purpose. . . . Transforming leadership is dynamic leadership in the sense that the leaders throw themselves into a relationship with followers who will feel "elevated" by it, and often become more active themselves."[9]

You can begin to be a "transforming leader" by clarifying goals, celebrating success, and giving control.

After you have developed Positive Power Builders for yourself, begin to develop springboards to success for your employees. This can be done by giving the Triple C Action Chargers to your employees; these are clarification, celebration, and control.

Clarification. If you boil management down to its two most essential ingredients, they are: (1) clarify expectations for results, and (2) go out of your way to celebrate people's contributions in reaching these goals. The first thing to do is to choose no more than 3-5 key goals yourself. Clarify them in terms of

expected results. Learn how to articulate them in all
sorts of ways. Then begin **talking** about them.
Remember that there are no real changes made by
writing. Although MBO's have been touted for the last
decade by many top managers as being a godsend, middle
and lower managers tend to treat them as a snowstorm of
paperwork to be endured, but nothing more. When people
ask you what to do, tell them what you're trying to
accomplish, not just that you're director of this, or
head of that.

Talk about your key results at every opportunity.
Begin with people who are closely linked to your
performance, whether superior or subordinate.
Regardless of whether you respect them or they you,
remember that your destiny is hooked into their
evaluation of your key results. In fact, more often
than not, in the normal American workplace which does
not have humanistic management, managers tend to view
these people as being less competent than themselves,
as having a lack of sensitivity or ethics, and even as
being less experienced than they themselves are. These
very negative feelings are generally explained by the
power that these people, who are closely linked to your
results, have over you.

Begin with these people. They are called your
"role set by some sociologists. If you are not in one
of the rather rare workplaces where humanistic
management has already become operative, it is usually
best not to ask your role set what they believe should
be done, but rather simply to tell them what you think
should be done. This will evoke one of three
reactions. They will agree, disagree, or not care.
For the present, don't deal with the "don't cares";
deal only with the people who "agree" or "disagree."
Get the "agrees" to help you, and begin to negotiate
with the "disagrees."

Next, recognize who the main people are in the
role sets of your role set. You won't have time to
give in-depth service to those peripheral people, but
if you're to be successful, you must recognize what
main pressures are being brought to bear on your role
set members. Once you begin to strongly articulate
your expected results, sensitively to service people in

your role set, and humanely to recognize the peripheral pressures, you being to move toward power **with** people.

Celebration of Success - Four Guides. If you study outstanding managers, you will notice that they build their organizations on strength. Although they recognize weaknesses, they spend minimal time on them, for time spent on trouble-shooting and problem solving detracts from the time available for capitalizing on strengths.

Sidney Harris, in his book, **Winners and Losers**, notes that losers don't know their own strengths and weaknesses, and they don't know what they want. If they discover weaknesses, they don't like to talk about them. Winners, on the other hand, know their strengths and weaknesses; they know that both are part of the same person.[10] They spend maximum energy on their strengths while merely managing their weaknesses. They're aware of their weaknesses, but they know that too much time on weaknesses lowers productivity, while concentration on strengths tends to improve both strengths and weaknesses.

You may be able to **maintain** an organization by trouble-shooting weaknesses, but you can never obtain breakthrough progress that way. Therefore, go out of your way to recognize the good things that people do. Inasmuch as is possible, ignore the things you don't want, for one of the least productive ways to spend your time is in talking about things you don't want. The better managers seem to go out of their way to reinforce people at least five or six times per day-- not five or six times to each subordinate, but spread out among all. That's the minimum. Some do a lot more. The important thing is to go visibly about the organization announcing its goals and mission, and to thank people for doing those things.

In rejoicing in the strengths and success of employees, there are four factors which are more critical than others; they are (1) advice, (2) specificity, (3) feedback, and (4) dialogue.

Giving Advice: When you need to give advice, it's best to do so just before it's needed. For advice that

is given further than about thirty minutes before it
can be used, or when it cannot be used, is usually seen
as punitive, no matter what your intention is. It's
deceptive. The employee says, "Thanks, I appreciate
that. I'll use it." However, research shows that deep
down, the person usually actually hates you for your
advice. The person feels bitter even though you were
simply concerned and trying to be supportive and
helpful. The reason seems to be largely because of the
timing.[11] Of course it takes discipline on your part
to time advice in this way, but it can pay huge
dividends.

There is a reasonably simple way that you can
practice this principle without tying up your day.
Separate the "good and bad" news. During a specific
evaluation observation, agreed upon in advance, discuss
only the good things. Your evaluation becomes a real
ego trip. You say, "These are the things I saw you
doing which were absolutely fantastic." At the next
observation, you meet again with the evaluatee, this
time just before the observation. At that time
suggestions are made for improvement. At the same
time, you arrange to give a signal when the improvement
on these items is made. This way, feedback is
immediate, the evaluatee's ego is fed, and suggestions
are given and accepted, for which maximal benefit is
possible.

You might also use a system of envelopes. You
might suggest, after the ego trip evaluation, that the
employee take the envelope in which you've placed a
suggestion, and open it only just before a certain
specified time when it can be used. If employees are
properly trained, this can work; if not, it is likely
to be misused. Some will forget. Some will open it
immediately and castigate themselves. Only about one
third will probably use the envelope as intended unless
you give training and practice in their use.

Specificity: When you give praise you have to be
specific. Generalized compliments, including glad-
handing and slapping people on the back, tends to
lessen your managerial image. People wonder why you're
spaced out--what galaxy you're from.

Also, keep your encouragement pure; don't mix the good and bad news, for if you do, people are likely to focus on the bad rather than the good. What happens if when you're invited out to dinner you remark to the cook that the filet was tender and tasty, but the broccoli was tough? Is the cook likely to run back to the kitchen to get you some more broccoli? Not on your life. What you get is one of two usually fundamental responses. The first is to avoid you because you were critical; you don't get invited to dinner again. The second is to avoid failure; the cook may not prepare broccoli again. If you want creative productivity, you must discipline yourself to stop with, "That was a tender and tasty steak." Period. But, you say, "What about the broccoli?" The time to talk about the broccoli is if the employee is about to damage himself, or if the progress of the organization is being seriously inhibited. Otherwise, it's just before the broccoli is about to be prepared again.

<u>Feedback</u>: The best feedback systems are those which let people know how they're doing at least every two hours on the job. This is of course extremely demanding criteria for feedback, and it may seem impossible. But, one of the really important elements of a truly dynamic workplace is to structure the system so that people know how they are doing almost immediately in relation to expectations. Ask yourself how you can tell often, throughout the day, how well you are doing. Feedback need not be personal, but it does have to exist if your organization's growth is to be progressive and breakthrough the normal rather static barriers.

A self-maintenance feedback system coupled with feedback from your superior is best. This can consist of quality control standards, timelines, narrative descriptions of standards and a "roving manager."

<u>Dialogue</u>: Another important principle in developing power with people is dialogue. When we open up our ability to see and accept solutions from employees as well as ourselves, we increase our power rather than decrease it. Possibilities, rather than impossibilities, are then expanded. Managers who believe that if they make changes based on the input of

employees, are not doing their duty, are out of place in today's workplace. They're placing self-imposed limitations on their potential.

Louis Tice tells of his experiences as a football coach when he prematurely locked on to limiting factors. He says that he got to know "everything there was to know about his football players"; he knew for sure that his ends couldn't catch, his quarterbacks couldn't throw, and that the team had absolutely no speed. He recalls that he was halfway through one season. His team was ahead by one touchdown, and his team was in a position to score again, which was unusual. The quarterback called time out and came over to the coach to ask if it might not be possible to throw the ball to Marty, an end. Tice, the coach, said, "What do you mean? You know we don't pass." But the quarterback pleaded; he said, "Marty's been open the whole game!" (The coach had locked on to his opinion that ends couldn't catch, and failed to see this.) When Tice rejected this suggestion, the quarterback repeated, "Look, Marty's not only been open the whole game, he's been open the whole season!" So, finally after another play where Marty was open, the coach finally "found it." On the next play, Marty was thrown a pass and got a touchdown. In fact, three more similar plays were run with three more touchdowns! The coach decided to talk to more players about their suggestions, which he got and used. The team changed its scoring pattern from one to multiple touchdowns per game. Why didn't the coach see these tremendous possibilities? Tice himself says, "Because I was so opinionated." When you lock on to stubbornness, you also lock out potential."[12]

What is it like in your workplace? What opinions and images have you locked onto? Do you believe that employees are not to be trusted with information, that they've given up, that things can't be done? Have you also limited Your-Own-Power because of Your-Own-Low-Self-Esteem? Do you believe that you're not really worth much if you don't already know everything? After all, you're paid to be the manager. You may even limit your potential more subtly by thinking that you ask for other opinions, when in fact, although you ask, you don't really understand those opinions.

You may also lock out potential by listening to suggestions and then saying, "But, we're already doing that," when the fact is that you're really not doing the critical 10%, and you've locked out an ability to see that 10%. Or, have you locked onto some mistake that an employee has made? Then, do you find it difficult to allow Eliza Dolittle to be anything but a flower girl? What more can you do to increase growth and productivity of the individual as well as the organization?

Control. In addition to clarification and celebration, good management is making a deal with people about results and how **they** are going to control what is to be accomplished, and then leaving them alone to create the ways to achieve those results. It is **not** controlling how your people do things. If you don't give them enough privacy, they won't be able to marshal their own resources and innovations. Keep the focus on results. Give your employees appropriate control, and don't meddle with their processes.

FINALLY: USE POSITIVE IMAGERY & ACTION

You can develop power that grows and grows as you develop it **with** people. The guts of this power are thought, emotions and imagery which you can develop through awareness, affirmation, and action. And the greatest of these is action, with the Triple C Chargers of clarification, celebration, and control.

VII

HUMANISTIC ENTREPRENEURS:

LITTLE THINGS COUNT A LOT

Good management ultimately boils down to two things - people and results. This means that great managers need to be humanistic entrepreneurs.

INTRODUCTION

This is a chapter of simple, separate and miscellaneous strategies to help you manage for double wins. If you're the kind of manager who learns best by simply applying principles from stories you've read, you may like this chapter best of all because it's long on stories and short on theory.

These strategies are **fusers** of selfishness and selflessness into synergy, and they are also **fuses** for igniting power with people. They are the little things that count a lot. If you still have any doubt about what "Leadership for Empowering People" is all about, this chapter will help to explain it in easy to understand stories.

These strategies are not the complete answers-- only starters. They're a bit like the couple in North Dakota in the days before cohabitation was practiced as much as it is now. It was late one Friday night when a young couple knocked on the door of the Justice of the Peace. Finally, a woman came to the door. The couple explained that they wanted to get married. The woman was sorry to report that the Justice wouldn't be back until Monday. Downhearted, the couple started to leave, then turned back and asked, "Well, couldn't you at least say a few words to tide us over the weekend?"

If you're having trouble practicing management strategies that marry the individual with the organization in a non-manipulative but entrepreneurial marriage that fulfills the needs of both, let this chapter tide you over. Let it give you a few words about ways to **empower** people until you can smoothly and unselfconsciously integrate the humane with the entrepreneurial.

There is a burning need within most of us to be a part of a group as well as a bursting drive to stick out. We all have the capacity to resonate to the harmony of teamwork as well as the call for individual heroism. We are all driven by selflessness as well as selfishness. The job of today's manager is fusion--the kind of fusion which links selflessness and selfishness, and the kind of fusion which fires controlled combustion, providing power both for individuals and for groups.

Detached, analytical and rational management is no longer enough. Today's superior managers get things done so that both employees and organization meet needs in ways which are mutually fulfilling. Today's great managers are generous visionaries who help guide people to innovative plans, creative risks, and high moral purposes. Instead of the old kingpin concept, today's outstanding managers live by a linkpin philosophy. This we have called **Humanistic Entrepreneurs**.

People will flood you with ideas, loyalty, and energy if you let them. They will identify deeply with their work if you give them the right kind of control. Common ordinary workers are likely to become heroic and to produce extraordinary results if you nourish and give them esteem. Self-generated quality control may even be rigorously practiced if you give meaning and trust as well as money. It all boils down to focusing on people as well as products--people in terms of customers, employees, owners/shareholders and communities; products in terms of innovation, action and quality. Humanistic entrepreneurs link these aspects together to transform people and products rather than just to maintain or contain them.

This concept of the humanistic entrepreneur is particularly important for public service organizations, a few of which overcome the handicap of bureaucracies, even though the public often does not think so. For example, a letter addressed to "God" arrived in a post office one day. It seemed to have been written by a child. A postal employee opened it. Inside was the following letter: "Dear God, I am George and I was seven last month. I don't have no Mom and Dad, don't have no job. Sis and me are both hungry. Could you send $300."

The postal sorter who read the letter soon let others in the office see it. They were moved. They passed the hat. They got $150, which was sent to the boy. The boy, upon receiving the $150, wrote another letter to God, asking that the money be sent straight to his house next time, because when it was mailed by way of the post office, $150 was deducted.

While this story illustrates the true generosity of many public service employees, it also portrays the image that many citizens have of them, and often for good reason. For instance, how many times have you gone into a post office, government office or public school and felt that people who met you didn't want to see you, didn't want to service you, and wished you'd go away? In spite of the fact that there are many public service employees who go out of their way to give service and to treat you as a "precious customer," the many who don't are remembered. They are probably the major reason why post offices, government service and public schools have recently had serious competition from private enterprise. On the other hand, humanistic entrepreneurs both from the private and public sector have linked customers, community, owners and employees and provided superior services and products.

Customers, community and employees all cry out for a meeting of their own needs. This is what humanistic entrepreneurs target--meeting these different needs in ways which are beneficial to all.

STARTER FUSES AND FUSERS

Ayn Rand said, "The first right on earth is the right of the ego." This describes the cult of narcissism which has swept our country in the last decade. While a certain amount of self love is necessary for people to be motivated to do their best, excessive preoccupation with self can easily be detrimental to self as well as society. Psychologist Shirley Sugarman, in **Sin and Madness; Studies in Narcissism**, writes about the vicious cycle of destructive narcissism. She says, "The ancient wisdom of both East and West [tells] repeatedly of man's tendency to self-idolatry, self-encapsulation, and its result: self-destruction."[1]

Western society has recently seen plenty of the seeds of self-destruction sown by excessive selfishness. Paradoxically, however, in the midst of this age of meism, seeds of selflessness have also abounded. It remains the manager's job to fuse these seeds in strong strains of synergy.

Several recent best sellers have developed the thesis of power over people. But there is also another case that needs presenting and that is the case of power **with** people. The objective of this chapter is to suggest strategies for developing power with people, and for reducing power used over them without being naive about the selfishness, exploitation, and hostility which abound around you. Power over people is finite with boundaries that must constantly be guarded. On the other hand, power developed with people is potentially infinite. If developed properly, it multiplies to everyone's advantage.

Alfred North Whitehead wrote that, "All of the progress of human kind can be summed up in the distance humans have traveled from force to persuasion." The suggestions in this chapter are not necessarily the greatest philosophical aspects of developing power **with** people, but they have been found to be some of the most helpful suggestions to many managers.

ACCOMPLISHMENTS AND POWER OF OTHERS

It is threatening to reinforce the power and accomplishments of others, for you fear that you might be embarrassed by their sterling performances.

Although you want your subordinates to do well you are also likely to be apprehensive about their success. If you let yourself be threatened, however, you are likely to engage in negative management. If you are a manager who guards closely your own power, one who tries to curb the power of subordinates by keeping them off-balance, by listening to gossip, by not letting them know clearly what you expect, by "dividing to conquer," and by not allowing them to outshine you in your own areas of weakness, you may be doing yourself more harm than good. If properly shared, power can grow and grow to the benefit of all power sharers.

A game, played by one of the authors at a leadership retreat, illustrates this. Groups were divided into two sides. The object was for each side to scheme in private and to attempt to win a contest over the other side. The contestants were left in the dark as to how to win except to be told that the basic rules were (1) to do no physical harm, and (2) to win. The surprise solution, however, turned out to be that the only way to win was to include the opposing side in the strategy in order to accumulate the winning number of points. Thus, only when a team decided to risk cooperation with the competition could it obtain the maximum number of points and win the contest.

Two of the most important ways to increase the accomplishments of others are through giving both recognition and authority. As obvious as this is, many managers fail to apply these principles to others even though they apply it to themselves. Some managers find it difficult to give recognition because of jealousy, some because of playing the macho role of being tough to impress, and others because of fear that liberal praise will result in swollen heads or swelling monetary demands. Regardless of how you feel, however, you can get better results by giving praise liberally than by withholding it.

Organizations in which lots of recognition and authority are given to their employees tend to have very low employee turnover. Although job changes occur for many reasons, people who are being fulfilled in their jobs are very reluctant to go out looking for new employment. Ask yourself the following questions to test how well you give recognition and authority to your subordinates:

_____ (1) Do I go out of my way to tell people how important they are to the company? (Or, do I take them for granted?)

_____ (2) How many chances do I give my subordinates to be really proud of themselves by giving them freedom to exercise authority in their own way? (Or, do I "diddle" in their processes? Do I give them a job and then come back and tell them to do it a certain way?)

_____ (3) Have I done my best to make jobs challenging and meaningful for employees?

_____ (4) Do I make their work as varied and interesting as possible? (Or, do I leave them where I can more easily exploit their abilities to my personal, immediate advantage?)

_____ (5) Have I eliminated as many unimportant rules as possible?

If any of your answers to these five main questions are "no" you are likely to be losing much more productivity than you win. If this is so, get your head out of the sand and change. Give employees control over their destinies. Give power to others as well as yourself. Live by dictums such as: "I win as you win." I am strong as your are strong." "I will hire to compensate for my weakness." "I will share power to the enhancement of all power sharers." "I will prize and publicize actions of employees who help others as well as themselves."

NEEDS AND ANXIETIES

The very core of successful leadership is committing yourself to finding solutions for the major needs and anxieties of the people you want to lead. Look at great leaders in recent times and you will see

that this is unmistably true. Where Hoover said the
depression was over, and failed as a leader, Roosevelt
made it clear that he recognized the problems of
depression and poverty, and said that he committed
himself unequivocally to the arduous task at hand.

Martin Luther King committed himself unreservedly
to justice, dignity and equality for his people, and he
did so in such a way as to invoke the least violence.
Not only did he feel this approach to be morally right,
but he also realized that the effects of violence would
repel the supporters most needed.

Eugene McCarthy contributed to Lyndon Johnson's
resignation from the presidency by clearly and
committedly calling for a halt to Vietnam--a major
anxiety at the time. In spite of the fact that Hitler
was repugnant to many Germans, he mesmerized them to
action by ardently pursuing solutions to their
anxieties of poverty, low self-esteem and fear of the
Jews.

John F. Kennedy recognized the needs of Americans
at a time when they were insecure about their place in
the world. In a larger sense, he appealed to the
entire Western world for truth and justice at a time
when these seemed to be in doubt. The he presented
himself as a person to solve the problems and committed
self and country to a search for solutions. Who can
forget his classic inaugural address and the vibrant
dedication in his voice as he approached the end of his
speech with these words: "I do not shrink from this
responsibility. I welcome it." Whether ethical and
humane, or evil and horrendous, if you dedicate
yourself to taking care of your followers' needs and
anxieties, you are on your way to becoming a powerful
leader.

DOGMA AND RESULTS

In being a humanistic entrepreneur, try not to
become so committed to an ideology or procedure that
you fail to achieve your humane goals. Don't tilt at
windmills, nor sacrifice results for dogma.

An illustration of this is in the Pamico Company's traditional demand for excellence on any company writing. The sales manager went to the president of the company to complain about his new salesman, Joe. "The man just cannot spell," he said, showing three telegrams from Joe.

The first telegram read: "Bos, jus sol $50,000. worth in Chicgo." The second read, "Bos, seling gong fin. Sol $75,000. in Detroit," and the third, "Bos, thes pepul grate. Sol $100,000. in San Fransco."

The sales manager asked, "What am I going to do? All the other salesmen don't even take him seriously." Quickly, the president wrote out a memorandum. "Post this for the other salesmen," he said. The president's note was succinct: "Congratulations Joe. And the res of you salsmen, les speling and more seling, ples."

Your priorities may not fall entirely in line with those of Joe's president, but few would doubt the necessity for results, not dogma, in such a case, at least to some extent. We hear that Joe has a secretary to "spel" for him now--in his own company!

You may erroneously have concluded that even though you are using a principle that doesn't seem to work, you still must follow it because it's good and it's more important than the result. Because of this, you may operate on principles such as: you must never seem to be unkind; you must never fire an employee if he or she is supporting a family; the individual is more important than the group, or individuals will be cooperative **if** you just do the right thing.

If you follow these kinds of naivete, however, you invite disaster. You can seriously damage an entire group of people by saving a wrongdoer. While you should certainly accentuate the positive conditions where it is called for, you also need to respond to the negative to whatever degree is called for by objective facts. While human relations writers such as McGregor assume a very high proportion of cooperative needs in people and organizations, there **are** conditions which allow the jungle principle of crass survival to operate. When this happens, you are foolish to

continue to hang on to "positive" principles that don't
work.

RATIONALIZING TIME

When changes are to be made, rationalizing time is
usually needed. While all of us like novelty, we also
like the tried and true things that we're used to.
Even when changes are suggested sensitively to
receptive employees, there is usually a need for the
"seed to grow." This means time to assimilate new
information into our systems of thought and action. It
means touching base with people so that there are no
significant surprises.

When you touch bases and talk about proposed
changes to employees, it gives people a change to
suggest better ways of change, or to marshal evidence
against the changes. It also provides opportunities
for employees to adjust to the changes. If then,
during this rationalizing time, the new ways cannot be
justified and supported, the changes should not occur.

If, on the other hand, you believe that people
should be made to conform to change in order to "show"
'em who's boss," you're very likely to be disappointed
at the results. Today's employees just do not respond
with positive energy to "show-'em-who's-boss" changes.
They are likely instead to become bitter, spiteful
"saboteurs."

FOOT-PRINTS AND BUTT-PRINTS[2]

Walter Jones, from Tacoma, Washington, started out
at the age of 104 to visit every one of the United
States. Three years later he was still driving toward
his goal as he traveled the rugged Alcan highway to
Alaska in his motor home. He was a man of action who
also carried his slogans with him. He had buttons
saying such things as: "Senior Power," "Gray Panthers,"
and "Off Your Butts." When asked why he had a button
saying "Off Your Butts," he indicated that most people
seem to want to make foot-prints in the sands of time,
and this can't be done sitting on their butts. This is

true in workplaces as well as for life in general. While most of us do seem to want to make foot-prints in the sands of time, many of us end up making only butt-prints.

It may be surprising how many companies which swear allegiance to foot-prints end up instead with more butt-prints than foot-prints. Bill Daniels, management consultant with American Consultant and Training Co., points out that organizations are interested in stability.[3] They're not really interested in change--change of any kind, even change to greater productivity. John Naisbitt, in **Megatrends**, indicates that while different studies reveal different data, there is general agreement that mature companies tend to be less productive than young, innovative ones.[4]

What this points to is the need for entrepreneurs today. Many years ago, a creative young risk taker worked in one of the old-time hardware stores which had the usual overload of merchandise that had not sold for years. This young clerk suggested a sale to sell off all these items at $ .10 each. The owner very, very reluctantly agreed. The sale was a complete success. From this, the clerk conceived of the idea of a whole store selling nickel and dime items. His name was F. W. Woolworth. Had F.W.'s boss not had a young man with foot-print itch, the old hardware store would simply have been maintained with butt-print passivity.

Failure to question present practices is one of the main reasons for organizational status-quo. While one of the authors was living in Germany, he heard the following story, which although he cannot vouch for its authenticity, makes a certain point. During an inspection of a British NATO battalion, one soldier in each gun crew was observed standing at complete attention during the entire exercise. A fellow NATO colleague from another country asked why, and was informed briskly by a Briton with stiff upper lip that this was simply the man's job. He always stood at attention when the gun was being fired. The colleague pushed, however, and asked why this "attention man" was needed. The answer could not be given immediately. After lengthy research it was ascertained that the job

of this man, way back, had been to hold the reins of
the horse!

FEELING AND THINKING

In getting a break-through-the-barriers mentality
in the workplace, an emphatic response to feelings
needs to come first, and an emphasis on rational
thinking second. Feelings are absolutely fundamental
to what happens at work. One of the problems of modern
management is that so many managers are oriented around
rational thought and objective analysis, while most of
society lives by "feeling oriented" behavior. This can
be called the "dilemma of the Left vs. the right
Hemisphere of the Brain." Your left brain hemisphere
contains the control functions for objective analysis,
and your right brain takes care of aesthetic, emotional
and integrative tasks.

American management is still excessively oriented
around such scientific management principles as
complete control of everything, objective analysis of
problems, scientific decision making, lowering costs by
making workplaces bigger, and getting quality control
by inspection. We over-emphasize a narrow emphasis on
thinking. To be effective today, we also have to
understand the aesthetic needs of employees, customers
and community, and to empathize with their feelings.

VALUES' CONSISTENCY

Superior salespersons first discover their
clients' needs and values. They then tailor their
product to these values for they know that people who
buy something, or engage in an activity, which is
foreign to their values, are likely to become unhappy
and a detriment to the salesperson's cause.

Employees and customers are similar. If they are
forced into actions which are inconsistent with their
values, they balk, become passive or negatively
aggressive, and productivity suffers. Therefore,
conmingle desire, concerns, and aspirations of
employees so that they see their endeavors as

consistent with their own beliefs, needs and values. Often, this requires unapologetic, straightforward selling. Sometimes it even takes a "conspiracy openly conceived." Whatever the means, the best organizational success results from employees being engaged actively in self-actualizing themselves according to their own values within the context of the organization's goals.

FALLING AND FAILING

You are almost bound to fall in one of two ways, either on your back, or on your face. Which will it be? All people who are good at anything know that in order to be good, you must take risks. If you take risks, you're going to fail sometimes. But, contrary to merely ordinary managers, if you're good you'll focus your energies on goals and risks rather than failures and fears.

How many mediocre coaches try to get their people on the edge of good performance by saying things like, "Now be careful, one mistake can make the difference," and it does! They lose on one mistake, rather than to keep trying and trying.

Babe Ruth was one of the greats who concentrated on present goals and negated past failures. During one double header he struck out seven times. Now, Babe Ruth was well known for reacting the same if he struck out or hit a homer. He would tip his hat, smile, and sit down. After one particular game, a reporter asked him how he could not even appear to be worried at seven strike-outs. He replied something to the effect of, "Why worry? It's the pitcher's worry. I get a homer about one in eleven times at bat. Sometime soon I'm due for a homer." We all know that even great batters have only about a one-third success rate at hitting. Yet most of us excuse ourselves from action if we fail just a few times. We say things like, "I guess I just don't have it; I'll quit."

How many failures did Helen Keller have? Did you know that Leon Uris, the author of **Exodus, Armageddon,** and **Trinity,** flunked high school English three times?

Are you aware that Lucille Ball, of TV's "I Love Lucy," tried unsuccessfully to become Miss America three times, failed at becoming a dancer with Radio City Music Hall, and lost the use of her legs for two years, before finally becoming famous with "I Love Lucy" at the age of 40?

If you are not able to let yourself fail, you also produce unnecessary stress for yourself. This is likely to result in a self-fulfilling prophecy, or even avoidance of risks altogether. Failure can refine you or destroy you; it's mostly up to you. You can learn what to do and what not to do, and you can learn determination and empathy from failure, or you can become cynical and passive. It's up to you.

FOLLOWING - ONE STEP AHEAD

In order to focus the energies and desires of your followers, you must articulate purposes which match their moods and needs. This means you can't be too far ahead of them, but that you must reflect their dreams. People can only be inspired to go where they want to go. You can, however, help people decide where they want to go. Consider the following example.

In a school district of about 40,000 population, it was obvious to the superintendent that integration was only a few years down the road. He brought citizen groups (both ethnic and non-ethnic) together in committees to research and evaluate all possible solutions. It even became a status symbol to attend education-related evening classes on this matter at the nearby university. Eventually, the citizen committees arrived at their recommendations which, by then, reflected their own dreams and convictions. Boundaries were redrawn without dissent, and harmony prevailed in the wake of reconstruction.

Successful political leaders also seem to follow-- a step ahead: F.D.R. in getting us out of the depression and into World War II; Eisenhower in getting us out of Korea and keeping us out of "cold wars"; J.F.K. in articulating the need for more vigorous leadership, and Reagan in trying to extricate pervasive government influence from peoples' lives. Regardless of whether people change or stay the same, however, the direction people will go must match their moods and needs. Successful leaders seem to follow--one step ahead.

Leadership is no longer merely orders passed down--if indeed it ever was. Rather, even visionary leadership is responsiveness, dialogue, and a tapping of moods and needs.

MOTION AND ACTION

Hemingway supposedly once said to Marlene Dietrich: "Don't confuse motion for action." Bill Daniels says that studies have shown that about one third of what most managers do is considered unimportant by other key managers in the company.[5] Still, this one third "motion" is continued with diligence and even worry, as managers consider it to be important action.

One of the main confusions of motion and action is in regard to people and things. Before Bill Jeffers was first given the top job at the Union Pacific Railroad, he was known as a people oriented manager. After Jeffers became C.E.O., an old friend--a train engineer--visited him with an operational suggestion. The engineer could see that Jeffers was not really concentrating on him, and finally reprimanded his old friend, who was now his superior, by reminding him that even the top boss should not get so busy as to be unable to concentrate on the little person who might have a good suggestion. Jeffers supposedly profited from this criticism.

INFORMAL COMMUNICATION

Current management experts agree that informal communication is necessary to maximizing productivity. The essence of informal communication is simply talking with each other easily and regularly. Real change is not brought about by writing memos and objectives, but by talking, by really knowing, and by reinforcing.

Great workplaces of the present are structured so that casual meetings among different populations of the organization are easy and even random. Salespersons, consultants, research and development people, and accountants sit and informally discuss possibilities. These communications are not cases of formal presentations, but rather people meeting in small rooms with blackboards or overhead projectors to get things done.

Contrast this with many institutions where managers who have offices next door to each other communicate largely by memos, and where the philosophy is that because people will misuse information, you must be very cautious in giving it. These are often organizations where perfection and experimentation are low. These are often the organizations which operate largely by formal committees and task forces. These are the workplaces where the vigor of ideas is distilled with bland, conformist thinking. The processes for getting things done are diddled with by superiors, and both managers and employees are left confused, bothered and bewildered.

Superior workplaces, on the other hand, are likely to have open, intense, and action based communication. There are apt to be only a few goals. Values are thoroughly known by everyone. Managers are visible. What it all results in is lots of high quality, informal communication where ideas are freely given-- mistakes and all--where experimentation is revered, and where adaptive action is cherished.

FREE LUNCHES AND GARDENS OF EDEN

People who seek perfect and free worlds with no complaints seek death. How many times have you heard, "There are no free lunches"? Yet how often do managers, as well as customers, try to get everything for nothing? A story about a lady with a washer illustrates this. The guarantee on a washer had just expired when a grating noise began. The owner requested a serviceman from the company where she had purchased it. A repairman arrived, and upon seeing the guarantee was no longer valid, attempted to get the owner to take out a long term insurance contract for repair. He said that there would be no cost for the present service call if the insurance was accepted. The owner, being appropriately cautious, said she wanted to consider it, and would call the man later.

At this hesitancy, the repairman blurted out, "Well, just remember if you want service at no cost, you have to pay for."

COMMITMENT, COMMONALITY AND COMPROMISE

Commitment to common goals is essential to high productivity: this means that people are then pulling in the same direction. In getting commitment to common goals, regardless of whether you simply tell people what the goals are, or forge them through participative management, one of the first things you need to do if you want people to swear allegiance to these common goals is to go about saying, "If we don't agree, you must have different information than I have. If we only had the same information, we would very likely reach the same conclusions." If we talk in a relaxed and open way, either agreement or agreeable disagreement is likely to be reached, either of which is likely to promote commitment, commonality, and compromise.

One of the best examples of how this has worked on a national level was the story of Austria, described in Chapter I. Between World Wars I and II, labor and management formed subcultures bent on destroying one another. After the second World War, however, they changed tactics. Labor, management, and government forged an alliance guided by the three C's of cooperation, consensus, and compromise. Instead of maximizing the different interests of particular groups, they committed themselves to conflict management which looked for collective concerns. As a result, Austria is one of the healthiest countries in the world economically as well as in people and welfare areas.

Leadership is easy when there are clear goals, or a clear enemy. For example, when Hitler was a clear threat to Western civilization, the allied leaders simply had to articulate that conviction and convey it to the people. But in present times, there are few unambiguous enemies, and there are few clear goals that everyone accepts, even in relatively small workplaces. Multiple expectations exist where different groups contend with each other to be heard. In this climate, good leadership means the three C's--whether commitment, commonality and compromise.

PRUDENT PERMISSIVENESS

Some well-meaning humane managers feel guilty if they do not respond positively and permissively to all their employees' requests, even when these employees make absurd demands. If you are one of these managers, perhaps it is because you fail to understand employees who take advantage of permissiveness.

These employees are often those who, as children and young adults, were allowed to be lazy and socially destructive. Or, conversely, they may have grown up in a heavily authoritarian environment. What often happens to these children when they become adult workers is that their energy becomes demanding and destructive. It is frustrating, but fascinating, to talk to destructive people. And it is astonishing to find out how deluded they are, honestly believing that they are justified in their destructive actions. Many of these people have also learned that they can manipulate some well-meaning and weak manager because of the manager's confusion, guilt and poor perception.

Humane management does **not** mean permissiveness to destroy. Rather, it means confronting advantage takers and calling a halt to their machinations. Bear in mind that they often consider themselves deserving of special privileges, and therefore feel that they deserve a disproportionate amount of time and attention.

EXPECTATIONS AND EXCELLENCE

Expect, and you shall receive. This powerful phrase is at least two thousand years old. It is simple, easy to understand, and yet many managers continue to make it work against themselves. One of our favorite studies about the power of belief comes from a certain workplace. Two new section managers were given two different departments. One manager was informed that his group had given trouble, that there would be problems with production. The other manager was told that he was to be in charge of one of the finest, most cooperative, high producing groups available any place, and that getting excellent results would be easy.

The fact was that the manager with "trouble" had been misinformed; each section was similar. In spite of this, the "bad" department began to develop problems, and production declined. The "good" department did superior work.

Set and maintain high standards of excellence in ways which elevate the mediocre performer and do not alienate the superior performer. Any manager who accepts standards of mediocrity out of fear of alienating the "common" person, has neither superior nor mediocre workers who will do very well. (This is one of the problems of the public schools today.) They will all be dissatisfied and the organization as well as individuals will suffer. Organizations and societies gain strength from the ability of their people to admire and respect (or at least not to dislike) superior people.

A particularly delicate and highly significant problem in a democracy is this one of egalitarianism. How much openly admitted superiority should be allowed and nurtured in a democracy? Should superior people be put on the defensive because of their superiority? What is the best way to minimize inferiority feelings by people in "lesser" or menial jobs? In America, this delicate problem is ignored by practically everyone. Yet, it must be confronted and solutions to the problem must be found, if we are to be leaders in the world. The dilemma of helping people of all abilities to be comfortable and productive is extremely complex. Even so, three simple rules will help to maximize benefits for all.

a. Prize and reward excellence for all, no matter what level of work, and decry shoddiness in work standards.

b. In teaching equality, don't raise expectations unrealistically by preaching the doctrine of "being able to do anything you really want to." This is a quick way to dashed hopes and troubled people. Rather, strive to help develop the unique talents of each person to the best of each one's ability.

c. Consider placing the very highly gifted in jobs where they won't have to engage too much in participative management decisions, for very highly superior persons sometimes are more likely to be stressed than the average person since they perceive ramifications of problems much more quickly than most.

IF YOU WANT TO DIE JUST GET BY

Maud Tole, at age 85, learned how to swim. She got her first driver's license at age 91. At 104, when she appeared on the Johnny Carson show and he asked her what she thought about remarrying, she said, "No, I don't want to get tied down." Bernice Warner joined the Kelly Girls at age 85. At age 94, she was hired full-time by Airborne Freight in Accounts Receivable. She supposedly also goes to the horse races every day they run. Her advice for keeping it up is relax, don't smoke, and have a cocktail before dinner and a glass of beer at bedtime, and have strong ancestors.[6]

Many people live for retirement. They feel that they're entitled to take it easy from some particular point on, and not really have plans and goals. In response to this, insurance actuarial tables show that there is a distinct difference between people who retire with plans and those who don't. Those who don't, live on the average, about 3-5 years after retirement. Those with vibrant, meaningful plans tend to live 15-20 years past retirement.

The same is true on the job. How many people do you know who retired at age 35, but just haven't bothered to file a pension plan? They continue to live out their lives in a sleepy state of existence for 30 years.

When we begin to just get by from one weekend to the next, when we begin to believe that our past accomplishments are more important than our future ambitions, we begin to die.

As each goal is reached, we need to look for new ones. That's what makes one great. When you believe you've "arrived," be careful; you're beginning to pack a pleasant, but fatal rut. When you get to that point, you're close to being a "has-been."

SIMPLE, SORT OF

Many managers fail because they are simplistic when they should be complex and complex when they should be simple. Here are some rules of thumb for simplicity and complexity. Be simple in making goals and values clear, and in going around "blessing" those who achieve those goals. Be complex in knowing what is happening and in understanding deeply. Be simple in keeping the focus and energy on just a few goals at a time which will result in great actions by many people. But be complex in never underestimating the things that can go wrong in operationalizing a few simple goals.

You may be a bright, sophisticated manager who is very adept at manipulating hundreds of variables in analyzing causes and effects. You may devour 300-page plan documents; but you may still be a mediocre manager unless you get your simplicities and complexities straight.

If you want to be a superior manager, focus with intensity on only a few goals, continually using a wide range of action devices to keep people from meandering into complex detours. The problem is to foster movement toward those few simple and clear goals that really count. Cut out the paper chases. Study complex issues informally and quickly. Have task forces that meet intensively for five or ten days, rather than those which meet intermittently for two or three years.

There is another aspect of the simple and complex. It has to do with communication. It is often difficult to boil down complex issues and messages to simple and concise statements, because most people can only take in little bits of information at one time, and like it or not, main ideas or slogans are springboards to action much more than lengthy memos or speechs.

There is no way you can be a real leader without offering a simple, eloquent message. No matter how complex the issue, you have to be able to boil it down so that everyone can understand and identify with it. This is sophisticated simplicity--Martin Luther King used his "I have a dream" and F.D.R. his "You have nothing to fear but fear itself."

There are two bases to cover here. First, relax your approach to complexities. When you approach a problem, take a hint from "The Wing" musical and "ease on down the road"--slowly. Don't worry about the solution until later; just let it evolve as you focus in on the research. Turn the problem over in your mind so that you see it from its different angles. Above all, mull it over calmly, as if you were entirely separated from it. An old-fashioned phrase was, "Sit and cogitate awhile."

View the matter from the standpoint of each person or group involved: workers, customers, Board of Directors, shareholders, top boss, and the press are a few possibilities. Try to put into a simple sentence or paragraph what each would feel. This is an inner sort of brainstorming where you just let your own knowledge and experience speak to you and give you a grip on the complexities involved. When you arrive at a pretty good understanding of the matter, you are ready to cover the next base--simplified communication.

In the same relaxed way, try to reduce the complex to the simple. Say to yourself,perhaps, "If I had to explain this situation to a newcomer who was just beginning in the field, how could I say it most simply and briefly?" After you have figured this out (and jotted notes down on it), then go to the next step. Be sure that you have kept your depth. In other words, reduce the complex to the simple, **but** do **not** lose the complex aspects which convey depth. Without the substance, people could misunderstand and feel that you are talking down to them.

If you worry about using few words, read Robert Frost. Many of his poems are complex, yet so simple that even children love many of them. Who would doubt the simple eloquence of this poet in his down-to-earth language? To use simple style but maintain the complex underpinnings is the highest form of sophistication. Carried to its extreme, this reduction to simple eloquence is the classic formula we find in Newton's law of gravity, or Einstein's theory of relativity.

One Step at a Time

We Americans are accustomed to doing everything at once. When social ills are finally recognized, we want to pull out the powerful societal penicillin, legislate quadruple doses, and heal society immediately. Although this type of healing is usually impossible, still many people expect it, and are frustrated when cures are not instantaneous.

One key to success is breaking goals down into manageable jobs, and then getting the jobs done. Effective managers may only accomplish two or three primary goals a year, but if they do them well, in the course of three or four years, they will be seen as blitzkrieg leaders.

Even though you are an entrepreneur, some goals must be reached one step at a time with each step visible for later perusal. You surely remember hearing the story of the Little Red Train that "thought he could." That little train faced the huge mountain with doubts; however, he "thought he could." Chugging along, one mile after another, he made it to the top of the mountain.

Issues Leadership vs. Trouble Shooting Management

Issues leadership means that you spend no more time than necessary on trouble shooting. It means that although you manage problems, you concentrate most of your energies on reaching far enough out into the future to be able to capitalize on opportunities and to prevent problems. This requires management that is highly active, adaptive, and futuristic. It demands intense analysis of issues, including descriptions and histories. In addition, sensitivity to community impact and other general publics is necessary. Legislative tracking may even be needed. Priorities must be given, and plans of action which include contingency alternatives must be provided.

Dynamic organizations address issues in ways which stimulate action. Static ones focus on maintenance and trouble shooting, or they study issues in ways which stultify action. One study revealed a $600 million company which had 325 task forces which had been operating for at least three years without accomplishing their missions![7]

Issues leadership requires that you are a tough minded pragmatist, who is also a bit of a philosopher, for you must be able to balance the part with the whole. Along with this is the occasional necessity to fight for what's right. Although humanists are sometimes reluctant to come out swinging, this kind of swinging is sometimes important if you are to be effective.

Excitement and Fun

The workplace that plays together stays together and works like hell. Much has been written lately about the quality of life in superior high tech companies. One characteristic that stands out is a zest for life and for work. McGregor described this ingredient of the Y type workplace way back in the '50's. It's now becoming institutionalized in more and more effective organizations. What we're mainly talking about here is the zest for work that comes from communicating informally, knowing purposes, agreeing

with values, knowing why things are being done, having
some control over what is being done, and above all,
having trust.

BREAK THE BULLIES

Even Maslow, one of the strongest exponents of
decency and democracy, said that "The correct thing to
do with authoritarians is to take them realistically
for the bastards they are and then behave toward them
as if they were bastards."[8] If you smile and trust
authoritarians (or any other tyrants or bullies) and
give them the keys to your vault, they will steal the
guns, hold you (the benefactors) hostage, and demand
ransom, considering you to be weak, stupid, and
spineless.

For example, Joe was a bully who took advantage of
other workers and even took advantage of his boss. The
manager for whom Joe could work well would have to
first "break Joe's back" and then affirm his authority
before he could become humane, strong yet kind, gentle
and appropriately permissive.

Sometimes, you have to stop tippy-toeing around
and be direct. In one small school district a super
health benefits contract had been negotiated which
required 100% employee membership. All employees
except Ob Stinut had signed up. Both his colleagues
and principal tried to persuade Ob Stinut to join, but
Ob kept declining. Finally, the superintendent asked
Ob to come to his office and said, "Here's your
contract for the health plan. Sign, or hunt another
job." Ob signed.

Later, when Ob was asked why he hadn't signed
sooner, he replied that he just hadn't seen what was in
it for him until then!

If the people you want to help haven't gone too
far, you can win them over to being democratic and
humane. However, if a certain line in psychopathology
has been crossed, no amount of "therapy" is likely to
be successful. A great problem is that actual
psychopathological situations are sometimes glossed
over with certain stupid kinds of "helpfulness." To

make this mistake can be fatal for you, your organization, and even for society.

SITUATIONAL LEADERSHIP

Many employee strikes have developed through raw power management which degraded the individual. In a communication session following one strike, the most impassioned plea of the strikers was to be treated as equals by managers. In this particular case, a large part of the problem was a kind of righteous ambivalence by managers who wanted to treat them as equals, yet not do so.

This illustrates a prevalent dilemma for managers in which it is easy to become hostage to your principles. Managers have been socialized to believe that equal treatment should be preceded by equal talent, or by equal time spent in work, or at least by equal commitment. When you are confronted by desires for equality by people who seem to violate these standards, you automatically believe the confrontation to be a dilemma of principles. At any rate, to be treated as equals is one of the loudest cries of new-age employees. It is also a cornerstone of humanistic management.

One way to treat people as equals is through situational leadership. In situational leadership, different leaders are nurtured for specific functions according to their expertise. The manager ideally is like the quarterback who calls signals and coordinates plays. In another sense, the situational leader is the most capable servant of the group. In any event, the manager shares power, assigns precise obligations, and ensures that things get done. Situational leadership is, in various ways, a positive challenge to hierarchical authority, an antidote to paternalism, and the antithesis of "bossism." Perhaps these are the reasons that the use of it has been so minimal.

STANDING OUT

To be a good leader, you must also stand out in some way--have commanding features which are associated

with you. Lincoln had his stove-pipe hat; Davy
Crockett, his coonskin cap; Ike, his huge grin; J.F.K.,
the charisma of a movie star. You too need an easy-to-
remember identity tag--a genuine one, of course. If
you don't have one already, develop it. Search
yourself. What do you like to do (or be) that doesn't
necessarily conform, but would be harmonious? Maybe
there is a saying you grew up on that you keep
reminding yourself not to say because it is colloquial.
Say it! Be colloquial when you feel like it. Be your
unique self, develop some feature to make you
memorable, and project easy firmness.

TAKING TOUGH PROBLEMS YOURSELF

Don't delegate all difficult problems, nor waffle
and weakly manipulate, but grab hold of them. Chief
Justice Burger has faced a good deal of adverse criticism because of problems in this respect. According to
the Supreme Court's procedure, the Chief makes
decisions on the court cases at hand. Then, if he is
in the majority after the other justices decide, he
appoints a justice to write the majority decision.
Otherwise, the senior justice of the majority delegates
the writing. According to Woodward and Armstrong's
book, **The Bretheren**, Burger has frequently refused to
decide until the other justices have rendered their
decisions. Then he has delegated the writing whether
he is in the majority or minority. This has led to
resentment on the part of the other justices of the
court.[9] Further, it may suggest to a watching press
and public a certain ineptitude as well as high-
handedness which has strained Burger's public
credibility.

TRANSCENDING

When you go beyond the narrow boundaries of
rational analysis of what is happening right now, and
begin to make intuitive leaps to perceive what can be--
to what the potentials of programs and people are at
their best--you begin to transcend the barriers of
"normal" management. Transcendence first of all
requires a belief in employees' potential greatness.

It also involves an ability to be absorbed in what is going on at a particular time. Watch a small child, for instance, looking at a crawling snail for five or ten minutes, oblivious of all else. When you, as a manager, begin to concentrate completely on a client, or an issue, and put everything else totally out of your mind, you begin to transcend "normal" managerial expectations. This concentration comes from an internal peace which can inspire loyalty, intensify focus on the really important things, increase efficiency, and maximize creativity. It is not the frenetic activity of the Type A manager who may get lots of motion, but also lots of wasted activity.

Transcenders are persons who break barriers of normal, constricting win/lose situations. They know that no one is better than everyone else for more than a little while. They realize that this makes everyone losers part of the time. Conversely, they know that everyone has different skills, abilities, and instincts, and can win at some things. They know that hope, not frustration, is the key to high productivity. Cooperation, more than competition, usually improves performance. Pride, rather than picking at oneself, motivates higher productivity. Relaxation and confidence, not fear and insecurity, are fundamental to doing one's best in almost everything, whether it's giving a speech, or working on the assembly line. On the other hand, needling, decisive, or cajoling managers who clearly believe in win/lose scenarios, lower dignity and produce tensions. And managers who actually say stultifying things like, "No matter how well you do in the first year, I won't believe you're good unless you can keep doing it at least two years," create discouragement. The results are invariably lower productivity, or even failure.

Transcenders change things, they don't just maintain them. They have fire in their blood to inspire others, even though they get advice from cooly objective experts. In tough times, when leadership is needed most, people don't respond to cold reason. They won't do something just because it makes sense. They must be stirred and excited--not just given a lecture on the complexities or impossibilities of the problem.

The transcender has a certain irrationality--a stubborn refusal to accept defeat and an infectious optimism. Listen to Churchill speaking at Dunkirk: "We will win the inevitable victory, so help us God." Leaders must be able to convince that all is not lost even when people fear it is; that the greatest victories are over impossible odds.

FAITH

There are two important aspects of faith. One is a confident belief in self or another being--one's God and/or another human being. The other aspect pertains to goals and perseverance. When we combine this power of confident belief with the single-minded pursuit of desired goals, we begin to tap enormous energy and power within ourselves.

Illustrating both belief and perseverance is the account of Florence Chadwick swimming the Catalina Channel. She set out on a cold foggy morning in 1952, committed to being the first woman to swim from Catalina Island to the coast of California. She had already earned the distinction of being the first woman to swim the English Channel in both directions. On this July morning, the water was so cold that her body became numb. The fog was so thick that she could barely see her crew in the nearby boats. Sharks even got so close several time that they had to be shot at, but she swam on and on.

After almost 16 hours in the water she decided to quit. Her mother and trainer, however, said she was close to land and urged her to swim on. But Florence could see only fog, and feel only indescribable fatigue and numbing cold. So, she was pulled from the water-- only one-half mile from the California coast. Later, she told reporters that if only she could have seen land, she might have been successful.

She strongly believed that she was defeated not by the fatigue or cold, but by the fog. The fog had dampened her vision, her reason, and her faith. Here we see one of the biggest challenges of faith--to keep on believing when the goals are obscure. Florence

Chadwick learned from her experience to meet the
challenge. Two months later in similarly dense fog,
she succeeded, and she even beat the men's record by
two hours. This time her faith helped her persevere;
it was like a beacon cutting through thick fog.

THIRTY-THREE "ONE LINER" SUGGESTIONS FOR DEVELOPING POWER WITH PEOPLE

Some of these short suggestions are merely boiled
down from the strategies you've just read. Others are
new. All can be helpful in developing power **with**
people as a humanistic entrepreneur. They are all easy
to remember and to have at your fingertips.

1. Don't interrupt employee's talk nor rush their thoughts.

2. Use valuable tools of communication such as paraphrasing, or summarizing that help employees to realize that you understand their views.

3. Don't fire a barrage of questions that makes you appear aggressive.

4. Stay away from quick, cliche-like answers that indicate you don't really have time to deal with employees' deep concerns.

5. Care deeply. Think of the most precious person you have ever known. Then treat all people as though they were that person.

6. Give advice more often than orders.

7. Concern yourself just as much with feelings as with ideas and words.

8. Make service your motto, and commence most of your contacts with, "How can I help you?"

9. Keep people informed (they're **down** on what they're not **up** on).

10. Be open to people and ideas, but don't vacillate.

11. Try always to engage in win/win, but not in win/lose situations. Understand that the domination/submissive approach is a one-way street with a dead-end.

12. Don't steer away from important personal feelings which need to be expressed nor distract others by diverting attention to things which are less important.

13. Try to ensure that all employees have the belief that they have a voice in whatever affects them.

14. Consider leaving a conflict unresolved but with increased trust and morale, that will help further negotiations.

15. Understand that mutual trust is one of the most important aspects of the workplace.

16. Test all things by the Rotary test:

    - Is it the truth?
    - Is it fair to all concerned?
    - Will it build goodwill and better friendship?
    - Will it be beneficial to all concerned?

17. Acknowledge and prize superior people and work, wherever they are.

18. Practice the Golden Rule of Gossip. Instead of gossiping, ask yourself if you would want that information passed on. The justification for gossip (and also sometimes for business decisions based on gossip) of "Where there's smoke there's fire" is often incorrect. In fact, where there's smoke, it may just be someone blowing hard on some moist bit of garbage and nothing more.

19. Practice the Golden Rule of Labeling. Label only as you would want them to label you.

20. Try to eradicate forever the diabolical we/they dichotomies. They are absolute anathema to humane management.

21. Strive to love persons unconditionally even when you find their actions undesirable. Commit yourself to practicing, "I love you because you're human, and I want to help us all to be productive."

22. Prize dialogue, not monologue. Try never to talk longer than one minute at a time when you talk with subordinates, unless you are informing them of something that is not really suitable for dialogue.

23. Look for complexities. Don't accept what seems to be at face value.

24. Learn how to compromise while simultaneously increasing your pride and self-identity. People sometimes say, "Either you can be yourself and keep your pride, **or** you can go along." If that is truly the issue, it means that disagreements are "win or give in." Why not say, "Other people do not have power to give or withhold pride from me. Only I can do that." Also, tell yourself, "My pride grows as I help others to be proud."

25. Don't get upset with imperfections in others. First, look carefully at the imperfections. Are they really detrimental to the operation of your company? If they are, then find some way to help the person do better. If it is more in the area of something that bothers you, forget it, and appreciate the enrichment of diversity instead.

26. Give employees as much freedom in their work as possible. Don't require conformity to narrow rules unless it's really essential to the company's operation.

27. Delay judgments about people. Instead of categorizing them on sight according to superficial and external criteria, suspend judgment. Search for reasons for your feelings

and others' actions.

28. Stretch your mind regularly by practicing "debate" in your thoughts. The debator must look carefully at all sides of an issue and be able to justify each side. Try this yourself. Instead of categorizing, condemning or praising according to past prejudice and experience, ask yourself what other sides exist, why, and how you can understand others and their points of view.

29. Read and listen to learn, not to refute others or to substantiate your own view.

30. Plan a one-year program for self-development for yourself. Go to plays, movies, and concerts you would not ordinarily go to. Introspect with yourself. Deepen your understanding of yourself and others. Do these things with an openness and diligence, not with half-hearted resignation.

31. Realize that the more work seems like play (as long as commitment to both organization and individual exists), the better off both the organization and the individual will be.

32. Don't let yourself get into the vicious cycle of believing the world is one vast persecution arena where the lions are out to get you so you must get them first.

33. Never punish employees or allow them to lose face when you can change behavior through positive means.

SUMMARY THOUGHTS ON CONNECTING "HUMANISTIC" WITH "ENTREPRENEUR"

In the folklore of business, is a question asked of Andrew Carnegie about which of the following was most important: workers, money or intelligence. Carnegie put things in perspective by supposedly asking, "Is there one leg of a three legged table that is most important?"

Further sharpening the perspective of humanistic entrepreneurs is a story about a child and a puzzle. One day, a child, becoming more and more bored, became more and more of a nuisance to his father. Finally, Dad, in exasperation, reached for the daily newspaper. Thumbing through, he saw a map of the world which covered nearly an entire page. He then cut that page into many different and complicated pieces, and said, "Here, put this together." Dad thought he would now have a long spell of tranquillity. But after just a few minutes, the boy called to his father to come and look. Sure enough, the paper was put together properly. Dad was astonished and asked how his son had been able to put the whole world together so quickly. His son replied that it was easy. "I found a big picture of a human being on one side of the paper. I simply concentrated on the person. When I put the human being together, the world was just right!"

REPLACE VICTORIAN BOSS HABITS

WITH HUMANE POWER STRATEGIES

The Manager's Golden Rule

When I am your manager, I try to imagine the kind of manager I'd like if I were you. Then I try to be that kind of manager.

INTRODUCTION

As a manager you can weaken your alter ego, whose name is "Personal Power" by serious managerial infections that keep you from peak performances. As with physical bacterial ailments, you may keep going without getting any better; you may even finally accept mediocrity as normal. You may blame workers, society, or the Supreme Court for your poor performance when, in actual fact, what you really need is to look at your Victorian Boss Habits. We've labeled such things as anger, blame, excessive approval seeking, and narrow responsibility as Victorian Boss Habits. If you have these kinds of old time managing habits, we believe that the only cure is a massive injection of the Golden Rule--of love, forgiveness and treating others as you want to be treated. The Golden Rule cure will help to reduce excessive selfishness, exploitation and hostility. It will help you to make people, not things, the key to productivity.

There are four main bacterial boss habits that keep managers from functioning fully: they are (1) excessive approval seeking, (2) blame, (3) narrow accountability, and (4) hostility and revenge. It's very easy to surround yourself with "yes people" who seek **approval** obsequiously, to **blame** others when things go wrong, to foster very **narrow accountability** because it's clear and precise, and to reinforce habits such as gossip which then produce **hostility** and **revenge**.

Like many in our society, you may have grown up with some "you should" beliefs. And what happens is that "you should" all over yourself. "You should" all over yourself by saying:

-- You should get **approval** at any cost.
-- You should **blame** the guy who screwed up.
-- You should only worry about getting employees to be **accountable** to their **boss** and **own** department.
-- You should get **angry**, get even and take **revenge** if you want real power.

These are all habits that the average manager has picked up. The problem is that the kinds of habits you allow yourself to have govern, to a large extent, the kinds of people who work for you, and the kinds of efficiency you get from these people. If you listen to obsequious employees as much as objective ones, give blame as easily as compliments, reinforce account-ability to single departments more than to the whole company, and allow yourself to get angry as much as you do to laugh, you're likely to be fostering a workplace that is infected with the illness of mediocrity. And any organization today with average managers and mediocre employees is in trouble.

You as a manager may be weakened by any or all of these diseases simply because you were exposed to them earlier in your life. You may not even realize that you have an infection, or that you're weaker than you need be. Take a simple test to assess the well-ness of your workplace and your self. Do you believe that:

1. If you let 'em get by with that, you might as well never try to enforce anything from the central office again.   Yes_____ No_____

2. People do not really want to cooperate; it's a dog-eat-dog world, and the best way to be an effective manager is to show 'em who's boss.   Yes_____ No_____

3. Someday I'll get even with those
   people who cross me.   Yes_____ No_____

4. Lots of times you just have to say,
   "That's none of your business."   Yes_____ No_____

5. You often have to **blame** people in
   order to get accountability.   Yes_____ No_____

6. It's O.K. to cloak critical messages
   to employees by saying things with a
   laugh.   Yes_____ No_____

7. Do you allow employees to bad mouth
   other employees?   Yes_____ No_____

8. My employees:

   -- Do less work than I think they
      should.   Yes_____ No_____
   -- Say things like, "You may
      remember that I suggested that a
      year ago."   Yes_____ No_____
   -- Seem preoccupied.   Yes_____ No_____
   -- Seem angry, or sometimes sabotage
      things.   Yes_____ No_____

     The number of "yes" answers will probably indicate
the extent of bacterial infection in either yourself,
your workplace, or both. Of course, it is possible for
a very healthy manager to come into a workplace with
employees who have acquired Victorian boss habits of
selfishness, exploitation and hostility themselves.
When this happens, it is a long haul to well-ness of
the workplace. And it is even probable that the
workplace will never be "well" unless the chief
executive officer is committed to this kind of health.

     The reduction of Victorian boss habits begins with
your mind. You must learn to control your thinking.
This requires awareness first of when you are behaving
in habitual, but counterproductive ways. If you can
catch yourself acting in these ways, you can then begin
to challenge the values at the bottom of your behavior.
It's not the reactions you **plan**, but the habitual

reactions you don't plan that are important. Many managers have to change their responses, and this requires thinking first, feeling second, and action third. In other words, when you **feel** yourself about to blame, or be obsequious, or get angry, stop and think carefully before acting.

At the heart of the way you think, feel and act, are your beliefs about what values are most important. If, for example, you believe that win/lose high-noon kinds of competition are bottom lines for people, you will likely try to develop raw power over people. On the other hand, if values such as esteem, respect, and affection seem most important, you will have a reason to develop power **with** people. We believe that human beings demand esteem and respect in any organized, satisfactory system, and that these qualities are sources of human joy, the language of human relations, and that they are desperately needed outcomes in any organization today.

In addition to general joy and improved human relations, there is another major reason for eradicating these infectious boss habits. It has to do with inappropriate stress. Obsequious blame and anger in particular, contribute to the kind of stress which can easily lower efficiency and overall work rather than to inspire better work. Obsequiousness, blame and anger can also even contribute to physical ailments such as ulcers, gastro-intestinal colitis, spastic colon, mild cardiac problems, angina, migraine headaches, asthmatic attacks and allergic reactions.

As you decrease some general illnesses of the workplace, you are in a position to begin to increase the strength of your alter ego, "Personal Power", as you make yourself and workplace more healthy.

Gerald Jampolsky, who has written a bestselling book called, **Love is Letting Go of Fear**, applies this concept to management as well as to all other relationships. Dr. Jampolsky believes that such emotions as blame, anger and excessive approval seeking are the result of fear, and that you can actually replace fear with love for everyone you come across in management (even those with whom you may have

problems).[1] [2] This, we believe, has immense possibilities for both job satisfaction and productivity.

While esteem, respect and appropriate motivation
can be generated by developing power **with** people, this
kind of power is stifled by Victorian habits.
Therefore, it would seem an important aspect of
developing peak performance in others as well as
yourself to reduce Victorian Boss Habits. Even while
practicing a system of self improvement which
emphasizes positive self-imaging more than negative
trouble shooting, there is also an important place for
awareness of these negative habits in order to replace
them with positive ones.

APPROVAL SEEKING

*Approval is seductive, elusive, dangerous **and** important.*

The Problem

As a boss, you are a little like a gladiator in
the ancient Coliseum of Rome. You are in a bloody
arena; a few slips and you've had it! On the other
hand, with courage, skill and strength, you may
overcome the lions and win the approval of the emperor
and the crowd. The paradox in your job, as in the
ancient arena, is that if you try mainly to win
approval from the emperor or the crowd, you're more
likely to slip and fall than if you try for skill,
strategy and survival.

As you study the phenomenon of approval, you find
that, based on initial impressions, only about two-
thirds of the people you meet approve of you on sight.
The other third will disapprove, citing such reasons as
the way you part your hair, speak, walk, dress,
supervise, or don't. What is important to remember is
that you can't please everyone. If you try, you will
please fewer people than if you strive to do your job
well. What you must do is to manage people in the very
best way you can, be concerned primarily about what
kind of a job you do, and let approval (or disapproval)
follow. The day that approval stops being a must and

begins too be merely a nice thing to have, is the day that both your management effectiveness and personal happiness are likely to increase.

The need for approval is strong for most managers, for not only is approval an integral part of your managing success, it is also a part of the warp and woof of American culture. You know that despite all the talk of rugged individualism in America, many kinds of conformity exist. A large percentage of all advertisements appeal to the desire for approval--and they work! Religious, political, and fraternal institutions make narrow approval boundaries paramount to their membership. Families frequently over-protect, over-expect, and overly-suspect their members, thus demanding mutual approval of neurotic habits and stultifying growth toward the independent and yet caring souls.

As a manager, you also have an additional reason for letting yourself seek approval seriously. For as manager, you must take certain rebukes from superiors and subtle rebuffs from subordinates. It is difficult to deal with these potential insults without getting caught in the traps of currying favor to gain approval or being belligerent to show that you are your own person. Still, how you resolve this dilemma can be one of the important factors which decides how effective you will be.

Approval seeking is also connected to stress, and when stress becomes excessive, functioning is decreased. Two major causes of stress are (1) fear of rejection, and (2) fear of failure. From this frame of reference, when you, as manager, reinforce the rejection and failure of employees who don't conform to narrow standards, you actually lower the functions of the workplace. When you, as subordinate, are overly concerned with whether your superior accepts you and sees you as credible, you are also likely to waste time and energy through stress which could be alleviated by the practice of a few simple strategies such as those in this section.

RECOGNIZE WHAT TO DO

RECOGNIZE WHAT JOB-RELATED SUPERIORITY SHOULD MEAN

The boss should be the most superior person in the group at getting people to do their best. This presupposes mutual respect between boss and employees, but does not mean that the boss will be the chief pin-up girl or boy of the workers. To be liked is nice, but respect is better--particularly the kind of respect which results from humanistic management. To be free of disapproval is impossible.

RECOGNIZE THE DIFFERENCE BETWEEN DISAGREEMENT AND DISAPPROVAL

Remind yourself that no matter what you do or say, some people are going to disagree with you, particularly before you have all tried to reach consensus together. Disagreement itself is not bad; it is war and hostility and sabotage that are bad. Disagreement doesn't even necessarily mean a lack of approval. In fact, one of the most healthy signs of friendship and genuine approval is the kind of relationship which allows for agreeable disagreements in trying to discover "truth."

RECOGNIZE BASIC REASONS FOR EXCESSIVE APPROVAL SEEKING

The basic reason for excessive approval seeking is a feeling of unworthiness. If you are a **manager** and you foster too much approval seeking by subordinates, it is likely to result in lower productivity in terms of energy, initiative and creativity directed toward the company's goals. On the other hand, if you are a **subordinate** and seek too much approval, it is likely because you feel unworthy and are trying to increase your esteem by approval seeking. Neither of these results of approval seeking is likely to be helpful to an organization. What is needed is a workplace centered on getting jobs done and taking care of peoples' needs without a neurotic focus on approval that exists in some workplaces.

TWENTY-TWO STRATEGIES FOR MANAGING APPROVAL NEEDS

1. Understand that some people will always behave in certain ways, no matter what you do. Some are always going to disapprove of you. And some will disapprove of almost everything anyone does--these people will never enjoy life fully. To these people even the most delectable happiness is a mistake, a surprise, or transient. There is at least one person with this attitude in every work force of any size. And yet, the amazing thing is that bosses often feel compelled either to get mad at them because of disapproval, or to try continually to get approval from them. Admit to yourself that their approval will never be yours and live calmly with this realization.

2. Ignore the frowning or sarcastic innuendoes when subordinates or peers are trying to manipulate you, or ask mater-of-fact questions about what they're saying. Smoke them out in disarming ways, but don't expect nor depend on their approval.

3. Don't be defensive by modifying your stand, or by apologizing, when others disagree with you. Learn to disagree agreeably. On the other hand, don't stick stubbornly to illogical positions. Both extremes are equally neurotic.

4. Don't oversell your accomplishments to get approval, for, if you do, people may suspect your strengths or resent you.

5. Don't undersell your achievements, hoping that people will recognize your accomplishments without being informed, for they may never find out what you've done. Another side of underselling can be false modesty, which can easily be the meanest species of pride.

6. Don't defend yourself against baiting disagreement. Just say, "O.K.," or "Oh," to the baiting person. Don't defend, and don't elevate the importance of the disagreement.

7. Stop prefacing comments by phrases such as, "I may be wrong," or "This is just my opinion." These often mean "Give me approval for my humility," or "I want to hedge my bet." The best approval comes from standing on your own two feet.

8. Thank people for making suggestions on how you can improve, but don't take offense at the suggestions.

9. Listen carefully to all people and react respectfully and sincerely, regardless of position or rank.

10. Try concentrating simply on how you feel at the moment when you feel tense in front of others. Tense people are prime candidates for neurotic approval seeking. Let yourself acknowledge silently that you feel tense; frequently tension then will dissipate or even disappear. You may also feel less need for approval as you feel more secure and less tense.

11. Ensure that your secretary does not react to problems in way which callers will feel to be signs of disapproval. This is so easy to do.

12. Never indulge in self-pity, just turn your mind to developing skill, courage, and power with people.

13. Admit to yourself that you, as well as other people, have some needs for approval; these needs only become destructive if you **have** to have the approval.

14. Don't try to get approval from people who are generally negative and disagreeable. Take care of their needs which Herzberg called "hygiene," and keep them from sabotaging an operation, but don't work for their approval. To do so would often sabotage the goals of the company.

15. Don't be habitually late for meetings, hoping to create the feeling that you are so busy that you must show up late. You're likely to get more disapproval than approval.

16. Don't be phony with your knowledge of a problem about which you really know very little, in an attempt to impress others.

17. Don't change your position just because your boss shows disapproval, but be certain your convictions are based on facts.

18. Don't believe that you've "blown it" by having a view contrary to that of your boss' view.

19. Don't believe that you **must** disagree with subordinates much of the time, or resort to other nonconforming actions, in order to establish your identity. This can be just as neurotic as having to be similar and having to have approval.

20. Don't act as though you agree when you don't.

21. Don't feel resentment because you've helped someone and have not been thanked. In other words, never expect thanks.

22. Don't gossip. The approval you get from the other gossips is like a double-edged sword.

APPROVAL: ASSET OR LIABILITY?

One old-style boss of a large corporation, J. R. Weakness, hired **no** employees in whom he could not find flaws. He believed that flaws in his subordinates would make them less secure and more in need of approval, which in turn would allow him to bind them closer to his own image and self, and thus get more loyalty as well as obsequiousness for himself. This was eventually disastrous for the organization as well as for Mr. Weakness, even though in the short run it was comfortable for J. R.

Today, higher sophistication in employees and technology demands more strength and professionalism in managers. As the new breed of people has become more difficult to manage, and as technology has become more complex, subordinates have had to be far more than merely loyal minions or colorful cronies.

It is obvious that people will react better to your leadership if they like you than if they don't like you. In fact, the ability to get people to like you in non-neurotic ways is one of the greatest assets you can have. What usually makes people like you is a good sense of philosophical humor, basic kindness, knowledge and appreciation of others' feelings, fairness, and conveyance of the feeling that all others are just as important as you. If you can practice these things, approval seeking will be turned into the highest kind appreciation **of** and **from** people.

BLAME

To make a mistake is natural, and to blame someone for it is human. But outstanding managers don't blame; they analyze and act.

Many people believe that if something fails, you should fix the blame fast. Find someone who is, or can be made to look guilty. Then punish or terminate! Blame is one of the easiest traps for managers to fall into. Blame most often occurs in organizations in which narrow fiscal results are all important and humanistic management is a frill. You might characterize these workplaces as driving at unsafe speeds, and running over anyone who seems to be in the way.

Blame is particularly a disease of middle managers because they feel put upon. But it also happens on the highest executive levels. When General Motors, Ford and Chrysler fell behind the Japanese car makers, the American reaction was "Who's to blame?" Detroit's executives responded by blaming customers, the government or assorted foreigners--everyone but themselves. Anxiety and frustration reign until someone says, "Let's stop blaming and start changing." You need to see that there is really no merit in blaming another person.

WHAT BLAME REVEALS

On a personal boss level, blaming others when

things go wrong, of course, reveals weakness, lack of responsibility, lack of control, and lack of humaneness. And yet, blame is an everyday, detrimental device that many bosses use, often unthinkingly. It's so easy to say to your superior, "Well, you know Lewis, he's just weak, and he just didn't carry through." Or, "It's the teachers' fault; they just won't call the parents when students misbehave."

When confronted with a difficult task, it's also easy to blame superiors. You might say to subordinates, "I can't figure out how anyone could expect us to do this, but you know how it is, someone has to look good."

In addition to superiors and subordinates, you can indict, with infinite ease, legislators, the public, clients, customers, etc.--in short, anyone--as the cause of your problems. You can almost always find someone external who plausibly is at fault for ineffectiveness with which you are associated.

The problem is a paradox. You, the boss, are supposed to be powerful and in control. Yet, you cannot be all that powerful if you allow external factors to exert more power and influence over the jobs for which you are responsible than you, yourself, exert. Therefore, if Lewis is weak, then do something to solve the problem or to compensate for it, but don't use Lewis as your excuse. If the legislators have passed some laws which make your job more difficult, then by all means do something to get the laws changed, but in the meantime, do not let yourself be stifled or ineffective, moaning and muttering about those jelly-brained politicians, judges, or whomever.

WHAT TO DO ABOUT BLAME

DIFFERENTIATE BLAME FROM REASONS

Never indulge in blame. Blame is condemning and defeating when managerial energy should be utilized in determining and correcting reasons for failure. Blame allows you to externalize influences so that you don't have to accept responsibility. Blame focuses fault on someone else. On the other hand, analyzing reasons for failure or ineffectiveness can help you to direct attention to the facets of the problem which need remediation, all the while accepting your own responsibility to get the job done successfully. You are boss, and you gain esteem when you don't blame.

RECOGNIZE SOME TYPICAL WAYS IN WHICH MANAGERS REDUCE EFFECTIVENESS BY BLAMING.

In trying to ensure that you do not fall into the "blame trap" by default, be sure that you are aware of some of the most typical indications of boss blame, such as the following:

1. Blame others for your own lack of action. Sylvia Hirsch is a person who didn't blame, but changed. When she was in high school, her home economics teacher labeled her as a person who was likely to fail. Two and one-half decades later, her cheesecakes sold for $8.00 each and Sylvia was making $250,000 per year baking them. Ms. Hirsch did not say, "My teacher says I can't cook, and so I'll blame my own inaction on her appraisal." Instead, she analyzed, acted, and became immensely successful.

2. Get to meetings or workshops late or not at all, allegedly because of the pressures from duty-- insidiously implying that your superior is to be blamed for working you too hard, or that the place is poorly organized.

3. Blame the union for not meeting management halfway in order to settle the contract. Blame them because they're not doing their part. (Of course, they're not doing their part; it's an adversary relationship. Why expect that they would be different unless it's changed to two-way problem solving?)

4. Blame people for being evil when their value systems disagree with yours, even though no violence or psychological harm is being done. Certainly seek sane morality where the happiness of the individual and the safety of the society are pre- eminent, but do not require allegiance to narrow dogma.

5. Get angry with yourself or others because of a lack of perfection. Perfectionism is one of the surest ways to unhappiness, loathing, and blame.

6. Be resentful toward a superior or subordinate while "suffering in silence." Blame them for your own failures. An example of this is the teacher who blusters about the administration not backing him even when the administration does, in fact, take strong action and does offer the teacher several alternatives. The problem for this teacher or for any other employee in business or elsewhere may be skewed perception, laziness, weakness or inflexibility. Even though this teacher may have been a lion-tamer at one time, he is now lazy, and wants to do little but blame others. In his flexibility, he also does not tolerate, nor even see the effectiveness of different approaches to problems.

7. Cast your decision making into sagas of right vs. wrong instead of preferable alternatives, then blame those you believe to be wrong. If the scenario is **right vs. wrong**, you are very likely to **have** to be right all the time, with all that implies--indecision and delayed decisions, trying to find the right choice, blaming others if something is ineffective, and even psychotic refusal even to see facts of failure.

8. Be reluctant to stop blaming others. The curious thing about blaming by managers is that you **could** do better, but you don't. Why? You get satisfaction for not improving. These rewards are things that mean a lot to you--things such as:

-- You don't have to improve yourself.
-- You don't have to acknowledge your imperfections.
-- You don't have to think for yourself.
-- You don't have to build self-confidence, for events are really beyond you anyway.

TEN STRATEGIES FOR REDUCING BLAME AND INCREASING EFFECTIVENESS

Now that you've reviewed some of the ways bosses reduce their effectiveness by blame, make a commitment never to blame again. The following strategies may help you.

     1. Keep a log with four columns. In the first column, record events which were largely successful because you made them so. In the second column, list events that were unsuccessful. In the third column, record any blame (indirect as well as direct) you gave others; and in the fourth column (in reference to the unsuccessful events), state when you did not blame others, but instead analyzed the problem and got to work on practical solutions.

     2. Take stock of how easy you make it for others to blame you. For example, take a look at how often you impose policy authoritarianly without giving the recipients of those policies a voice in the policy making. Why not develop a practical kind of participative management?

     3. Practice not blaming others and keep the record mentioned in Item 4. Do this with ever-increasing proficiency. Even when people give you excuses to blame, don't. For example, even when your secretary maintains that your boss makes it hard on you, try to give responses which show that you, in the final analysis, control your own destiny--responses such as: "Anytime there may be difficulties, I have options such as. . . ."

     4. Go ahead and blame someone. Go ahead and write your blames. Does that change anything? Does it make you more effective? What disadvantages does this have, such as making you seem too weak to stand on your own two feet to get things done, etc.? Then compare the results of spending time on blame vs. eradicating blame and starting to work immediately on an action plan to solve the problems.

     5. Say to yourself, at times of disappointment, things such as, "I have been ineffective in . . . (be specific), and I will do . . . (be specific), to be more effective next time." In this way, you do not blame others, and you do not castigate yourself--you improve!

6. Don't be stifled by the "should be's." Don't "should all over yourself", and become upset to the point of being immobilized because people don't do the things we want them to do. For example, during one recent strike, all managers witnessed activities which surprised them immensely. Some managers let themselves become incensed with union activities to the point that good employee/boss relations could never be re-established. Other managers became, if anything, more effective than usual during the strike (as well as after it, too). The effective managers accepted what had to be, understood contradictory views and actions, and non-judgmentally separated the temporary reality from what they **wanted** it to be. These managers had learned to be adaptable and to roll with the punches without being wishy-washy.

7. Learn from the great people you know, or read about, but don't be discouraged or demoralized because they seem to be so much better than you, for it's a diabolical form of blame to stifle your own actions because of idealized images of perfectionism. This can happen, however, if you worship others in ways which actually repudiate your own self-importance.

8. Never blame things on "them." Never use the "great, gray they." Never say "I'd like to, but **they** won't let me." Or, "How can we do that when **they** say. . . ." This is not only unprofessional, it is also cowardly!

9. Tell yourself over and over again (if necessary) to practice the Golden Rule in blame. Be humane, and don't blame, as you do not want to be blamed.

10. Don't subvert the Golden Rule either. Unfortunately, some people, when reproaching others unnecessarily, say, "Oh, I **am** behaving according to the Golden Rule. If I **had** made a mistake, or had done something that bad, I would deserve to be blamed, but I haven't." These people often are serious neurotics who cannot allow themselves to admit to self-imperfections.

HOLISTIC AND MUTUAL ACCOUNTABILITY

BROAD VS. NARROW ACCOUNTABILITY

A farmer once took a pumpkin to the fair. The pumpkin was exactly the same size and shape as a one gallon jug. He had formed it that way by placing a jug over the plant once it had begun to grow. Although he had an interesting freak, he did not have a fully developed plant. You can put one gallon jugs over employees in your own work plant by requiring very precise but narrow accountability. You can easily believe that you have well shaped-up workers, when in actual fact, you have grotesque and weak parodies of the growth you could have.

One of the strengths in much of present-day Japanese industry is that there is widespread responsibility by workers for their company's products; this is shown in working overtime without pay, staying with one company for a lifetime, and in widespread commitment to helping others in the organization. Likewise, in these workplaces, executives feel responsible for much more than merely paying hourly workers' wages; there is also a deep concern for the employee's total welfare. The results are holistic and mutual concern, loyalty, and job mastery both for employee and manager.

You have holistic and mutual accountability as you get people to expand their horizons and productivity, to think together, work together, be responsible to each other, and to pull together. There is no way to accomplish these things if managers and employees have only narrow and precise responsibility and account-ability. There must be a spirit of pervasive and mutual concern for the general outcomes of the organization, as well as for precise individual responsibility for specific tasks.

At a time when atomistic characteristics of our society often stifle productivity, and in some cases dampen responsible democracy, it is particularly important that managers stress the whole as well as the part. This is not easy when the first priority of millions of individuals is to do their own thing, to be beholden to no one, or at least to be only narrowly accountable.

In fact, you can create stunted dwarfs in one gallon jugs merely by acting in habitual American ways. You can stress that managers should fight for their turf--argue or make recommendations and decisions merely on the basis of their own departments, rather than the entire organization. You can fail to give employees an important voice in their work. You can focus too narrowly on your company's products and exclude the concerns of your people and community. You can also pay salaries to people who do things on the basis of narrow accountability.

On the other hand, you can inspire people to unlimited growth; one place to begin is with holistic and mutual accountability. You might think of holistic accountability in terms of this poster that one of the authors once saw.

WHO ARE YOU TO THINK THAT YOU CAN CHANGE THE WORLD?

Who?	Who?	Who?	Who?	Who?	Who?
	Are	Are	Are	Are	Are
	You?	You	You	You	You
		To	To	To	To
		Think?	Think	Think	Think
			That?	That	That
				You	You
				Can?	Can
					Change
					The
					World?

People have the potential for so much drive,
energy, and impact when you use the unlimited power of
holistic accountability rather than one gallon jugs of
"usual accountability." But you have to reach for the
"world" rather than just your jug. Goethe said, "Treat
people as they are, and they remain that way; treat
them as though they were what they can be, and we help
them become what they are capable of becoming."
Holistic accountability is one of the secrets unknown
and unpracticed by many managers.

The more that individuals in a workforce or a
nation are interrelated, the more they need personally
to be dedicated to caring for the total enterprise, and
not just to separate segments of work or their lives.
Tuskegee Institute, a large private black college,
illustrates holistic accountability in instilling in
students financial accountability in repaying college
loans. In the last fifteen years, the federal
government has allocated huge sums of money and low
interest loans to college students of the past
generation for college costs. Large numbers of these
students default. In fact, the gross failure of
students to repay loans has resulted in the current
policy of not making loans to students attending
colleges with a student default rate of more than 25%.
This has not been a problem at Tuskegee, however; in
fact, Tuskegee has had a higher percentage of students
repaying loans than has Harvard. Almost 95% of
Tuskegee students have repaid their loans. This makes
Tuskegee students' payback rate one of the highest in
the nation, in spite of the fact that their students
come from families averaging less than $12,000 per
year. Tuskegee has gotten its students to realize that
not paying their debts is likely to result in a loss of
this privilege for future generations. This is
holistic accountability.

THREE IMPORTANT ELEMENTS OF ACCOUNTABILITY

There are three important elements of holistic
accountability: reciprocity, pervasiveness, and precision.

RECIPROCITY

Employees must be accountable to managers and vice versa. Managers themselves must be accountable to clients or customers, peers, and other executives in the official hierarchy. Each has some power to enforce claims. For example, peers can help, neglect, or ostracize their colleagues. Superordinates can be supportive, hostile or indifferent. Subordinates can befriend or tolerate managers, and clients and customers can respect a business or they can make a claims office into a living hell. The fact that the bosses, other executives, clients and peers may be in conflict with one another does not mitigate the need for accountability. There should be concern for feelings and opinions as well as for facts and hard data.

PERVASIVENESS

For accountability to seem fair, it has to include all major elements of the organization--in short, to be pervasive. To be pervasive, accountability must have at least four main aspects: (1) cash, (2) things (material and equipment), (3) deeds (impact on people), and (4) results (both process and product). Accountability must be seen as a cooperative endeavor involving bosses, workers, policymakers, and the client, or public at large.

PRECISION

The possibility of precision in accountability often raises grim panic because of obvious difficulties. For example, educators ask how they can be responsible for Johnny's learning when he spends 1,000 hours per year watching T.V., etc. True, but there are many times when we can be precise and should be. At other times, we must remember the classic analogy with the President of the U.S. He is accountable for so much, but can control relatively so little. Educational and other organizational leaders must foster cooperation in accountability, using as much precision as possible while at the same time tolerating ambiguity.

WHY ARE WE NOT HOLISTICALLY ACCOUNTABLE?

We may be able to explain why American and European managers have been too narrow in the sense of accountability by right/left brain concepts. The left brain is the domain of linear thinking--reading, decoding math, and hard data. It dominates the process of linking decision making to well-organized relevant information. Even the casual observer knows that American management executives have tended to be dominated by left brain operations. In contrast, the right brain is the domain of holistic thought--giving us full perspective by showing the whole. Conceptualization, feelings and emotions, wordless thinking, intuition, poetry and music, and beauty take place in the right brain.

Most American management has not been dominated by the right brain. This may be one explanation for so much recent failure in personnel management. Our society has become more interdependent, and correspondingly there has been a need for more holistic understanding. The workers and employees in our society have also been engaging in more self-actualizing pursuits, which involve aesthetics and other right brain activity. Yet, managers are still trying to motivate them with left brain, segmented appeals.

A MODEL FOR BUILDING HOLISTIC ACCOUNTABILITY AND RESPONSIBILITY: REPLACING COLLECTIVE BARGAINING WITH COOPERATIVE PROBLEM SOLVING

Within the concept of holism, one of the greatest challenges today is to melt away the threats, force and fragmented accountability fostered by adversary-oriented collective bargaining, and to set up holistic problem solving, trust, responsibility, and accountability instead. This is a tough task. It takes tremendous courage, but it can be done. One place pioneering in this is a school district in Livermore, California, where the superintendent, and the teachers' union representative have risked high-stakes failure in order to try to forge cooperative and integrative problem solving from competitive and adversary collective bargaining. The following model represents part of their successful work.[3]

IMPORTANT PRINCIPLES FOR MOVING FROM AN ADVERSARIAL TO A PROBLEM-SOLVING MODEL

Principal One.

Move **FROM** these Assumptions & Actions	**TO** these Assumptions & Actions
-- Win/lose, we/they mentali- ties where each side fights to gain at the others' expense.	-- Integrative action
-- Expectations of the other side's being unreasonable and nasty, and therefore be rejected.	-- Exceptions of rationality
-- Settings where feelings are angry and hostile.	-- Cooperative problem solving
-- The traditional collective bargaining strategies of:	-- Problem-solving strategies of:
-- No priority demands	-- Straightforward priority issues
— Extreme positions	-- No extreme positions to show compromise

-- "Throw-away issues"	-- No "throw-aways" which
	    make negotiations a
	    guessing game

— Impasse when items cannot
    be agreed upon (and where
    frustration and hostility
    reign)
	-- Study committees where
	    mutually beneficial
	    solutions are emphasized.
	    (This also allows a large
	    number of people to
	    participate.)

-- Outside professional district negotiators who tend to be viewed with distrust and suspicion by teachers or other employees.

-- In-house management negotiator who is skilled in inter-personal communication, problem solving, and conflict resolution. The in-house negotiator also has greater commitment to the resolution than an outsider, and this is less of a threat.

— No structured contact between management and and the employees' union or management and unions.

-- Executive (closed-door) meetings between the board and the employees' representatives. In this way, teachers would not feel that their positions were filtered incompletely to the board through the management representative.

Principal Two. Ensure That The Following Aspects Exist.

-- Intelligent, sensitive, and honest leadership by both management and employees consistent with classroom and business ideals rather than leadership with threats and angry rhetoric.

-- Conflict resolution and problem solving maintained away from the bargaining table.

-- Mutual respect for each other's positions.

-- Open and shared communication to avoid misunderstandings: The superintendent-boss and the union president are both invited to each other's council meetings and workshops so that questions can be asked and creative dialogue can occur.

-- Grievances are now viewed as means of addressing a problem rather than as power struggles.

**Principal Three.   Other Aspects of An Holistic
Problem-Solving Negotiation Model Might Include:**

-- A "facilitator" chosen by popular vote of the
union and management members who trains all who
are interested in communication and problem
solving.

-- A "crap detector" who interrupts whenever
anyone at the bargaining table begins to engage
in subversive influences.

ANGER

"I don't get mad, I get even."

Whether you get mad or get even, both responses
are hostile, and either response is likely to do you
more harm than good in today's workplace. Don't stoop
to hostility and you may conquer.

Whenever you get angry, or become hostile, it's
because, for the moment at least, you feel somewhat
incapable or inferior. It may be that some poor soul
will not respond to your superior logic, or it may be
that you realize at some level of consciousness or
unconsciousness that the other person actually has
superior logic this time.   But regardless of the
situation, hostility always seems to result from
feeling incapable or inferior. Hostility results from
a threat to status, and one of the immutable laws of
life is that anyone who allows feelings of inferiority
to result from status threats will feel hostile.

So what? You may say: "It still feels good to get
angry every once in a while." That may be so if you
are unenlightened, or if your simple refusal to accept
that anger is the result of inferiority. But if you
allow yourself to accept the fact that hostility
results from inferiority, you will be unlikely to
continue to maintain that anger feels good, for that
actually is an admission of doing "less well" than
someone else.

It is also important to realize that you can't be angry and have peace of mind at the same time, and that peace of mind is a very important asset in making good decisions in complex situations. This certainly does not mean you should repress your anger. You should recognize it when you have it, and you should own it, but then begin to choose whether or not to be angry. One of the best ways to choose not to be angry is to change your viewpoint in looking at others. It's customary to see people who disagree with you, or who may seem hostile, as attacking you. This usual point of view, however, can easily cause anger. Often times you won't even realize that you're angry. A better way of looking at hostile people is to see them as fearful, and an alternative way of viewing disagreement is to see what you can learn. In both these instances, try communicating love, and respect and openness.

What we want to emphasize is that hostility problems can be greatly reduced simply by the way you look at others. You can eliminate inferiority feelings, and you can make yourself and others happier and more productive, as you replace inferiority and hostility with love and respect. Five basic strategies for doing this follow.

FIVE STRATEGIES FOR REDUCING HOSTILITY

1. EMPATHIZE, ESTEEM, AND BE SOMEWHAT EMOTIONAL

Help others to overcome hostility, and do so yourself by overcoming inferiority. One way to do this within yourself is by not giving other people power to make you angry. The most effective ways of helping others to overcome hostility are (a) by empathetic listening and understanding, (b) esteeming, and (c) by building self-respect.

A good example of how to do this is found in the way a high school principal dealt with a very hostile lady. Mrs. Bitcher was a perpetually angry and defensive lady who visited a certain school often, each time with fire "spewing." She was a flaming terror. She had even once been forcibly removed from the school. Shortly after a new principal arrived at the school, Mrs. Bitcher stormed in. The principal didn't have time to ask her into his office, she was already there! She launched into a diatribe against the school. The principal listened for about half an hour, focusing empathetically on what Mrs. Bitcher was saying. For the second half hour, the principal was able to ask questions and get a dialogue going. The outcome was that Mrs. Bitcher became a great supporter of the school and principal, seemingly because someone cared, was not worried about being "insulted," and reached out with emotional empathy and esteem.

2. BE NEITHER VICTIM NOR VICTOR, BUT SYNERGIZER

A natural reaction to the hostility from others, because it is entwined with inferiority, is to attempt to be the victor in trying not to be the victim. The problem with this, however, is that the victor can end up as the victim by being despised. The thing to do is to escape the victor/victim syndrome, and become the synergizer--the one who promotes cooperation through fusing selfishness with selflessness.

Two examples. First, an example of what not to do. Mrs. Bellows called the principal. She was very upset; she castigated the school for her child's problems, and even erroneously blamed the principal for not returning her call. A natural reaction at this point would be to hang up. But to do so would not solve the problem; if fact, it would invite greater hostility and perhaps a call to the superintendent.

Another example was Mr. Badger, who was illogical, uninformed and pretentious. Some people might recommend gently nudging Mr. Badger into a corner with logical but ever so slightly arrogant questions such as, "Oh, so you think. . . .?" But to do so might easily result in loss of face for Badger, and hatred toward the nudger. The secret in both these cases was not to get caught up in a power struggle in which either a victim or victor would have to emerge, but rather to increase the satisfaction of both parties by generating cooperative, synergic energy and creativity for the future problems.

Four Rules for Synergy with the Bitchers, Bellows and Badgers

a. Almost all persons, no matter how extreme, consider their reactions to be justified.

b. Extreme persons almost always blame others when something is wrong.

c. If the manager cannot help disturbed people, the manager will be blamed and may even be hated.

d. The manager will be most effective by "reaching out" (rather than by replying in kind). Effectiveness is in being magnanimous, generous, empathetic, even a "semi-therapist." Help to find genuine solutions. There is no way a manager can lead when hated and despised.

3. INCREASE OTHERS' RESPECT LEVELS

There are several ways that this can be done. You can be the butt of a joke. You can elevate the other person's position (without being phony). One thing not to do is to alibi, for alibis rob the other person of credit for his criticism. On the other hand, the person whose esteem you elevate becomes increasingly trustworthy and loyal.

4. DON'T MAKE A GNAT INTO A HIPPOPOTAMUS

One of the easiest traps for managers to fall into is that of allowing certain irritating people to be bigger and more important than they really are. Tantrums by anyone can get to you and ruin a whole day, or even contribute to ulcers. Needlers and meddlers can create exasperation. Yes, gnats can be bothersome, but they're only a real problem if you, yourself, make them into hippos.

Everyone sometimes needs "trigger mechanisms" to help control reactions to gnats, particularly when one is just beginning to take charge of controlling his or her reactions. One manager found that "think gnats and hippos," when irritators tried to create stress, was all he needed. Think, "flick with a finger," or take a fly swatter to them, but don't get out the 105

Howitzer. You'll only make a fool of yourself.

5. YIELD NOT TO REVENGE

Don't let the temptation of revenge ruin you or reduce your effectiveness. Don't let decisions about persons you dislike be influenced by your disapproval. Even among the best superiors, very few indeed have conquered this problem. Ms. Sharp was a popular, young and attractive female teacher who was the cheerleaders' sponsor at a large California high school, with two first and two second squads of cheerleaders. During the annual and traditional initiation of new cheerleaders by those leaving, things got out of hand. Decoration on the new girls' garments went way beyond the bounds of even permissive propriety. Rather wild actions followed the bawdy suits. These things were distasteful enough as they were, but they could easily have been handled with a quiet, "Go change clothes." However, the sponsor had long harbored special disapproval of one particular girl, whom she had discovered was the hapless hatcher of the plot. Within five minutes of the initiation's beginning, the instigator had been hit with a tirade of abuse from the sponsor and within five hours, had been served with a letter of dismissal from the squad. Due process, of course, necessitated an investigation. The final result was merely a letter of reprimand to the cheerleaders and reinstatement to the squad of the girl who had originated the plot and who fanned the fickle fun.

When fantasies of revenge are released from their dark cages, they are hard to catch and cage again. It's usually easier to learn how to change these savage reflexes to sane and measured action, than it is to repair the damage after they fly amok.

TWELVE OTHER WAYS TO FAIL BY MERELY BEING HUMAN

CAST ASPERSIONS

Bad-mouthing, or casting aspersions, can be done in many ways. The **quasi-joke** is one way. For example, there is the wife who makes a suggestion to her husband with a giggle, then says she was only half serious. The not-so-hidden message is that, "I don't like what you're doing, but I don't really want to take responsibility for saying so politely and clearly, so I'll cloak it in this way." Some managers use this tactic, thinking it's an innocuous way to deal with a problem. Actually, it usually belittles the manager by making him seem to be weak. It is also a put-down to the subordinate's ability to cope with honesty and candor.

A second way bosses belittle is to use **derogatory terms** such as stupid, dumb, slow, awful, etc. You can call persons sloppy, precipitous, unthoughtful, but never cast direct aspersions upon their intelligence.

A third means of belittling is to **hound the capable person**. Some managers seem to exert their own superiority over people who are actually superior in some ways to them. An example is the defensive assistant site manager of a department store. An energetic young M.B.A. was hired for purchasing. This person managed to make some terrific buys from which the store stood to gain much. The assistant manager found small points to criticize and hounded the potentially outstanding employee into resigning and going elsewhere.

A fourth, sometimes unthinking, way to belittle is to **criticize an employee in front of others**. It may be because of the pressure of duties, the availability of the mistaken person, a lack of self-discipline on the part of the boss, or simply because the boss believes this to be an effective way of getting employees to shape up. It seldom works in the long run, however, for it creates embarrassment, resentment and hatred.

IGNORE SOME PEOPLE

Do you believe it's better to ignore people than to disagree with them and constructively criticize them? Do you ever allow an employee to become a white cipher in the snow? Silence, isolation, or even minimum communication, all discourage commitment and productivity. Find ways to give each of your employees some complete and undivided attention. During this

time, listen with absolute empathy. Show complete
concern. But don't just ignore them until they goof;
don't alienate with inattention.

PLAY FAVORITES

Personal preference is completely "human," but to
be "human" in this way, is to err. There was once a
chief executive officer of a rather large organization
who played the game of favorites. It was not enough to
be good and to be loyal; one also needed to be
obsequious. In fact, he came to be known rather widely
as King Louis XIV, with all the court and court games
that the Sun King and Versailles imply--who's in favor
now and who's out? People stayed close to the throne
so as not to lose favor, even though jobs suffered, and
minions with little real job ability but lots of
"games" ability survived and were promoted over those
with superior job ability and inferior "games" ability.
Needless to say, the "kingdom" was rife with plots and
counter plots; many people didn't stay long, and
business, of course, suffered greatly in the long run
because of the reigning mediocrity.

Another boss--principal of a large high school--
made a similar mistake, though from very different
motivations. Whereas the Sun King was a defensive and
benevolent despot, who seemed to thrive on unsettling
people, the principal was 100% ethical. He simply
believed that the "righteous" should have more
privileges and more of his time than the curmudgeons.
His end was unfortunate: At an early age he had to
resign, for playing favorites divides the house, and a
"house divided against itself cannot stand."

SHOW SELFISHNESS

You can deflate and demotivate employees simply by
being normally selfish. While it is natural that your
own interests are paramount over those of others, if
this is obvious, employees will believe that you're
only manipulating them for your own advantage. Are
you?

It is also natural that the manager be superior,
but if this superiority is shown in selfish ways which

detract from an employee's dignity, you will almost certainly damage your own effectiveness in the long run. If, however, there seems to be need to show that you, the boss, do actually have some particular expertise in order to gain or maintain respect from subordinates, then a demonstration of that superiority may very well be in order.

Hold the Good Back

Many a good executive has failed to nurture maximum growth in subordinates. This can be a curse on you. If word gets around that good employees working for you were not notified of promotion vacancies, or were not really helped to get better jobs, then you are the real loser in the long run.

Be Sly

Sly promises, sweet talk, double talk, baloney, jargon and phony praise, are likely to damn and doom you. Everyone dislikes being disillusioned in these ways. People are offended and insulted by being considered stupid enough to be hoodwinked, and yet some bosses still believe that they can profit by deceptions—sometimes slight and subtle, and sometimes massive and bold.

One manager, a back-slapping though charming boss, speaks of contacts he does not have, promotions he cannot produce, and threats he cannot carry out. This produces resentment and bitterness.

Another manager is phony by not accepting compliments. Somehow, you know that he always thoroughly realizes his own part in successful endeavors, but he won't acknowledge them. This becomes a put-down to the complimentor and a deception by the boss.

Be Insensitive

You can easily reduce your effectiveness by being insensitive. One disastrous consequence of insensitivity is to think that only the "big" things are important. Often it's insensitivity to the small things which causes failure. For example, you can **talk now and think later**, and fail. If you are to be promotable (or even survivable) in most organizations today, you must learn not to make rash statements even when provoked. For example, one manager, when confronted by strikers who were getting nasty on a very hot day said, "Let the traitors burn." Within nine months he resigned because of not being able to heal the strike wounds. Another manager, in a similar situation, took iced Kool-Aid to the strikers. Within three months his school was back to normal.

You can be insensitive by tightening up and making demands when a worker is dispirited, instead of listening carefully. When you see someone who seems to be lacking energy, you can ignore the possible cause of lethargy and make matters worse. One Army lieutenant did these things, thus driving too hard and overworking his people. Even though he was capable, and one of the most "gung ho" men in the Army, he was forced out of the service within two years of making 1st Lieutenant. When you forget feelings, and rely too much on money, duty and efficiency, you are likely to fail.

VACILLATE

You can vacillate for any one of several seemingly good reasons. You can waiver or fluctuate because of real complexities, because of trying to be humane and not hurt someone, or because you don't want to be stubborn. But the fact is that you will not be very effective if you do not conquer vacillation. Learn how to make decisions quickly and correctly; if you don't, get more training or stop trying to be a manager. For without confident decision making and actions, you cannot have confident employees and efficient workers.

MAKE NUMBERS EVERYTHING

At a certain university psychology department, which is statistically oriented, there is a phrase: "If you can't put it into numbers, the hell with it." Some executives, as well as universities, put too much credence in numbers--in output figures, performance charts and comparison statistics. As important as objective comparisons are, you just **cannot** put

everything into numbers. When you **do** use these data
with your subordinates, try using the following guides
so you will not misuse numbers: (1) use them as
advisory adjustments to other data; (2) make
comparisons privately; (3) make data collection and its
use, the result of mutual agreement according to
mutually agreed upon goals.

SAY NAY

Dr. No was a manager who often rejected employees'
requests. He didn't say no directly, but the result
was somehow no. Needless to say, this dampened energy
and creativity; all but the most energetic were also
somewhat passive.

One of the puzzles to many managers is that they
say that they want to get all the new ideas and energy
they can from employees, and yet this doesn't happen.
For example, one manager we know makes much ado about
liking and encouraging new ideas and high energy from
employees. The problem is that he also has a way of
making people feel small and insignificant if their
ideas disagree with his, or if he doesn't understand
them. Furthermore, this particular manager doesn't
seem to realize that he is putting down potential
contributions; he seems to think he is only engaging in
energetic and objective exchanges about the merits of
the ideas.

In order not to fall into the trap of dampening
creativity and energy, it might be wise for all
managers to check themselves occasionally on this.
Here are four simple guides to use.

1. Most important of all, do others see you as
the kind of person who builds esteem in employees by
nurturing them and their ideas? Or, do you have a
reputation for being the hard hitting person who
sacrifices sensitivity for action? Do you say things
like, "This is not a social worker organization, you
know."?

2. Take a hard look at your feelings and beliefs.
Do you feel at a gut level that you should play devil's
advocate most of the time rather than to reserve that

role for carefully selected times?

3. Look carefully at your body language as well as the way you say things. Do others see you as using "imperious" waves of the hand, or insulting inflections of the voice?

4. Look carefully at how you may be turning people off, if they:

- do less work than you think they should
- seem somewhat passive
- say things like, "You may remember that I suggested a solution to that a year ago."
- seem preoccupied too much of the time, or
- seem angry.

When leaders help to create an open and accepting work atmosphere, which supports and relies on constructively energetic workers, both leaders and workers benefit. Employees are likely to regard this atmosphere as one which is compatible with their own basic needs and beliefs, and to self-actualize both themselves and their organization.

LOWER YOUR STANDARDS

Despite many pressures for mediocrity, do not allow low standards to debase your organization, for if people who pursue mediocrity are allowed to have key positions, those with high standards will either leave or reduce their energy and creativity.

BE EXCESSIVELY REFLECTIVE

Reflective bosses probe deeply. They can easily spend too much time on theorizing, for the social, psychological, political, and philosophical issues are indeed complex and do not lend themselves to neat answers. In fact, sometimes answers just do not seem to be available at all. These cautious bosses operate on the periphery of action and contemplate the dilemmas. In the end, because of a paucity of evidence, they are stymied, actions are stultified, and a well-worn record for inaction is spun.

FINALLY, NO MORE "GOOD OLD DAYS"

The good old days will never return, and you must get rid of the good old Victorian boss habits which served those good old days. The facts of modern life demand that you be a student of complexity without being stymied by inaction, humane without being soft, and tough without being insensitive. Blame, anger, narrow accountability and building loyalty from too much one way approval and administration are passe.

PART THREE

A PHILOSOPHICAL BASE

FOR UNDERSTANDING

THE PAST, PRESENT AND FUTURE

IX

THREE MAJOR PROBLEMS OF THE WORKPLACE

SELFISHNESS, EXPLOITATION AND HOSTILITY

(A PHILOSOPHICAL BASE FOR UNDERSTANDING THE WORKPLACE)

> *"Yea, they are greedy dogs that never have enough, and they are shepherds that cannot understand; they all look to their own way, everyone for his own gain, from his own quarter."*
>
> *Isiah: 56:1*

MANAGER QUOTIENT

Now that you've read eight chapters about empowering others through leadership, take a hard look at yourself. Have your basic beliefs about the roles of the manager changed? To help you assess your beliefs, indicate either agreement or disagreement with each question or statement. Force yourself to make one of the two choices. First, there are ten questions oriented around actions. Next, there are ten statements composed as beliefs.

ACTIONS

Yes   No

_____ _____ 1. Do you serve your superior better than your subordinates?

_____ _____ 2. Do you use individual competition, pitting individuals within your work organization against fellow workers to build energetic work and healthy morale?

_____ _____   3. Do you consider it unnecessary and inefficient to get agreement by subordinates on all major goals and changes which affect them before the goals or changes become operative?

_____ _____   4. Do you consider it almost inevitable that when there are disagreements some will win and some will lose?

_____ _____   5. Do you usually work for immediate commitment when trying to "sell" an idea or program rather than to take it easy and provide "rationalizing" time?

_____ _____   6. Do you focus on only two options for the marginal employee: fire or punish?

_____ _____   7. Do you frequently talk for longer than one minute at a time unless informing employees of something that is entirely unsuitable for short statement or dialogue?

_____ _____   8. Do you usually use more positive and warm emotional influence with people you naturally like than with those you don't?

_____ _____   9. Do you attempt to "divide and conquer?"

_____ _____ 10. Do you act basically as though your concerns are not the concerns of others and vice versa?

BELIEFS

Agree   Disagree

_____ _____   1. The desire for high wages is **not** usually one of the greatest needs in the work place today.

_____ _____ 2. The greater the degree of interdependence in a society, the greater the need for individuals to be self-disciplined.

_____ _____ 3. Personal power is probably the single most important aspect of management for the democratic leader.

_____ _____ 4. The desire to be "in" on things is one of the two or three greatest needs for employees today.

_____ _____ 5. All normal humans have strong needs to relate cooperatively to other people.

_____ _____ 6. High morale alone does not cause high productivity.

_____ _____ 7. Almost all people need a feeling of wholeness between themselves and their work world.

_____ _____ 8. One third of all people you meet are likely not to like you on sight.

_____ _____ 9. One of the biggest problems of bosses is that managers tend to be "left brain" people (linear, hard data) whereas society has become "right brain" (aesthetic, feelings, wordless thinking, etc.).

_____ _____ 10. Money is generally less effective than esteem in motivating people.

Your Manager Quotient Score

If you responded "no" to all the action questions and "agree" to all the belief statements, you may already be an effective and humane manager. The frequency to which you responded positively to the action questions and negatively to the belief statements, however, should be an indication of the extent of your problems in practicing effective humane management.

For eight chapters you've been reading about many practical strategies to help you **empower** others, and thus to make your own power limitless. Now look at the few philosophical concepts that tie all these strategies together. We believe that there are three major problems which explain almost all low productivity and job satisfaction; these are selfishness, exploitation and hostility. We also believe that as you try to overcome these problems through a general commitment as well as through the use of the strategies found in this book, you stand a good chance of reaching a breakthrough kind of productivity. Therefore, we urge you now to go beyond concrete techniques to a more abstract understanding of what we believe **Leadership to Empower Others** is all about.

INTRODUCTION TO SELFISHNESS, EXPLOITATION AND HOSTILITY

It used to be that if you asked people what they most wanted from life most would say money. Now, if you ask people the same question, they increasingly say things like, "To be in on things.", "To be happy.", "To feel needed.", "To be helpful.", "To have peace in life." While gold watches and material things used to be the most powerful motivators, usefulness and being a part of things now seem to be even greater needs among employees.

The best way to be successful today is to help others to win because when they win, you win too. The problem is that most managers are still looking out too much for number one. A certain manager recently said, "I don't have stress, I make it." While this statement in isolation may seem extreme, it was made by a typical manager of an American public service organization with about 500 employees and an annual budget of 16 million dollars. Although the man who said it is usually affable, he is also consistently guilty of exploiting his employees. The results are easy to see. Employees respond to what they believe to be insufficient care about themselves by their own kind of insufficient concern about the workplace and productivity is lowered.

We believe that careful analysis of what has happened in many American workplaces is that three basic characteristics, which are fundamental to almost all people problems today, have been allowed to get out of hand; these are excessive **selfishness, exploitation** and **hostility**. This belief will be supported through much of this chapter. These three characteristics are complexly and cancerously related. Look at it this way: Excessive selfishness multiplies exploitation which then results in hostility. It is a simple formula: $eS \times E = H$, but it wreaks complex havoc.

In Japan these characteristics do not seem to be serious problems to managers. Instead, cooperation, help and widespread caring seem to characterize the much publicized Japanese modern workplace. Pascale and Athos point out in **The Art of Japanese Management** that even criticism is viewed by employees as leading to personal development. The manager is not seen as a selfish, exploitative person, but rather as a kind of coach who helps to train, nurture and bring out the best qualities in employees.[1] While Americans do well with the inanimate elements of management, a surprising numbers of managers fail miserably when it comes to coping with people. The Japanese simply out-manage us in the area of people skills, and we believe that the basic reasons for this are too much selfishness which then results in exploitation. When there is exploitation of employees, there is bound to be some level of hostility.

Everyone knows that employee productivity suffers when hostility reaches the point at which substantial energy is directed away from the task at hand. What happens is that as people become more preoccupied with getting as much as possible, as soon as possible, for as little as possible, the stage is set for excessive selfishness. This drives exploitation madly on. This in turn results in widespread hostility, and productivity is lowered. In a real sense, as selfishness has become more pervasive, employees have become less productive. This is not as it was supposed

to be. The original scenario called for self interest
to drive individuals on to great productivity and
higher standards of living for all. The missing
ingredient, however, has been sufficient selflessness
to produce cooperation, trust, loyalty, collective
responsibility and concern.

EXPLOITATION

Human history is filled with the degradations of
exploitation and fixations for counter-exploitation.
In fact, a large part of history is the study of how
people have gained power, used others selfishly for
their own ends, and then in turn have been revenged by
those they have used.

In America, we have been curiously conditioned to
exploit others, but at the same time to respond to
exploitation to ourselves with anger, aggression and
revenge. It's as though as a society, we have set
ourselves up to chase our own tails. We cannot
logically both exploit and revenge exploitation without
going in circles and wasting billions of tons of
energy.

Why does our society live this illogical kind of
life? The basic philosophical justifications we give
stem from those of the evolutionists' survival of the
fittest, or the creationists' belief about original
sin. The evolutionists say that humans have survived
in primitive times with a kill or be killed hostile
aggression and that vestiges of this primitive instinct
remain. The creationists say that people exploit
others basically because they are sinful and bad.
Original sin is impossible to stamp out, and so is
exploitation, so live with it.

While there may, of course, be considerable truth
to both, the point is that all too many people live by
the dictum, "Exploit or be exploited." Experience and
logic show that while it is true that many exploiters
now exist in our society, if we are to survive in a
world of limited resources and educated and well-fed
workers, we must stop these ridiculous chasings of our
tails. We must stop simultaneously exploiting and

prosecuting exploitation. This is not a cynical view of our society, but rather a description of one of the contradictions by which much of society lives. Many people assume that a certain easy compartmentalization exists which allows people to exploit and to be exploited simultaneously; they assume that nature is simply operating naturally when the strong use the weak, that somehow the unfortunate exploitee has a high tolerance for being dumped upon.

Catastrophic mistakes have been made through this and similar assumptions. The human heart cries out against such debasement. For example, Marx wrote that, "Society will pay for my carbunkles," and it has!

Exploitation tends to stigmatize its victims as inferior. Exploitees then tend to conform or to be exaggeratedly defensive, to be apathetic and do little, or to be hostile and destroy the place. Both alternatives are ill advised. Encounters because of exploitation often evoke terrible animosities and create enormous problems of coexistence. At best, productivity is lowered.

It is increasingly difficult both for managers to be strengthened by weakening the workers, and for workers to win all-out power struggles by marshaling their forces. Both management and labor have equal rights in the American system, and each gains by cooperating productively, rather than by competing exploitatively. How to do this? First, look at some popular forms of exploitation; second, at a fundamental cause of exploitation, selfishness; third, at one of the major reactions to exploitation which is hostility; and fourth, at some principles to guide solutions to problems of selfishness, exploitation and hostility.

SIX COMMON EXPLOITER/DESPOTS

Almost all bosses who exploit others, do so because they believe it is the best way to get their jobs done. Very few exploiters are red devils with pitchforks. Most are successful leaders in government, industry and business, but they operate on erroneous beliefs such as:

-- Idealism is naive and in order for people to be productive, they must be coerced.

-- Bosses gain the most power when they use force.

-- In fact, force is the only real power.

-- A truly humane society is impossible.

-- You've got to **get** others before they **get** you.

-- The main cause of poor performance by any particular race is really the result of the lazy side of human nature.

There are many other erroneous assumptions which could be enumerated, but suffice these to begin the list. There are also many descriptions which could be given of bosses who exploit employees and thus, reduce potential productivity and job satisfaction. We've chosen to name six which we believe will describe how selfishness, exploitation and hostility are reinforced in the workplace to the detriment of all concerned.

The blood-and-guts despot. This is the thoroughly obvious and obnoxious despot--the general who slaps the sick soldier, the father who forces his son with a strained ankle back into the game, or the manager who exploits either his company or his employees. Although few of these wolves **without** sheeps' clothing remain presently in management positions, many **with** sheeps' clothes survive.

The charming despot. This is the boss who is charming, but mean. This person says, "I don't get mad, I get even." Astute people somehow realize that behind the smiles of charm and persuasion lurk deep feelings of revenge. It's a personal matter; one must do what is desired or suffer the consequences. This should not be confused with the "surgical action" of the effective and humane manager taken when remediation fails to correct the ineffective employee.

Jerry was a charming boss. His smile was broad; it enveloped his entire face. His eyes lit up, and warmth seemed to radiate from inside him. But Mr. Hyde, as well as Dr. Jekyll, lived inside Jerry's soul. To cross Jerry meant "death" even if it took years. Charm was used for getting what Jerry wanted. Jerry was a hater as well as a charmer.

Another kind of charming despot is the nice and busy person--always nice, never seeming to become a Mr. Hyde, never too busy to **seem** to be interested in an employee, but always too busy to really help unless it is clear that the employee will return that help in kind.

The benevolent despot. Although the benevolent despot **can** have charm and superior knowledge, these characteristics are not necessities. The benevolent despot is fundamentally a cynic and a liar. He doesn't really believe in the self-governing ability of people. He doesn't even believe in people, although he talks about helping them. The benevolent despot always pretends to know what is best of the employee; all they must do is trust him and let him make the decisions.

Joe was a benevolent despot. He was head of a large government agency. He kept all the reins of power he possible could, until the agency was malfunctioning because too many decisions were stacking up for him to make. He died of a heart attack in middle age.

The puppet-puller despot. Some bosses use much of their power as an unseen but strongly manipulative force behind the scenes. They use people as puppets. Often these bosses become puppet-pullers out of fear. They believe they do not have enough talent to lead by example, and so they get behind the scenes and pull the strings. One form of this is the leader who waits for things to disintegrate, then picks up the puppet pieces, reglues them, and attaches his own strings to the reglued pieces. Another form of puppet string puller is the behind-the-scenes horse-trader.

The puppets pulled by these despots often don't realize their strings are being pulled, but somehow they do dance to their master's tune. There's a gross indignity to this; they've been used.

The superior despot. These are the persons who act kindly toward all, but feel disdain for most. They may make superior investments or have superior knowledge or skills. Bosses frequently use these reasons to excuse the exploitation of many in the cause of few. It makes a certain kind of sense, because the boss who has invested much more money or time or energy in the business, may feel that he or she should call the shots, even if it means exploitation. Besides, the reasoning goes: "Those lazy workers are liable to ruin things if you let 'em." The counterproductive problem is that this is likely to become a self-fulfilling prophecy in which potentially energetic people are driven to laziness. The "superior" despot is thus locked into erroneous and inferior logic.

Short-term, or hit-and-run, despot. The short-term despot may easily be all of the above, with an additional talent for hitting and running. Sometimes the blessings of God are even invoked to describe this despot. "God made me charged with energy to get things going; not many people can do what I can do." The problem is that many people may be destroyed under the guise of God's blessings. Often, these despots are shallow people. They may say, "I'm not interested in theory. Just tell me what you want done." Short-term despots often confuse motion for action, and while short-term profits may look good, short-termers often have to get out before long-term effects appear.

Unfortunately, many organizations build in short-term exploitation by managers. For example, managers' performance evaluations and rewards often are based primarily on short-range indices. When this happens, managers are likely to be more exploitative both of people and resources than if the emphasis is on the long-term future of managers, workers and the organization. The logic is to make quick bucks and get big bonuses.

SELFISHNESS -- THE ROOT CAUSE OF EXPLOITATION

We believe that the root cause of exploitation is excessive selfishness. In one sense, this is a disease that afflicts and addicts executives in masses; i fact, it sometimes seems to assume plague proportions among people with authority. It is a curse to families, and it has cast a pall over schools as well. It is like a cancer. It begins from small spot-like beliefs, but it can spread to engulf the functioning of the entire organization. The symptoms of the disease are complex, but the result for an organization is simple. Relationships are ruptured, and the heart of productivity is ripped into fragmented pieces. As Yeats said, "Things fall apart, the centre cannot hold. The blood dimmed tide is loosed."

THE AGE OF MEISM

Although we have not yet devised a machine capable of measuring the soul of any particular historical period, there seems to be little doubt that the past decade has been characterized by excessive self-centeredness. People have seemed to care too much for themselves and too little for others, for work to function at its most effective level. An old-fashioned word for this is selfishness; a new term is meism. Regardless of what you call it, however, "things fall apart, the centre cannot hold," when there is too much emphasis on the part to keep it in balance with the whole. Self-interest itself has always been a major factor in any society, for people are naturally more concerned about themselves than about others, and well they should be. That much is fine. Self-interest can provide wholesome motivation, pride, and perseverance, but pursuit of self-interests to the detriment of others ultimately leads to trouble. Problems develop at the point where people practice the kind of concern for self, which is harmful to society or to the organization as a whole; our society seems to have reached this point.

To illustrate this, look around you at the towering phantom of Changed-Employee-And-Society. While most workers used to be rather poorly educated, frightened and obedient, many are now rather sophisticated, secure and independent. A study by Opinion Research Corporation says that 70% of employees now believe that they need not take orders from a supervisor if they disagree.[2] While most employees used to be loyal and obedient to their bosses, work hard for money and survival, and respond rather submissively to force, many now believe in the psychology of entitlement: they are loyal to a lifestyle rather than a job. They are more skeptical, diverse and better educated than ever before. They expect to be prime movers, active rather than passive, and persons rather than things. Many workers are only slightly interested in the organization for which they work, and some are downright hateful toward it. These employees have taken on the tenor of the times, sometimes seeming to be contradictory polarities of personalities, rather than teams of people striving toward the same goal.

INTERDEPENDENCE <--> INDEPENDENCE

Theoretically, at least, all people could be as self-centered as they wish as long as there was no interdependence. As interdependence increases, however, accommodating one's self-centeredness to others also needs to be increased if destructive conflicts are to be avoided. What has actually happened in America in the past couple of decades is that we have become increasingly interdependent through technology and living together, while simultaneously pursuing more diversity and independence in order to do what we want. This is insane. It has resulted in difficult problems for managers and society as a whole.

If John Naisbitt is right in his book, **Megatrends**,[3] this trend will continue. For all of the ten "mega issues" which he defines for the '80's involve in one way or another, moving toward ever more diversity and decentralization on the one hand, while becoming ever more interdependent members of one world on the other. These movements are on a collision course.

INTERDEPENDENCE, ANONYMITY, AND SURROGATES

Adding to the problems of self-centeredness and interdependence has been the anonymity of large communities and workplaces. What we now have is an anonymous interdependence with surrogates to solve problems. Even though we are now trying to reduce this anonymity by such actions as decentralization, participatory democracy, self-help networking, and multiple options for living and work, we also cling to old style, anonymous ways of solving problems, where it's easy for selfishness and exploitation to reign and increased hostilities to result. Surrogate negotiators who represent management, battle surrogate negotiators for employees in a kind of anonymous master/servant jousting. Unions and management are anonymous adversaries. Lawyers, in increasing litigation, reinforce the feeling that selfish settlements can be made by surrogate people removed from the problem, if you can only get the right attorney. These kinds of things up the ante of selfishness, exploitation and hostility.

We try to solve the problem of interdependence through anonymous surrogates. It doesn't work very well. What are needed are managers who reduce selfishness and exploitation through their daily action. Some top executives have even stripped themselves of "perks" from reserved parking spaces on up, in setting an example of reduced selfishness.

EMPTINESS AND ESTEEM

As workplaces and communities have become larger, and people more mobile, churches, communities and families have met fewer and fewer needs of the individual for identity, esteem and affection. As this has happened, people have been left with feelings of emptiness, which they have tried to fill with self-centered pursuits. But these don't solve problems of social or industrial productivity very well. What is needed is for work organizations to help employees fill their needs for identity, esteem and affection, through humanistic management. But first, three kinds of self-centeredness that seem to have contributed to productivity problems.

THREE CURRENT KINDS OF SELF-CENTEREDNESS

This might at first seem to be simplistic, for

there are, of course, many kinds of self-centeredness. If, however, you tried to boil these down into a few which have recently caused the most trouble for the workplace, you might very well come up with the same basic three we have chosen. They are: excessive emphasis on **self-fulfillment, subgroup fulfillment,** and **Short-term management interests.** All of these influences began with the very best of intentions, but have lately begun to tear at the very center of productivity and sometimes even society.

SELF-FULFILLMENT

Self-fulfillment is a noble goal. In its finest sense, it embodies working toward high kinds of happiness, productivity and sensitivity. The logic of self-fulfillment goes something like this: develop and love yourself, and then you will be able to love others as well, but you only have responsibility for yourself, so live all of life with that thought in mind. Self-fulfillment has only recently been a promise for many people; it used to be the province only of the rich, or the very brave. Submissiveness and conformity used to be the norm for most people when there was little question but that "average individuals" had to be subservient to higher authorities. In this century, however, "average individuals" have been given undreamed of chances for self-growth and development, as well as for putting higher authorities on the spot without having to accept much responsibility themselves.

Millions of modern individuals have pursued self-fulfillment through such varied means as developing talents, increasing self-awareness, raising conscious-ness levels, living present moments, meditating, asserting themselves, sensitizing themselves to inner and outer space, screaming primaly, parenting singly, practicing new sex roles, and a host of other ways. The logic of most self-fulfillment is sound as far as it goes. The problems are (1) that it often doesn't pay sufficient attention to other people, and (2) its emphasis frequently results in excessively selfish pursuits. When people are strongly encouraged to look out for themselves and get all they can, it becomes easy to ignore their mutual interdependence with others, and to upset the delicate balance between self and group that is necessary for most workplaces to function well.

SUBGROUP FULFILLMENT

There are two particular kinds of subgroup fulfillment that began for legitimate and high-minded needs, but which are now contributing to excessive adversary relations, rather than cooperative problem solving. These are pluralism and special interest groups.

Pluralism. This has been a large movement among many ethnic groups to reassert ancestral languages and cultures, which began in the 1960's from needs for tolerance, acceptance and job opportunities. These are, of course, fundamental needs, and they must be met if our society is to be strong. Pluralism began with the goal of providing in America a mosaic of cooperating cultures, differing lifestyles and languages within the broad boundaries of U.S. nationhood. The reasoning was that by maintaining old cultural identities, newcomers would adapt more positively to American ways and ideals. This goal has desirable aspects, even though it seems to be reversing the historic motto "E pluribus unum", one out of many. The problem is, however, that pluralism does not seem to be working as planned. What actually seems to have happened is than divergent groups have felt even more intensely their own divergences than ever before; this is detrimental to the solidarity of the workplace, as well as the country.

This is not at all to infer that minority groups should be neglected, nor allowed to have a second-class place in our society, for no society will work at its best when any particular group is given secondary status. Rather, this is to say that both minorities and majorities must empathize with the problems of each other, and commit themselves to maximum cooperative problem solving and minimum adversarial confrontation and litigation if problems of society and productivity are to be solved.

Special Interest Groups: As America has become

more "anonymously independent," individuals have felt a kind of laryngitis of democracy--a lost voice among a mob of shouters. The quick solution for many has been to restore their voices by going to the doctors of loud, but narrow special interest groups. While certainly a lost voice can thus be found and then amplified, that voice is also distorted. It has only partial timbre. It rings with the sounds of only part of the body. It reflects inaccurately the original voice with its needs for a holistic approach to life, health, and society. In the workplace, one of these special interest groups is the labor union.

Granted, there have been ample reasons for employees to create organizations such as labor unions, for exploitation of employees in the past without power groups such as these is well known. The challenge now, however, is to change the nature of collective bargaining from adversary to cooperative relationships, while increasing the true problem-solving of both employees and employers.

The labor union is only one of thousands of special interest groups that have failed to capitalize on the overriding interests that bind producers and consumers, and even people in general. These special interest group promoters lobby for everything from animal rights to religious rights. While no value judgment is given here on the relative worth of any particular one of these special interest groups, the judgment is made that many groups--managers as well as employees--seem to be acting more and more in terms of their immediate and narrow interest, rather than to commit themselves to worthwhile results for society as well as themselves.

MANAGEMENT SHORT-TERM INTERESTS

As relationships between manager and employee, and between producer and consumer have become more remote, it has become easier for managers to pursue short-term interests to the long-term detriment of employees, organization and society as a whole. As managers have engaged in "planned obsolescence," they have fostered production of low quality goods and squandered the confidence of consumers. As managers have promoted near monopolies in manufacturing **or service**, they have sometimes concomitantly caused a disregard for customer or client complaints. And where near monopolies have reigned, managers have gotten a certain license for their own mistakes and excesses.

As widespread selfishness, short-sightedness and power of both the managers and employees have converged, the consequences have hardly been what was originally planned. Fewer jobs, rather than more, have been generated or maintained as consumers have bought foreign imports. Many workplaces have become cauldrons of discontent or places of passivity; and many people have lost faith in the social system and workplace themselves.

What is needed is a balance between the concerns of individuals and those of the organization and society. The balance is now wobbling precariously, particularly as applied to the world and society.

HOSTILITY

Hostility can be a problem of the first magnitude for managers when it results in energy being directed away from productivity or against the manager. Hostility is tied to two problems: (1) inferiority and (2) stress. First, inferiority. Inferiority is fundamentally a defensive and primitive biological reaction. People or animals who are threatened by physical harm or loss of self-respect instinctively react with fear, followed by a desire to fight or flee. Hostility is universally the same; it results from a threat to status. Dislodge your dog or cat from its comfortable corner, and watch the hurt pride swell up in your pet's face. Make fun of your spouse's over-concern about weight, and suffer the consequences. Fail to understand and appreciate the intellectual superiority of one of your sensitive subordinates; if this results in that person feeling put-down or made to feel inferior, you may get inefficiency or even sabotage for the rest of your work-life together.

MAJOR CAUSE OF HOSTILITY

Not many things are nearly universally certain in human behavior, but you can be almost sure that feelings of inferiority will produce feelings of hostility.[4] It operates for mother and child as well as for managers and union negotiators. For example, if Mom's superior logic fails to achieve the desired results with 3 year old Johnny, Mom may well become hostile if she feels incapable of getting Johnny to do what she wants. Managers and employees likewise get angry at each other when they feel incapable of getting the other person to understand them, or to do what they want. In the final analysis, hostility has almost nothing to do with who's right or who's wrong, but who feels inferior.

Hostility is also linked to excessive stress, which then contributes to lower productivity. Whenever you have any one or more of the following, you have stress: anger, anxiety, depression resulting from defensiveness, or guilt. All of these are tied right back to hostility. Anger **is** hostility. Anxiety is fear of failure or rejection. Depression from defensiveness is a result of the dichotomy of winners and losers. And guilt is a by-product that many exploiters work to produce in exploitees--"make 'em feel guilty if they don't conform to my narrow standards," so they will conform.

What stress does is to reduce the degree to which you can function. Lange, the psychologist who is an expert on stress, says that when you have a stressful exchange with someone, it takes your body about four hours to restore itself to its normal level of endocrine hormonal secretions. This not only means a shorter life; it also means less productivity.

RELATIONSHIP OF HOSTILITY TO SELFISHNESS AND EXPLOITATION

Now relate hostility to selfishness and exploitation. Exploitation is fundamentally the separation of superiors from inferiors. Superiors win, and inferiors lose. Superiors feel great. Inferiors feel hostile. Hostility then often results in wasted or misdirected energy.

We can help solve this problem by disciplining selfishness so that exploitation and counter-exploitation will not produce hostility. This needs to begin with managers. For as long as managers practice, "Give me all I can get as soon as I can get it for as little as possible," employees will do the same. A vicious cycle is likely to begin. The end result will then be lower productivity.

What to do about selfishness, exploitation and hostility? Abraham Maslow called the answer Eupsychia (Yoo-sigh-key-a).[5] Ruth Benedict called it synergy.[6]

ONE ANSWER TO SELFISHNESS, EXPLOITATION AND HOSTILITY: INTEGRATE THE INDIVIDUAL AND THE ORGANIZATION BUILD EUPSYCHIA WITH SYNERGY

EUPSYCHIA

Abraham Maslow first coined this awkward word theoretically to define a graceful and productive group of people on a sheltered island, for the goals of these people were to be psychological health for the individual, as well as productivity for the organization; these were of approximately equal importance. The process by which people would be helped to reach these goals was called eupsychian management.[7]

Eupsychian principles have been embraced with much enthusiasm by humanistic managers, for these principles echo with the sound of the twin virtues to which humane managers subscribe--improvability both of the individual and of society. The improvement of **either** the individual or the society tends to improve the other and to begin a cycle toward utopia. However, Eupsychia is **not** meant to be utopian--not perfectibility--rather, it is meant to be a **real** possibility, real improvability. Eupsychian management emphasizes the principles of trust, openness, harmony, the desire to achieve, and most importantly, cooperation with others as well as self-actualization.

This is perhaps best described by another unusual term--synergy. Even though the word synergy has been popular in the past, it identifies a concept that is particularly important now.

SYNERGY

Synergy was first used in a social context by Ruth Benedict, a sociologist who studied primitive tribes, and who also taught at Bryn Mawr forty years ago. She searched for conditions which promoted generosity, friendliness and openness.[8] In looking for these characteristics, she studied climate, geography, technology, heredity, population density, wealth and ways in which people related to each other. She concluded that the main factor determining synergy was the way two or more people combined their actions. She called this social synergy. She found that some groups institutionalized stinginess, suspicion and hostility; this she called "low synergy" interaction. She also saw that other groups had institutionalized generosity, openness and friendliness; she labeled this "high synergy" interaction. Benedict believed that the characteristics of people in any society were developed by the way they acted in that society.

A close look at American culture reveals both low and high synergy characteristics. While it's easy to see hostility, suspicion and stinginess, anyone can also see goodwill, trust, cooperation, mutual concern and openness. The question is, do we reinforce suspicion, distrust and law of the jungle through our management practices, or do we reverse this trend?

The much touted Japanese workers and managers probably best exemplify synergy today as they build trust and loyalty for their common good. Our present system of American confrontation functioned reasonably well as long as we had substantial surpluses and economic growth. That was when we could all get a share of the action if we really tried. That was when this country ruled the world militarily, economically and spiritually, and when we had unlimited resources. Things have changed, however. We have dwindled our leadership with startling rapidity. It is now unlikely that we can profit much from continued classic confrontations. What we need is eupsychia and synergy where esteem, trust, cooperation, open-mindedness and power **with** people are built.

SOME EXAMPLES OF OVERCOMING SELFISHNESS, EXPLOITATION AND HOSTILITY IN MANAGEMENT

A long-term example of solving problems by the collective responsibility and intelligence of the people themselves is in Switzerland. One particularly important characteristic of Swiss citizens is that they tend not to evade their own problems and pass them on to great leaders as we do in America. Rather, there is a sense that one's own voice can have an appreciable bearing on issues. All voters meet as a legislative body in each Swiss canton (state) and vote directly on issues which affect them.

Conventional wisdom has it that Switzerland works so well because the country is small, surrounded by mountains, and has escaped the ravages of war. This, however, begs the question. Ireland, Belgium and the Lebanon are small, yet all have bitter quarrels, either with neighbors or among their own citizens. In Switzerland, monumental problems have been prevalent which could have caused war, but somehow they've been solved. Different people of different religions have learned tolerance. Good housing, comprehensive public services, and fine education, which compliment democracy, have been provided to all citizens. In the final analysis, the Swiss people may actually have kept out of Europe's wars because of their good sense.

On the whole, the Swiss have found brilliant solutions to difficult problems. John Kenneth Galbraith, in **The Age of Uncertainty**, states that there are three reasons for this: (1) The Swiss are much more interested in results than in principles. Defense of rights which result in the extinction of persons is a rather poorly developed instinct in Switzerland. (2) There is a deep sense of community, which results in a feeling that the interests of the canon, or state, have precedence over the interests of individuals, parties, or organizations. (3) Each citizen's voice and vote is meaningful. These three principles describe three basic conditions necessary in American workplaces today.[9]

Another Western country which provides a good example of citizens working together to overcome problems of greed, exploitation, and hostility is Austria. While almost all other countries in Europe are struggling with recession, unemployment, inflation and trade deficits, tiny Austria, with no outstanding natural resources, except beautiful scenery, has insulated itself from the economic turbulence of its neighbors. Austria in 1982, had an unemployment rate of merely 3.4%, and an inflation rate that was only half that of its close neighbor Germany. For twenty years, Austria has had no major work stoppages.[10]

How has Austria done this? Peter Zdrahal, Director of the Austrian National Bank, says: "It's a question we often ask ourselves, and there is no simple answer, but basically it rests on two main factors. The first is simple good management of the economy. The second is what we call our social partnership between industry and labor, trade unions and employers, chambers of commerce. It's [an] arrangement that has . . . constant discussion and negotiation . . . to control both wages and prices on a voluntary basis."[11]

The key element of Austrian economic performance seems to be the employee/manager partnership. To understand this, State Secretary of Austria Seidel says, that ". . . when Austria became a nation again after World War II, there was a very strong and national conviction that the whole country had to **work together** come what may, if we were to avoid what happened after the first war."[12] An agreement was reached between labor unions and employers, completely apart from the government, that the unions would agree to hold down wage demands if the industrialists would hold prices down. These agreements have been upheld in negotiations ever since.

There is another important aspect of Austrian economic success, and that is long-term plans and actions. For example, there is still almost $100 million in Marshall Plan counterpart-fund loans available at low interest rates to Austrian industry, because it squirreled away its counterpart money (part of the terms of Marshall Plan aid), while other countries spent the money on short-term projects such as construction.

While Switzerland and Austria seem to be long-term examples of what can happen when there is a pervasive commitment to this kind of management, other examples are becoming available where a similar kind of management has been installed. Nissan, the Japanese car manufacturer, claims that American workmen are producing cars that are as good or better that Nissan cars made in Japan.[13]

Year after year, Delta Airlines has been one of the most consistent money makers among airlines. Delta considers the key to be service, and the key to this service to be a motivated and friendly work force. Pascale and Athos believe Delta's managerial style and subordinate goals embodied in the philosophy "the family feeling" are largely responsible for the achievement.[14] That Delta has overcome the greed and hostility that is often found between management and employees was shown a couple of years ago in the case of an airline purchased partly for Delta by its employees. In the latter part of '82, Delta badly needed another airplane, but could not finance it. Delta's employees "passed the hat" and helped buy an airplane for their company.

Matsushita Electric Company has grown from a humble beginning in 1918 to rank presently among the fifty largest corporations in the world. While Matsushita managers have always been tough minded, pragmatic, and energetic, they have also committed themselves to meeting the needs of the society, their customers, executives and employees. While Matsushita is dedicated to making profits, the company is also just as interested in spiritual values. Matsushita has interwoven hard edged efficiency with human values to produce a company with pervasive cooperation and high synergy.[15]

Knosuke Matsushita, the founder of the company, and certainly one of Japan's most successful businessmen and sought after lecturers, has just opened a School of Government and Management, with over 23 million dollars of his own money to train leaders for the 21st Century. The dominant theme for his three-year rigorous graduate school is to define the essential qualities of human beings and the disciplines that help society to endure. Matsushita wants his scholar-managers to provide the kinds of businesses and societies which will be servants of people and not their masters.[16]

These are examples of how management of power **with** people works. But the real test of whether **both** managers and employees can mutually benefit each other and the entire society in America, will occur (or will not), as thousands and thousands of local-level managers in schools, business, and government, practice (or do not), principles and strategies which change what executives do and who they are.

IMPROVING YOURSELF

It is not easy to think and act in new ways. You are accustomed to a certain set of thoughts, and you usually act in ways which are congruent with those thoughts even though you're not accomplishing what you want to. It requires a great deal of work to unlearn habits you've already learned. Learning new technical skills may be relatively easy, but learning **not** to do the wrong things may be more difficult.

We have found that only 5 to 10 percent of managers who read a book such as this will do much to improve themselves, unless they do more than just read about what to do. Among managers however who go beyond this to conscientious and systematic teaching of themselves to improve, about 90 percent can improve themselves substantially.

If you want to be among the 90 percent, you need first to be aware of what needs to be done. It helps also to understand some theory. You need to imagine what you want to do. You need to practice. And last, you need to give feedback to yourself on how well you are doing, and to modify strategies to suit your own styles and needs. As you read this book, think of it in these stages:

Stage 1: <u>**Awareness of Problems and Goals**</u>. If you want to make maximum progress, first identify your problems and goals.

Stage 2: <u>**Demonstrate Strategies to Reach the Goals**</u>. Find, and try, an idea or strategy which fits the problems or goal. If, for example, you are working with a tennis coach, this is the stage at which a demonstration is given to you on how to serve. In this case, however, you're demonstrating to yourself.

Stage 3: <u>**Image Positive Power Promises Which Will Help You to Reach the Goals**</u>. Use the conscious, subconscious, and creative subconscious parts of your brain to help you.

Stage 4: <u>**Practice**</u>. Imaging is great, but it's not enough. Practice the strategy 15-20 times in various situations, taking care not to be too concerned if you're a bit awkward. This stage is particularly crucial, for it is at this point that so many people give up and revert back to old habits, because old habits are natural and they seem for the time being to produce even better results. Now, you begin to realize that building new skills, as difficult as that may be, is easy compared with the problem of the integration of new skills with surrounding habits and external demands.

Stage 5: <u>**Feedback, Modification, and Integration**</u>. This is when the crunch begins, for there is a strong tendency to respond in the old ways. It's like the tennis player who wants to improve, so he attends a tennis camp or reads a book. He learns and tries new serves and strategies; he feels awkward. He plays a game and reverts to old habits because of being unwilling to lose a few games in the present, in order to improve the future. If you let yourself revert to old habits, you're making an educational cripple out of yourself regardless of how much ability you have. You have to be strong enough to let yourself be vulnerable enough to make some mistakes in the cause of progress.

Like Olympic class archers and pistol shooters,

you also need to work toward the place where you have integrated the skill so you can easily visualize and "pull." Changing the way you manage and lead people is never easy. You must practice and practice, for mastery means getting good at something, not just thinking about it. When you were growing up, did your parents sometimes say, "But if your life depended on it . . ." or, "If you were to get $1,000 for doing something, you would get it done, even if it meant hours and days of work." It was, of course, true, and it is the same now.

If you see the stakes as high enough, if your personal character is strong enough, and if you see the goals as possible, you will do what is necessary to reach those goals. Don't let yourself be deluded by the myth that "leaders are born" and that you can't really improve very much no matter what you do. Or, don't make the opposite mistake of thinking you can improve yourself easily merely by reading a book or attending a weekend training session. No one grows instantly. If you want to become a better manager in today's world, first accept that you are capable of controlling and maximizing your own growth. Then, diligently practice the principles and ways suggested in the remainder of this book. No matter what the particular emphasis of each chapter, keep all of these five strategies in mind, and use them systematically. For example, in the next chapter about imaging, keep thinking practice, feedback, and modify as well.

CHAPTER IX IN A NUTSHELL

Many of the worst problems in the workplace today come from excessive selfishness, exploitation, and hostility on the part of both bosses and employees. Even though these problems are complexly related and have been developing for thousands of years, one of the best ways to look at them is through the simple statement, "Excessive selfishness helps generate exploitation which results in hostility." (eS x E = H).

Unless there is a balance between self-centeredness and society-centeredness, "things fall apart; the centre cannot hold." The more interdependence there is among individuals in a society, the more self-discipline is needed for self-centeredness. However, what has happened recently has been that as individuals in our society have become more dependent on each other, they have simultaneously tried to exert more independence. With this kind of pulling apart, the center cannot hold. Three major contributors to this selfish contradiction have been self-fulfillment, sub-group fulfillment movements and short-term interests. These selfish aspects of our national life have recently resulted in imbalances which have been detrimental to the workplace as well as to society as a whole. Solutions lie not in neglecting the individual, the sub-group, or the society, but in integrating the needs of all. Hostility results from feelings of inferiority. In relating hostility to exploitation, you see that exploitation is fundamentally a dichotomy which forces people into categories which are considered inferior or superior. Inferior status produces hostility, which results in wasted and misdirected energy. The basic cure to eS E H, is through synergy. How to do this is what this book is all about.

Finally, managers are in the best positions currently to integrate needs of employees and organizations, and to create atmospheres where generosity, openness, and friendliness, replace selfishness, exploitation and hostility.

X

FROM FEUDALISTIC DOMINATION

TO LEADERSHIP FOR POWER WITH POEPLE

INTRODUCTION

Before the eighteenth century, there was little
need for theories of how to manage organizations, for
the established church was about the only continuous,
complex organization with much importance. Today,
however, organizations of every kind permeate, and even
dominate, our society and individual lives.

In early industrial organizations, the owner was
in absolute control of his workers, operating much as
the feudal lord of the manor did. But over the past
200 years, this has gradually changed to a sharing of
control as the owner/bosses have become professional
managers, and workers have become more respected and
powerful. The organization which was once an entity
unto itself, consuming people for the accomplishment of
its goals, has given way to organizations where people
have achieved varying degrees of control over their own
destinies.

These changes began with the Industrial
Revolution, and have been influenced strongly both by
collective bargaining and modern management systems,
the most important of which are bureaucracy, scientific
management, and modern human relations management
movements.

THE INDUSTRIAL REVOLUTION

The intellectual, scientific, political, and
industrial revolutions appeared almost at the same time

in the 17th and 18th centuries. They began in Europe, but soon spread to the New World as America developed. The Industrial Revolution was brought about by the development of power machines for which factories were built, and in which large numbers of people were employed. All this resulted in sudden and huge increases of production.

Factories gradually replaced the "cottage" system in which a merchant furnished raw materials to the home of the worker, who then constructed a product and sold it to the merchant, who in turn marketed the product. Because factories, with their speedy machines, produced goods much more efficiently than individuals could produce them at home by hand, the workers in factories were paid higher wages than those at home, and the "cottage" system gave way to an ever-growing system of industry. At the same time, an era of disconnected specialization began for workers. While prior to the industrial revolution workers commonly made all of any product, they now made only subparts of products. With this anonymous interdependence, began some of modern management's greatest problems.

Adam Smith, in <u>Wealth of Nations</u>, published in 1776, described this specialization when he wrote:

"One man draws out the wire, another straightens it, a third cuts it, a fourth points it, a fifth grinds it at the top for receiving the head; to make the head requires two or three distinct operations; to put it on is particular business, to whiten the pins is another; it is even a trade by itself to put them into the paper; the important business of making a pin, is, in this manner, divided into about eighteen operations, which in some manu-factories, are performed by distinct hands, though in others the same man will sometimes perform two or three of them. . . ."

With the interdependence of tasks and positions came a regimentation of behavior, which was different from the kinds of discipline necessary for most previous jobs such as construction, agriculture, military operations and small shop and cottage life. For example, everyone started and stopped work at the same time. Also, the hierarchy of bosses and supervisors was greatly enlarged. And perhaps most important, the social distance between factory worker and owner was now far greater than that between journeymen and master craftsmen of the Middle Ages.

Exploitation of workers was widespread. In 1835, factory workers in America worked an average of 78 hours per week, and employee practices were frequently unethical. Gross misuse of child labor was common; children often worked 12-15 hours per day in English coal mines of the early 1800's.

All in all, of course, the Industrial Revolution created great increases in output, goods, and capital. Commerce grew by leaps and bounds, and owners and entrepreneurs profited tremendously. The rub, however, was the worker. Labor was considered a commodity to be bought and sold, and the prevailing governments which largely lived by a laissez-faire philosophy, did little to correct the injustice. Many seeds of our present labor/management dissensions were not only sown, but also nurtured to gargantuan growth by these insensitivities.

COLLECTIVE BARGAINING

It was inevitable that sooner or later workers would react strongly against this debasement, and also attempt to improve their lot in life. Worker associations began and spread from factory to factory. In 1786, Philadelphia Journeymen Printers, because of a wage cut, called the first recorded strike in the history of American artisans. In 1779, actual collective bargaining was attempted by the Philadelphia Journeymen Cordwainers (Shoemakers) with their employers. The result was a lockout of the workers, followed by a negotiated settlement between the worker's union and the employer's association. This was then followed by a court case in which the Cordwainers were found guilty of criminal conspiracy to raise wages.

Meanwhile, about the same time, 1800, the English Parliament, in reaction to a number of violent strikes, declared trade unions to be illegal. An era of jockeying for position by labor groups then began both in America and England. It was not until 1842, in the Commonwealth vs. Hunt case, that a Federal court ruled that labor organizations were not evil per se and that they might have honorable as well as destructive objectives. After this court case, the right to organize and bargain collectively was gradually established. It was almost 100 years later (in the National Industrial Recovery Act of 1933) that legislation in America affirmed the right of workers to organize and bargain collectively.

Regardless of one's philosophical predilections, it should be obvious that an adversary--us/them--modus operandi between employees and bosses was not only established but accelerated by short-sighted and selfish managers and judges.

There have been, however, since the middle of the 19th century, a host of management systems designed to correct the inhumane and impractical attitudes and practices during the rise of big business in the United States. We will look briefly at the most important of these under three main headings: first, Weber's bureaucracy; second, the "scientific movement"; and third, the human relations schools of management.

MANAGEMENT SYSTEMS

BUREAUCRACY

During the 19th century, as tasks became more complex, industry, government, and business had increasing needs for consistent and efficient "professional" managers to run things. Rather quickly, forms of management and leadership developed which were subsequently described by Max Weber, the German sociologist, as bureaucracies. According to Weber, there were three types of authority: traditional (reverence for traditions), charismatic (devotion by followers to a magnetic personality), and rational (supremacy of impersonal law and order). Weber described the chief characteristics of bureaucracies as being: (1) job specialization, (2) hierarchical authority, (3) objective written record which could

help keep official acts segregated from private life,
(4) training for expertness and objective examination
for the qualifications, (5) full-time administrators,
and (6) regulation of official decisions and actions by
rules and policies, so that capriciousness was
eradicated or at least lessened. Managers themselves
began to have some security from inordinately
capricious decisions from their bosses, and workers
even began to gain a few rights.

Even though the mention of the term bureaucracy
today often elicits unpleasant and sarcastic comments,
the principles of bureaucracy emphasize rational
decision making, efficiency in work, trained experts
who are qualified for their jobs, and impersonal
relationships guided by objective rules which promote
rational and consistent pursuit of the organization's
goals. Weber's work in emphasizing fairness,
universality and training set the stage for the
Scientific Management Movement.

SCIENTIFIC MANAGEMENT MOVEMENT

Around 1878, Frederick W. Taylor, the most famous
name associated with this movement, developed what he
called the four great underlying principles of
management. These principals, which he included in his
book, The Principles of Scientific Management, were:
(1) the development of a true science, (2) the
scientific selection of workers, (3) the worker's
scientific education and development, and (4) the
initiation of friendly cooperation between the
management and the men.[2]

In line with his first principle, Taylor tabulated
job activities and simplified peoples' tasks on the
basis of motion, material, and equipment analyses.
Thus he changed the way foremen and workers operated
from the trial-and-error methods of the past centuries.
In line with the second principle, scientific
selection, he selected people who had particular skills
for specific jobs. In the third principle, training
and development, he trained people for jobs rather than
to continue the centuries-old practice of letting
people choose their own work methods and train

themselves as best they could. The fourth principle emphasized by Taylor was an almost equal division of work and responsibility between management and workers. He emphasized planning by management and worker-management cooperation, as well as a provision for the worker to share financially on an increased productivity basis.

Through these principles, Taylor immensely increased production at his Bethlehem Steel Company from 12.5 long tons per worker day to 42.5 per worker day. Other improvements also resulted in drastic improvement in efficiency along with greatly reduced costs.

In general, the Scientific Management Movement emphasized the importance of management planning down to the smallest detail in factory and business operations, and careful and systematic selection and training of workers. Although these were the major emphases of the Scientific Management Movement, workers were by no means forgotten. Not only did Taylor stress the sharing of economic gain with the workers, but he also emphasized recognition of superior performance. He truly led the way to an even greater humanitarian emphasis in the Human Relations Movement.

HUMAN RELATIONS MOVEMENT

WESTERN ELECTRIC

The Human Relations Movement began in the 1920's and early 1930's. This era was ushered in by the now classic ten-year-long experiment carried on by Elton Mayo at the Hawthorn works of the Western Electric Company in Illinois. Mayo, more or less in line with the Scientific Management Movement, was studying the effects of certain kinds of lighting on productivity when he discovered it wasn't really the mechanical physical conditions after all that stimulated workers to maximum productivity, but rather the human and psychological aspects of their working conditions. As workers no longer saw themselves as isolated and manipulated individuals, but instead saw themselves as participating members of congenial, cohesive work groups with feelings of importance, their affiliation, competence, and mastery caused the work itself to increase. One of the most famous conclusions from this experiment was that attention to workers' increased productivity more than environmental manipulations. This became known as The Hawthorn Effect.

MAYO & WESTERN ELECTRIC

Mayo, in his book published in 1933, The Humane Problems of an Industrial Civilization, also drew other conclusions which have become foundation principles of the Human Relations Movement. One was that some of the most significant factors affecting organizational productivity result from studying and understanding interpersonal relationships developed among people on the job, not just from pay and working conditions. Another conclusion was that routine and tedious tasks in an environment over which one has no control result in a feeling of helplessness/victimization.[3]

Mayo also found in his long experiment that many managers believed that workers were basically contemptible--Mayo called this the "Rabble Hypothesis."

These managers made certain negative assumptions about workers which were detrimental to both individuals and industrial growth. They assumed that society consisted of hoards of people whose only concerns were self-preservation and greed, that people were fundamentally dominated by physiological, safety, and greed needs, desiring to satisfy baser instincts and make as much money for as little effort as possible.

TASK AND RELATIONSHIPS

The staff of the Ohio State Leadership Studies, in the 1940's and 1950's, attempting to identify dimensions of leader behaviors which were effective and ineffective, eventually narrowed their work to two broad dimensions: Initiating Structure, and Considera- tion. These were described by Stogdill and Coons in the Research Monograph, "Leader Behavior: Its

Description Measurements."[4]

Initiating Structure refers to the way the leader defines the relationship between himself and members of the workplace and establishes patterns of organization, channels of communication, and procedures for getting things done. Consideration refers to friendliness, mutual trust, respect and warmth in the relationship between the leader and his staff. Leader behavior data were gathered by the now famous LBDQ (Leader Behavior Description Questionnaire) which has 15 items relevant to Initiating Structure and the same number for Consideration. The Ohio State staff plotted leader behavior appreciated by others on two axes seen on the left-hand grid. Later, Blake and Mouton came along and with their book, The Managerial Grid, superimposed their description of task and relationship leader dimensions, as seen in the right-hand grid. These axes represent the attitudes of leaders themselves.

Effective leaders usually have high scores on both Initiating Structure and Consideration, and ineffective leaders usually have low scores on both dimensions. Maximum attention both for people and production is the most desirable leader behavior, and minimum attention to both is usually least desirable.

THE HUMAN GROUP

George C. Homans, writing The Human Group, seemed also to build on Mayo's study regarding workers' inter-personal relations, developing a model of social systems to explain the power that an informal group has on its members. He described three elements in a social system: (1) activities (tasks performed), (2) interactions (behavior occurring between people performing tasks), and (3) sentiments (attitudes that develop between individuals and between groups). All three of these elements are closely related; change in one element causes change in the others. A spiral effect occurs. Thus, as positive interactions occur, more and more goodwill is achieved until an equilibrium is reached. As the spiraling process continues, people tend to become more alike in sentiments and actions.[5]

"Group" expectations develop. Peer pressure causes group members to conform or to leave the group. Various penalties are at the group's disposal, from gentle chiding to harsh condemnation; witness, for example, the aftermath of a strike. It should be noted, however, that groups have power that is positive, as well as detrimental to the organization. Mayo found how dynamic and positive informal groups can be in furthering the organization's goals.

THEORIES X AND Y

McGregor, writing in <u>The Human Side of Enterprise</u>, in 1960, believed that management practices needed to be based on an accurate understanding of human nature. He was keenly aware that actions result directly from the assumptions one makes about fundamental issues. He believed, in line with Mayo, that managers who perceived most people as wanting to be directed, not wanting responsibility, were inaccurate in their assumptions. He further thought that those managers (whom he called Theory X people) caused immature behavior and low productivity, whereas Theory Y people contributed to workers' self-growth and the organization's output. He therefore reasoned that a primary task of management was to bring out this potential in individuals by creating conditions in which properly motivated people could achieve their own goals while accomplishing the goals of their organization. McGregor's X assumptions closely parallel Mayo's "Rabble Hypothesis." Theory X and Y assumptions follow.

List of Assumptions About Human Nature That Underline McGregor's Theory X and Theory Y

Theory X	Theory Y
1. Work is inherently distasteful to most people.	1. Work is a natural as play, if the conditions are favorable.

2. Most people are not
   ambitious, have little
   desire for responsibility,
   and prefer to be directed.

2. Self-control is often
   indispensable in achieving
   organizational goals.

3. Most people have little
   capacity for creativity in
   solving organizational
   problems.

3. The capacity for creativity
   in solving organizational
   problems is widely distri-
   buted in the population.

4. Motivation occurs only at
   the physiological and safety
   levels.

4. Motivation occurs at the
   social, esteem, and self-
   actualization levels, as
   well as physiological and
   security levels.

5. Most people must be closely
   controlled and often coerced
   to achieve organizational
   objectives.

5. People can be self-directed
   and creative at work if
   properly motivated.

(Hersey and Blanchard, p. 54)[6]

McGregor believed that there was no inherent
difference between work and play except that play was
internally controlled and work was externally
controlled--one had to work; one could, but did not
have to play. Various kinds of conditioning produced
the belief that work was a necessary evil rather than a
source of personal challenge and satisfaction.

MOTIVATIONAL HYGIENE THEORY

Herzberg, Mousner, and Snyderman studied engineers
and accountants to discover what things made them
satisfied or dissatisfied on their jobs. In their
book, The Motivation to Work, they concluded that
people have two different categories of needs that are,
to all intents and purposes, independent of each other.
Each category of needs has different effects on
peoples' actions. They are listed below.[7]

Motivation and Hygiene Factors

Hygiene Factors	Motivators
Environment	The Job Itself
Policies and administration Supervision Working conditions Interpersonal relations Money, status, security	Achievement Recognition for accomplishment Challenging work Increased responsibility Growth and development

Herzberg and his co-authors discovered that when people were unhappy with their jobs, they were preoccupied with their work environment. They called these hygiene factors (as related to the medical meaning, preventative and environmental) and concluded that their primary function was to prevent dissatisfaction and work restriction. However, the meeting of these hygiene factors does little to motivate improved performance.

On the other hand, people who were happy with their jobs considered factors in the work itself to be motivating. Needs in the second category thus were called motivators as they seemed to result in challenging people to superior performance.

When Maslow's hierarchy of needs is superimposed on Herzberg's schema, Maslow helps to identify needs or motives, and Herzberg helps to articulate goals and incentives needed to satisfy these needs. (See following illustration.)

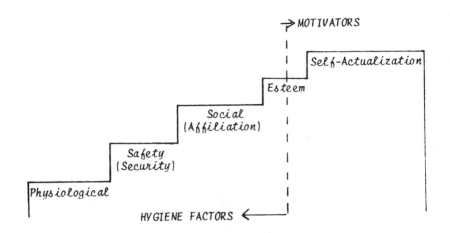

Herzberg's Motivators and Hygiene Factors superimposed on Maslow's hierarchy of needs.[8]

Herzberg's work is rich in implication for the full functioning of both people and organizations. Illustrations of effective use are given throughout this book.

LIKERT'S MANAGEMENT STYLES

Unlike McGregor's polar view of management, Likert dealt with a continuum of management styles from System 1 through System 4 in his books, The Human Organization[9] and New Patterns of Management.[10]

System 1 is exploitive and autocratic; System 2 is benevolent and autocratic; System 3 is consultative; and System 4 is true democratic leadership. System 1 is typified by no managerial confidence and trust; System 2 by a condescending confidence and trust; System 3 by a substantial but incomplete confidence and trust, and System 4 by a complete confidence and trust in its subordinates.

Likert's studies of high and low producing organizations consistently showed high producing organizations identified as System 2 or 4, and low producing organizations as System 1 or 2. Likert is convinced of the overall superiority of a System 4 type leadership, but recognizes that differences in the kind of work, in industrial traditions, and in employee skills and values may indicate that optimal leadership modes will be different than those identified under System 4. At the same time, however, Likert's intentions are to help leaders and organizations move from System 1 to System 4, or in other words, from immaturity to maturity as soon as possible.

Another of Likert's emphasis for the manager is that of the "linking pin." This means that each supervisor in an organization is a vital member of two groups: the one above him in which he acts as a subordinate and the one below him in which he acts as a supervisor. He thus forms a pin liking these two organizational structures.

Whereas classical organization theory perceives a supervisor primarily as a channel of communication and authority from the top to the bottom, Likert's structure has an upward orientation with each supervisor forming a point of articulation and communication; to the groups supervised beneath him, to other peer groups and to the layers of organizational consideration and decision above. Another important emphasis of this theory is that the basic building block of the organization is the group, with the resulting emphasis on group psychological and sociological factors.

INCREASING INTERPERSONAL COMPETENCE

Chris Argyris, in Interpersonal Competence and Organizational Effectiveness, has attempted to ascertain why so much Theory X management still seems to exist, despite overwhelming evidence that it does not work as well as Theory Y management. He has concluded that a large majority of people are treated to poor, shallow, and mistrustful relationships which result in phony expressions of feelings and "decreased interpersonal competence." He theorizes that a significant reason for this state of affairs is that most managers cling to what he calls a

"Bureaucratic/Pyramidal Value System" which is alien to theory of management assumptions.[11]

Argyris believes that the B/P Value System promotes distrust, rigidity, conflict, and a decrease in organizational success in problem-solving. On the other hand, the H/D (Humanistic/Democratic) Value system results in increased interpersonal competence, intergroup cooperation, flexibility, and organizational effectiveness.

Two Different Value Systems as Seen by Chris Argyris

Bureaucratic/Pyramidal Value System	Humanistic/Democratic Value System
1. Important human relation-ships--the crucial ones--are those related to achieving the organization's objectives, i.e., getting the job done.	1. The important human relationships are not only those related to achieving the organization's objec-tives, but those related to maintaining the organiza-tion's internal system and adapting to the environment as well.
2. Effectiveness in human relationship increases as behavior becomes more rational, logical and clearly communicated; but effective-ness decreases as behavior becomes more emotional.	2. Human relationships increase in effectiveness as all the relevant behavior (rational and interpersonal) becomes conscious, discussible, and controllable.
3. Human relationships are most effectively motivated by carefully defined direction, authority, and control, as well as appropriate rewards and penalties that emphasize rational behavior and achievement of the objec-tive.	3. In addition to direction, controls, rewards and penalties, human relation-ships are most effectively influenced through authentic relationships, internal commitment, psychological success, and the process of confirmation.[12]

Argyris believes that in many organizations the needs of individuals and organizations are still incongruent because management creates child-like roles for the workers. On the other hand, managers who are committed to helping people become mature, will help employees to move from passivity to increasing independence. Other qualities of the mature person are awareness and control over self, being active, having deep and strong interests, and occupying an equal or superordinate position. In this environment, trusting and authentic relationships are integral. The manager who takes into account the full complex of needs of each individual and the organization will be the one who is most successful.

SITUATIONAL LEADERSHIP

All human relations movement studies cited in this section have emphasized, in one way or another, the need for careful attention to people. It is only natural then that an attempt be made to systemize a leadership conceptualization which articulates the key variables in all situations where leadership is needed. This Hersey and Blanchard attempted to in the late 1960's, working at the Center for Leadership Studies, Ohio State University. Their book is <u>Management of Organizational Behavior: Utilizing Human Resources.</u>[15] Their attempt is mainly limited, however, to the maturity variable. Their basic concept of Situational Leadership Theory is described in their book as follows:

"*As the level of maturity of their followers continues to increase in terms of accomplishing a specific task, leaders should begin to reduce their task behavior and increase relationship behavior until the individual or group reaches a moderate level of maturity. As the individual or group begins to move into an above average level of maturity, it becomes appropriate for leaders to decrease not only task behavior but also relationship behavior. Now the individual or group is not only mature in terms of the performance of the task, but is also psychologically mature. Since the individual or group can provide their own "strokes" and reinforcements, a great deal of socio-emotional support from the leader is no longer necessary. The individual or group at this maturity level sees a reduction of close supervision and an increase in delegation by the leader as a positive indication of trust and confidence."* (p. 163)

Focusing on the leader behavior relevant to the task-maturity level of the follower, this theory is illustrated by the curvilinear relationship in the following figure.

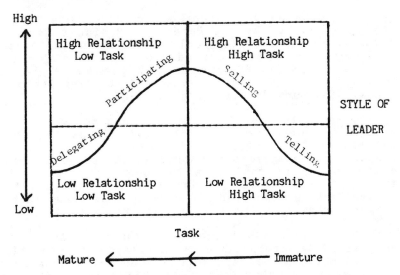

Maturity is defined by Hersey and Blanchard as the "capacity to meet high but attainable goals, . . . willingness to take responsibility, and education, and/or experience." Maturity is also confined to one task. Thus, for the employee who was "mature" in filling out forms, but immature in handling a distraught customer, the adept "situational manager" would apply different influence to the two behaviors.

This theory has easy applicability to parent-child relations as well as to superior-subordinate situations.

Connections Among These Human Relation Systems

Mayo, in the 1920's and 1930's, searching for ways to improve the work environment (which was very much a part of the currently popular scientific management) actually proved the importance of paying attention to people, thus beginning the human relations movement. In studying circumstances external to the worker, he discovered that the internal factors such as work competence, environmental mastery, and affiliation needs were the really significant ones.

Building on Mayo's work, the Ohio State Studies staff, organized by the Bureau of Business Research almost immediately after World War II, studied leaders' behavior. This study extended from the mid 1940's to the late 1950's. Two main components of leader behavior were isolated; these were Initiating Structure (task), and Consideration (relationship).

Homans, in the 1950's, noted that the workers in groups can make or break the boss; that the group determines the power of the leader. He reminded students of management that this should be just as much cause for exhilaration as for despair. About that time, in fact, a well-known Broadway musical, "The Pajama Game" popularized his theme of the happy factory workers breaking all the production records.

In the late 1950's and early 1960's, McGregor re-emphasized the importance of the leader's perceptions and assumptions. Perceive people as being capable of being self-directed, capable, self-actualizing, and they will be. However, McGregor did not seem to take into account in his theory the general nastiness and psychopathology of some people.

This lack may have accounted for Herzberg, in the late 1950's and early 1960's, stressing in his motivation-hygiene theory that some people--those fixated at hygiene levels of development--can never be motivated to do as much self-actualizing. One must simply try to insure that the "hygiene people" don't destroy things.

Likert, in the 1960's, extolled the merits of developmental stages. Managers should develop themselves and their employees from immature to mature, along the lines of System 1 to System 4.

Argyris found dismayingly in the early 1970's that most managers were still basically X people. This was in spite of the last 30 years' recommendations to managers to be Y people--to go beyond one-sided manipulation of workers, to commingle sincerely the needs of workers and the organization. (In other words, "tokenism" in meeting workers' and employees' needs was not enough.) Argyris then stressed that managers must meet the full complex of employees' needs.

Hersey and Blanchard sought, in the late 1960's and early 1970's, to provide a systematic conceptualization of how leadership should vary with situational differences. Their theory was labeled "Situational Leadership," and it gave a good framework for the leader to follow in using various behavior styles appropriate to maturity which was their main variable.

About the same time, after 30 years of research, Fiedler articulated his "Contingency Theory Leadership," which stressed the leader-follower variables of relationship, power, and structure.

Hersey and Blanchard and Fiedler's works describe several leadership styles, each of which, used separately or in combination, works best for specific kinds of situations. Managerial effectiveness results from appropriately matching a particular style to the idiosyncratic characteristics of a particular situation.

The four leadership variables of Hersey and Blanchard (maturity) and Fiedler[14] (relationship, power, and structure) are indeed important. They are also considerably more sophisticated than previous systems. That they are useful for managers is beyond reasonable refutation. Even so, these systems do not include enough of other extremely important variables such as expectations of followers, peers, and superordinates; perceptions; specific aspects of motivation; changing realities of power and the new breed of worker; interpersonal tensions; communication problems; and the great contemporary need to rebuild commonalities--communities of interest.

While all management systems have what might be called an arc in the circle of management "truth," some arcs are larger than others. No management system encompasses the entire arc encircling truth, and it is doubtful if one ever will. The effective manager will borrow practices from various theories. Power with People management is simply another arc which emphasizes the importance of helping the individual to be fulfilled as well as the organization to be efficient and productive in ways which foster widespread cooperation.

XI

THE FUTURE

WHAT WILL YOU DO ?

Lord, grant that I may always desire more
than I can accomplish.

Michelangelo
(1475-1564)

There are three basic kinds of managers. The first is the "Que sera sera" manager. He or she believes that not much improvement is possible by direct effort. These people simply hope to find a niche in which they can maintain the status quo, strike it rich luckily, or at least not be too miserable.

The second type of manager is the traditionalist. He or she hopes and works for a return to old-time autocratic boss powers.

A third type of manager is the one described previously as an effective manager. He or she accepts the present and optimistically works to change it, being actively committed to building widespread cooperation from local work sites to national life. Although many people believe this is impossible, our very existence on earth today is a reminder that humans have made startling changes in their history in the interests of survival.

All the way through this book you have found strategies which have been designed to help managers change and survive in today's changing work-world. In this chapter you will find first, six fundamental transformation strategies; then, you will find a grid which describes traditional and humanistic manager behaviors and attitudes for what we consider to be some of the most important aspects of managing people.

SIX FUNDAMENTAL TRANSFORMATION STRATEGIES

1. PERVASIVE VS. PIECEMEAL

One of the problems of people who want to improve things is that they use piecemeal, patchwork kinds of approaches when what is called for is total, pervasive commitment to change. Piecemeal approaches probably won't work for two particular reasons. First, partial changes in a system generate powerful forces which try to restore the system to its **former** state. Second, piecemeal approaches tend to be approaches of the timid who may be trying to find easy panaceas without deep commitment. These people may say, "Well, I'll try it and see." But what is needed is total commitment.

A chicken and a pig were talking one day. The chicken said to the pig, "Isn't it marvelous? We provide breakfast for people all over the world. You give the bacon and I provide the eggs. Isn't it fun?" The pig looked down at the chicken with somewhat less enthusiasm and replied, "It may be fun for you, but for me, it's total commitment!"

In addition to commitment, we must give up the notion of a Messiah or some great leader taking care of everything and requiring no effort on our parts. The only way we can get pervasive change either in our society, or within an organization, is through many leaders and bosses on all levels working slowly but surely together, with appropriate divisions of labor and acceptance of responsibility. Even though humanistic entrepreneurs are needed to point the way, it's up to the many thousands of followers who become leaders in their own rights to correct the wrongs in the work-world.

2. REDUCING EXPLOITATION AND HOSTILITY AND FUSING SELFISHNESS WITH SELFLESSNESS

The most important place to begin is with yourself and your beliefs about power. In order to help both yourself and others to maximize personal growth as well as to master job skills, you must first decide that we need not have winners and losers in the usual sense. We can all be winners. After that decision is made,

you are in a position to use persuasion instead of
force, to maximize the accomplishments of others, to
increase the power of others, to treat people as equals
and to develop situational leadership, and to resist
power struggles and work for long-term results in your
uses of power.

When you decide that we need not have winners and
losers, you can begin to heal the disease of
authoritarianitis and to enlarge your power base
through developing power <u>with</u> people rather than <u>over</u>
them. By not having to have winners and losers in the
conventional sense, you can also begin to eradicate
hostility which inevitably is exacerbated by the
win/lose cycle (this is where the losers feel inferior,
then hostile and revengeful, and try to get even with
the winners). By being non-exploitative, non-hostile,
and by fusing selfishness with selflessness, you can
save much negative energy which is counterproductive to
the organization's goals. You can build cooperation
and productivity.

3. <u>INTERPERSONAL RELATIONS</u>

As long as adversary relations are fostered in our
labor/management relations, we will have neither
individuals nor organizations which will be as healthy
as they might be. While creative disagreement is
always to be reinforced, adversarial disagreement is
usually debilitating to all except neurotics or
lawyers.

Presently, both out legal system and our
collective bargaining practices are dominated by
adversary relations. Skills of debate and criticism
are actively emphasized. Truth becomes blurred,
negative feelings rise; and real, lasting problem-
solving abilities diminish.

On the other hand, what we must have to survive
well in either local business or international
relations is interpersonal practices which become a
gateway to cooperative problem resolution.

4. HUMAN RELATIONS

No manager is likely to have much success in installing effective humanistic management as long as he or she views people as basically lazy, full of violence, incorrigibly selfish, and incapable of running their own lives. While it is true that values can be engineered in any society so that negative personal traits come to the forefront, it is just as true that personal qualities such as energy, responsibility, long-sightedness, peacefulness, co-operation, and success in running their own lives can also operate widely throughout society. The assumption in this book is that healthy people want to cooperate, to love and be peaceful, to gain esteem through worthy works, to lead and be led in order to find order and integration in their own lives and fulfill themselves.

When we begin to change from dominant values of rugged individualism, cut-throat competition, narcissism, and separateness to values such as community, mutual concern, service, love and peace, we will begin to develop high synergy workplaces and societies where both people and productivity will bloom. People will then be seen by the boss as ends as well as means, and bosses will be seen as helpers of the employee as well as the organization.

This is the climate in which a contagion of trust can spread, creativity can be fostered, and security can be built. Humanistic motivation will be natural and helpful both to employees and to bosses. And the boss will be the best servant.

5. ORGANIZATIONAL FORMS

Organizational forms which concentrate power, planning, and decision making in a few hands, that discourage personal initiative and personal responsibility for most people, that maintain considerable distance between bosses and employees, and that encourage short-term success at the expense of long-term health and success will have to be changed. Even though organizational form is not within the scope of this book, it is mentioned in passing because it is an essential part of success in a humane management system. By and large in the 1980's, organizations, in order to be successful, will have to provide better coordination than traditional forms of organizations have done; they will have to encourage creativity, personal initiative, and personal responsibility.

6. THE GREAT PURPOSE

If you ask many truly great leaders how they get their greatest satisfaction, you will often hear something like, "Helping others to fulfill themselves." Making money can make life comfortable, and being popular is nice, but helping others is surely one of the ultimate satisfactions. This means making a real difference in the world, improving the quality of life, and being kind to others. You, as boss, are in a privileged position to do these things--to help others fulfill themselves.

The most important thing about life is the sacredness of life itself. If you are really human, you want to give dignity to human beings. It troubles you to see anyone dealt with disrespectfully. You see each individual as being an end in himself or herself. You believe that everyone deserves respect and dignity. You don't groove on gossip; instead, what your neighbors do doesn't really make much difference to you so long as they are not being unkind or destructive to those around them. You watch yourself when talking with others to avoid letting yourself be drawn into casting aspersions. You will always try to practice a reverence for others as well as for yourself. And the Golden Rule is certainly one of your mottos.

People with a sense of great or ultimate purpose have a real sense of mission--a cause that transcends mere monetary rewards or power. Helping others is not tied in with sick manipulation or control over others, but rather, it means to help others enjoy the excitement of fulfilling themselves in the highest sense of the term--in pursuing truth, justice, dignity, and beauty. This sense of cause includes giving trust and being trustworthy. It means expanding minds beyond parochial boundaries, which restrict one to a tiny fragment of humanity. And this sense of mission, of course, involves an infectious attitude of fun and enthusiasm.

EMPOWERING PEOPLE MANAGEMENT VS. TRADITIONAL MANAGEMENT GRID

Following is a grid, or chart, on which to check your own present beliefs and behaviors regarding various aspects of management. Since only two categories are being used, some statements describing traditional management may at first seem to be extreme. However, if you look closely, we believe that you will see that most managers you know will fit roughly into these classifications.

While 35 aspects of management are given, this list is largely arbitrary. There could be many more. As you read through this grid, you will no doubt see yourself often in both categories. This is only natural, although most of the time you will probably see yourself predominantly on one column or the other.

The important thing to do is to think creatively about your philosophy of management. Become more sensitive about what you do in all situations. Ask yourself if you are truly satisfied with the way you act and react. Are the results really what you want. If not, convert your reactions to entrepreneurial, humanistic actions. **Lead to Empower People.**

CHARACTERISTICS OF

POWER WITH PEOPLE	TRADITIONAL MANAGEMENT

Trust

Involves competence, interest, and integrity. One of the most important aspects of attitudes and behavior. It is to be obtained at almost any honest cost.	Mainly involves boss competence. Monitoring and policing are more important than trust, as people are not really to be trusted anyway.

POWER WITH PEOPLE   TRADITIONAL MANAGEMENT

Spiritual Management

This can help criticism to be perceived as training, job transfers as character builders, pushes for efficiency as genuine desire to maximize winning for all and productivity as tied to the social good.

Seen as "soft" and impractical.

Consensus Decision Making

As much as possible, try hard for consensus. The time spent trying to get consensus can be very well spent. One can get some of the best decisions through consensus if you know how.

It's absolutely unrealistic to get consensus. It usually means the lowest denominator decisions. The boss should make the decisions. That's what he's paid for.

Authoritarianism

It's a very tempting but tricky drug of power to managers that is very often misused. It often stultifies the growth of individuals and organizations.

Successful bosses are almost always autocrats.

Right and Left Brain Management

Right brain activities are just as important as are left brain activities. (Right brain has aesthetic, holistic, empathy functions.)

Left brain activities are more important in management. (Left brain has analytical, objective and linear thought, and mathematics functions.)

POWER WITH PEOPLE   TRADITIONAL MANAGEMENT

Openness

Be open. Keep closed only on   Play cards close to your chest
matters which must be secret.   most of the time. Survive.
Don't just survive, but also
improve things. Crusade a
little.

Service

As boss, be the best servant.   Serve your superior & yourself--
                                       that's your only real objective.

Competition

Very complex issue. Should be   Actually, rather simple.
used so as not to create   Simply reward those who are
jealousy, harsh criticism, and   the best. If they're
gossip. Should be used in the   aggressive, good. If this
larger context of cooperation   creates anger and jealousy,
toward ultimate and mutual goals.   that's because the dullards
                                        don't like it when they lose--
                                        they should just work harder.

Participative Management

Make decisions after each person   Use P.M. to manipulate.
who will be affected by the
decisions has a real opportunity
for input into the decision.

Social Relations

Maximize social relations (while   Minimize social relations, or
also ensuring employee commitment   at least control them, or
to productivity). Often today,   they'll ruin you. People
because of anonymity, we need for   naturally gossip and as the
the workplace also to be a social   boss, you are prime bait.

The Future   330   A Philosophical Base

POWER WITH PEOPLE	TRADITIONAL MANAGEMENT

organization. Capitalize on the fact that most employee attitude changes are made throughout the day as employees go about their work and their talk.

Therefore, divide to conquer.

Esteem

Esteem is both internal and external. It involves personal feelings of competence as well as personal power and feelings by others that you have prestige.

Esteem is something to be bought with money or promotions.

Exploitation

It's a plague.

It's practical; life is the survival of the fittest, and this involves exploitation.

Manager/Leader Power

Empowers employees: mostly used with them.

Focus is on power used over employees.

Group Power

The manager increases group members' power and helps to guide the use of power for humanistic goals.

The boss frequently tries to curtail group power because he sees it as a threat. The boss sometimes tries to manipulate group power to further the goals of the organization. This boss says things like, "The employees aren't going to tell me what to do, how to spend the money, or what decisions to make."

POWER WITH PEOPLE   TRADITIONAL MANAGEMENT

Winning

Strive for internal winning. Minimize win/lose situations. Maximize win/win situations.	There are only winners and losers. If you're not one, you're the other. External winning, such as objects (trophies, etc.) and money, are emphasized.

Strong Leadership

A humanistic entrepreneur--one who gets things done for the good of all concerned.	One who accomplishes the goals of the organization without much regard for the individual employees. Much exploitation.

Organizational Forms

Flatten the hierarchcies. Promote as much dialogue all through the hierarchy as you can.	Keep rather rigid line and staff forms. Hold communication to the lines, much as one finds in military organizations. Colonels talk to colonels, privates to privates, etc.

Creativity

Nurture it in all employees.	Nurture it in the specially creative people, and cut even them down if they rock the boat too much or suggest spending much money.

Emotion vs. Objectivity

Be emotionally involved with employees to the extent of appreciating and empathizing in professional ways. Try to	Emphasize objectivity over emotion, believing that emotion may cloud the ability to act.

The Future   332   A Philosophical Base

maintain objectivity, but also
include considerable emotion.

Setting Goals and Objectives

Set them for the mutual benefit   The employee has to fit the goal.
of employees as well as of   Benefits for bosses, but not for
organization.   "lowly" employees.

Long-Term vs. Short-Term Goals

Long-term almost always has   Short-term and expediency
precedence.   frequently have precedence.

Relationship Between
Individual, Workplace and Society

Interrelated in an holistic way.   Only worry about the workplace.
Maximize connectedness.   Minimize connectedness.
                                         Employees don't really exist for
                                         the boss outside production
                                         lines. To a large extent, any
                                         relationships such as these are
                                         only for philosophers.

Permissiveness

Let the average, non-neurotic   Keep reigns on almost all
employee have as much freedom as   employees.
possible. But for the people who
are prone to take advantage,
build safeguards to keep them
from doing this.

POWER WITH PEOPLE	TRADITIONAL MANAGEMENT

Needs of Employees

Commit yourself to meeting these in ways which will satisfy the employee, the organization, and the society.	Use these to get more for the organization. Only regard the individual as you have to for increased production.

Threats and Punishments

Threats and punishments often cause more harm than good. They should be used very cautiously.	There should always be a threat of punishment. Punishment should be given quickly if the employee goofs.

Hostility

Try to eradicate it by raising esteem, for lack of esteem (shown in inferiority) almost always causes hostility.	Live with it, or decrease it when really necessary. The emphasis is on not allowing hostile people to show their hostility, rather than on "curing" the hostility.

Build Self-Respect in Defensive People

Absolutely.	It's not really the boss' business.

Work Itself and Meaning

Meaningful work is important to the person's self-image. If the workers sees an unsatisfactory image of himself portrayed through his work, he tends to feel inferior, then hostile, and productivity tends to fall.	Meaningful work is just not very often possible. Don't worry about it.

CHARACTERISTICS OF

| POWER WITH PEOPLE | TRADITIONAL MANAGEMENT |

Money

Often it is not as important as esteem. It must be put into perspective. The use of money as a motivator is complex.

Absolutely basic and central to motivation. Its use as a motivator is simple.

Teach and Coach

Spread your help and love to everyone you can. Certainly teach and coach those who have more talent than you, for if you do so out of love (and they are not neurotics), they'll usually benefit you too.

Teach and coach a select few. Don't teach and coach those who are better, or they'll take over. Pull them down to a lower level where they are no threat.

Morale

A genuine commitment to help people have higher morale because they are human beings and part of the human family we all work in. Morale's use in the organization seen as complex. You don't just build morale for productivity.

To be used to manipulate. No really widespread commitment to helping individuals to be happy per se. The use of morale is simple--to increase productivity directly.

Accountability

Holistic and reciprocal (as much boss to subordinate as vice versa).

Mainly one way--from subordinate to superior.

General Speed of Implementation of Change or Progress

"Leap" only occasionally. Usually take one step at a time. Touch all bases. Build solidly and stay.

Leap a lot. Benefit yourself and opt out.

The Future   335   A Philosophical Base

Employee's Perceptions and Expectations

Central to getting things done. Humanistic Management is basically good interpersonal relations, and fundamental to interpersonal relations are perceptions and expectations.

Peripheral. To be used to manipulate.

Communication

Emphasizes mutual talking and mutual understanding. Emphasizes as much talk from the bottom up as from the top down. Emphasizes both horizontal and vertical dialogue.

Emphasizes orders. Emphasizes dialogue as "horizontal" plan, but not on a "vertical."

CONCLUDING THOUGHT

All a teacher or writer or manager or anyone can do for you as a manager is to lead you toward some attitudes or strategies which may help you to be more effective if you sincerely assimilate them. To go beyond dissatisfaction with yourself as a manager, you must strike out on your own, cultivate your own growth, and nurture your own talents to be better than you have ever been before.

BIBLIOGRAPHY AND NOTES

Introduction

1. Kahn, H., & Pepper, T. The Japanese Challenge: Success or Failure of Economic Success. New York, New York: Crowell, 1979.

2. Pascale, R.T., & Athos, A.G. The Art of Japanese Management. New York, New York: Warner Books, 1981, p. 23.

3. Sullivan, H.S. The Interpersonal Theory of Psychiatry. New York, New York: Norton, 1953.

4. Dyer, W.W. Your Erroneous Zones. New York, New York: Funk & Wagnalls, 1976.

5. Pascale, R.T., & Athos, A. G. op. cit.

6. Ibid., p. 164.

Chapter I

1. Pascale, R.T., & Athos, A.G. The Art of Japanese Management. New York, New York: Warner Books, 1981.

2. Ouchi, W. Theory Z. How American Business Can Meet the Japanese Challenge. New York, New York: Avon Books, 1981, p. 108.

3. Cooper, M.R., Morgan, B.S., Foley, P.M., Kaplan, L.B. "Changing Employee Values: Deepening Discontent?" Jan/Feb. 1979 Harvard Business Review, p. 117.

4. Ouchi, W. op. cit.

5. Murdy, L. Trust Killers. Compiled by L. Murdy from articles, books and students. University of Southern California, 1985. This list is printed by the kind permission of the author.

6. Murdy, L. <u>Receiving Criticizm</u>. Compiled by L. Murdy from articles, books and students. University of Southern California, 1985. This list is printed by the kind permission of the author.

7. Murdy, L. <u>Giving Advice</u>. Compiled by L. Murdy from articles, books and students. University of Southern California, 1985. This list is printed by the kind permission of the author.

8. <u>AEsop's Fables</u>. (No editor). New York, New York: Grosset & Dunlap Inc., 1982. pp. 3-4. Library of Congress Cd. #47-27068.

9. Ibid. pp. 61-62.

10. Naisbitt, <u>Megatrends</u>. New York, New York: Warner Books, 1982. pp. 200-201.

11. <u>AEsop's Fables</u>. op. cit. p. 192.

12. Watson, T.J. <u>A Business and Its Beliefs: The Ideas That Helped Build IBM</u>. New York, New York: McGraw Hill, 1963. pp. 4-6.

13. Phillips, J.R., & Kennedy, A.A. <u>Shaping & Managing Shared Values</u>. McKinsey Staff Paper, Dec. 1980 p. 1.

14. Peters, T.J., & Waterman, R. H. <u>In Search of Excellence: Lessons from America's Best Run Companies</u>. New York, New York: Harper & Row, 1982. p. 281.

15. Ouchi, W. op. cit. pp. 193-222.

16. Ibid., p. 218.

17. Peters, T.J., & Waterman, R.H. op. cit. p. 318.

18. Ibid., p. 285.

19. Ouchi, W. op. cit. p. 194.

20. Ibid., p. 195.

21. Ibid., p. 214.

22. Ibid., p. 216.

23. Ibid., p. 214.

24. Ibid., pp. 214-215.

25. Ibid., p. 196.

26. Ibid., p. 215.

27. Ibid., p. 216.

28. Pascale, R.T., & Athos, A.G. op. cit., p. 288.

29. Ouchi, W. op. cit., p. 216.

30. Ibid., p. 218.

31. Ibid., p. 214.

32. Ibid., p. 198.

33. Ibid., p. 215.

34. Ibid., pp. 214-215.

35. Ibid., p. 215.

36. Ibid., p. 214.

37. Naisbitt, John. op. cit., p. 190.

38. Ibid., p. 181.

39. Ibid., p. 202.

Chapter II

1. Sigband, N. Communication for Management and Business. Glenview, Ill.: Scott, Foresman and Co., 1982.

2. Naisbitt, J. Megatrends. New York, New York: Warner

Books, 1982.

3. Sigband, N. op. cit.

4. Bruner, J.S., & Tagiuri, R. The Perception of People. In G. Lindzey (Ed.) Handbook of Social Psychology. Cambridge, Mass.: Addison Wesley, 1959.

5. Moawad, R. Increasing Human Effectiveness. Tacoma, Washington, United Learning Institute, 1981. (VTR)

6. Dyer, W. W. Your Erroneous Zones. New York, New York: Funk & Wagnalls, 1976, p. 1.

7. Getzels, J.W., Lipham, T.M., & Campbell, R.F. Educational Administration as a Social Process. New York, New York: Harper & Row, 1968.

8. Frankel-Brunswick, E. Intolerance of ambiguity as an emotional and perceptual variable. Journal of Personality, 1949, 18, 108-143.

9. Mazor, P.P. & Bush, F. E. The relationship between principal's self-perception and management style as observed in United States dependents schools (Doctoral dissertation, University of Southern California, 1976). Dissertation Abstracts International, 1976, 36, 7078A.

10. Orban, R. (Ed.) Orban's Currenty Comedy. Wilmington, Del., The Comedy Center (Publisher) Aug. 31, 1983.

11. AEsop's Fables (No editor) New York, New York: Grosset & Dunlap Inc., 1982. pp. 130-131.

12. Daniels, W. R. Key Behaviors of Effective Managers. Presentation at Twelfth Annual ACSA Conference, San Diego, CA, March 23, 1983.

13. Cohen, D.J. Listening Skill Development. Workshop Presentation for Simi Valley Unified School District, Simi Valley, CA, Feb. 1982.

14. Sigband, N. op. cit.

15. Sigband, N. op. cit.

16. Sigband, N. op. cit.

17. Cohen, D.J. op. cit.

18. Sigband, N. op. cit.

19. Naisbitt, J. op. cit., p. 200.

20. Sigband, N. "Do You Listen When You Hear?"
    "Executive Programs", University of Southern
    California School of Business Administration, 1982.

Chapter III

1. AEsop's Fables. (No editor) New York, New York:
   Grosset & Dunlap., 1982. p. 41.

2. Bremson, D. Coping With Difficult People. Garden
   City, New York: Anchor Press/Doubleday. 1980.

Chapter IV

1. Stallings, D. This Kaleidoscope is derived from the
   Needs-Sensing Kaleidescope originated by Dr. Dina
   Stallings for her Leadership Program at Riverside
   City College, Riverside, California.

Chapter V

1. Shook, R.L. Ten Greatest Salespersons. New York,
   New York: Harper & Row, Publishers, 1978.

2. Murdy, L. Excuses for a Closed Mind. Compiled by L.
   Murdy from articles, books and students.
   University of Southern California, 1985. This list
   is printed by kind permission of the author.

3. Wyckoff, J. Personal Problem Solving. Manuscript in
   preparation, 1983.

4. Georgiades, W. Class notes from Critique of
   Research, C & I, Course #792, University of
   Southern California, 1977.

Chapter VI

1. Hersey, P., & Blanchard, K.H. Management of
   Organizational Behavior: Utilizing Human Resources.
   Englewood Cliffs, New Jersey: Prentice-Hall, Inc.,
   1977.

2. Pascale, R.T., & Athos, A.G. The Art of Japanese
   Management. New York, New York: Warner Books,
   1981, p. 246.

3. Moawad, R. Increasing Human Effectiveness.
   Tacoma, Washington, United Learning Institute,
   1980. (VTR)

4. Cousins, N. Anatomy of an Illness as Perceived
   by the Patient. New York, New York: W.W. Norton
   & Co., 1979.

5. Moawad, R. op. cit.

6. Daniels, W.R. Key Behaviors of Effective
   Managers. Presentation at Twelfth Annual ACSA
   Conference, San Diego, CA, March 23, 1983.

7. Tice, L. New Age Thinking for Achieving Your
   Potential. The Pacific Insititute, Seattle,
   Washington, 1980, VTR #26.

8. Ibid.

9. Burns, J.M. Leadership. New York, New York:
   Harper & Row, 1978, p. 19-20.

10. Harris, S. Winners and Losers. Allen, Texas:
    Argus Publishers, 1973.

11. Daniels, W.R. op. cit.

12. Tice, L. op. cit.

342

Waitley, D. (Writer & Narrator) Audiocassette.
Seeds of Greatness. Chicago, Illinois:
Nightingale-Conant Corporation. This cassette
series is built around self-imaging psychology.

Waitley, D. (Writer & Narrator) Audiocassette.
The Psychology of Winning. Chicago, Illinois:
Nightingale-Conant Corporation. This cassette
series is built around self-imaging psychology.

Chapter VII

1. Sugarman, S. Sin & Madness: Studies in
   Narcissism. Philadelphia, Penn., Westminster
   Press, 1976.

2. Moawad, R. Increasing Human Effectiveness.
   Tacoma, Washington, United Learning Institute,
   1980 (VTR).

3. Daniels, W.R. Key Behaviors of Effective
   Managers. Presentation at Twelfth Annual ACSA
   Conference, San Diego, CA, March 23, 1983.

4. Naisbitt, J. Megatrends. New York, New York:
   Warner Books, 1982.

5. Daniels, W.R. op. cit.

6. Moawad, R. op. cit.

7. Ouchi, W. Theory Z. How American Business Can
   Meet the Japanese Challenge. New York, New
   York: Avon Books, 1981.

8. Maslow, A. Eupsychian Management. Homewood,
   Illinois: Richard D. Irwin, Inc., & The Dorsey
   Press, 1965, p. 72.

9. Woodward, B., & Armstrong, S. The Bretheren.
   Inside the Supreme Court. New York, New York:
   Avon Books, 1981.

Chapter VIII

1. Jampolsky, G.B. Love is Letting Go of Fear. New York, New York: Bantam Books, 1981.

2. Jampolsky, G.B., writer and narrator. Love is Letting Go of Fear. Chicago, Illinois: Nightingale-Conant Corporation, 1985, Audiocassette.

3. Kolar, J., Croce, L.R., & Bardellini, J.M. "Integrative Bargaining in One California School District." Phi Delta Kappan, Dec. 1981, pp. 246-247. "Important Principles for Moving from an Adversarial to a Problem-Solving Model" is printed by kind permission of the authors.

Chapter IX

1. Pascale, R.T., & Athos, A.G. The Art of Japanese Management. New York, New York: Warner Books, 1981.

2. Cooper, M.R., Morgan, B.S., Foley, P.M., Kaplan, L.B. "Changing Employee Values: Deepening Discontent?" Jan/Feb. 1979, Harvard Business Review, p. 117.

3. Naisbitt, J. Megatrends. New York, New York: Warner Books, 1982.

4. Layden, M. Escaping the Hostility Trap. Englewood Cliffs, New Jersey: Prentice-Hall, Inc., 1979.

5. Maslow, A.H. Eupsychian Management. Homewood, Illinois: Richard Irwin, Inc. & The Dorsey Press, 1965, p. xi.

6. Craig, J.A., & M. Synergic Power, Beyond Domination, Beyond Permissiveness. Berkeley, California: Pro Active Press, 1979, p. 123.

7. Maslow, A.H. op. cit., p. xi.

8. Craig, J.A., & M. op. cit., pp. 123-124.

9. Galbraith, J.K. The Age of Uncertainty. Boston, Mass.: Houghton Mifflin Co., 1977, p. 326.

10. Cook, Don. "Tiny Austria Manages to Avoid Slump." Los Angeles Times. November 7, 1982, Part VI, p. 1.

11. Ibid., Part VI, p. 1.

12. Ibid., Part VI, p. 4.

13. "America vs. Japan. Can U.S. Workers Compete?" U.S. News & World Report, Sept. 2, 1985, p. 43.

14. Pascale, R.T., & Athos, A.G. op. cit., pp. 287-288.

15. Ibid., p. 39.

16. "Leaders for the 21st. Century?" Time, April 28, 1980, p. 81.

Chapter X

1. Smith, A. Wealth of Nations. Vol. I. London: Methuen & Co., 1950.

2. Taylor, F.W. The Principles of Scientific Management. New York, New York: Harper & Brothers, 1911.

3. Mayo, E. The Human Problems of an Industrial Civilization. New York, New York: Macmillan, 1933.

4. Stogdill, R.M., & Coons, A.E., (ed.) Leader Behavior: Its Description & Measurement. Research Monograph No. 881. Columbus, Ohio: Bureau of Business Research, Ohio State University, 1951.

5. Homans, G.C. The Human Group. New York, New York: Harcourt, Brace & World, Inc., 1950.

6. Hersey, P., & Blanchard, K.H. Management of Organizational Behavior: Utilizing Human Resources. Englewood Cliffs, New Jersey: Prentice Hall, Inc., 1977, p 54.

7. Herzberg, F., Mausner, B., & Snyderman, B. The Motivation to Work. (2nd Ed.) New York, New York: John Wiley & Sons, Inc., 1959.

8. Ibid.

9. Likert, R. The Human Organization. New York, New York: McGraw Hill Book Co., 1967.

10. Likert, R. New Patterns of Management. New York, New York: McGraw Hill Book Co., 1961.

11. Argyris, C. Interpersonal Competence & Organizational Effectiveness. Homewood, Illinois: Dorsey Press and Richard D. Irwin, Inc., 1962.

12. Ibid.

13. Hersey, P., & Blanchard, K.H. op. cit.

14. Fiedler, F.E. A Theory of Leadership Effectiveness. New York, New York: McGraw Hill Book Co., 1967.